Artificial Intelligent Techniques for Wireless Communication and Networking

Scrivener Publishing
100 Cummings Center, Suite 541J
Beverly, MA 01915-6106

Artificial Intelligence and Soft Computing for Industrial Transformation

Series Editor: Dr. S. Balamurugan (sbnbala@gmail.com)

Scope: Artificial Intelligence and Soft Computing Techniques play an impeccable role in industrial transformation. The topics to be covered in this book series include Artificial Intelligence, Machine Learning, Deep Learning, Neural Networks, Fuzzy Logic, Genetic Algorithms, Particle Swarm Optimization, Evolutionary Algorithms, Nature Inspired Algorithms, Simulated Annealing, Metaheuristics, Cuckoo Search, Firefly Optimization, Bio-inspired Algorithms, Ant Colony Optimization, Heuristic Search Techniques, Reinforcement Learning, Inductive Learning, Statistical Learning, Supervised and Unsupervised Learning, Association Learning and Clustering, Reasoning, Support Vector Machine, Differential Evolution Algorithms, Expert Systems, Neuro Fuzzy Hybrid Systems, Genetic Neuro Hybrid Systems, Genetic Fuzzy Hybrid Systems and other Hybridized Soft Computing Techniques and their applications for Industrial Transformation. The book series is aimed to provide comprehensive handbooks and reference books for the benefit of scientists, research scholars, students and industry professional working towards next generation industrial transformation.

Publishers at Scrivener
Martin Scrivener (martin@scrivenerpublishing.com)
Phillip Carmical (pcarmical@scrivenerpublishing.com)

Artificial Intelligent Techniques for Wireless Communication and Networking

Edited by

R. Kanthavel, K. Ananthajothi, S. Balamurugan

and

R. Karthik Ganesh

Scrivener
Publishing

This edition first published 2022 by John Wiley & Sons, Inc., 111 River Street, Hoboken, NJ 07030, USA and Scrivener Publishing LLC, 100 Cummings Center, Suite 541J, Beverly, MA 01915, USA
© 2022 Scrivener Publishing LLC
For more information about Scrivener publications please visit www.scrivenerpublishing.com.

Wiley Global Headquarters
111 River Street, Hoboken, NJ 07030, USA

For details of our global editorial offices, customer services, and more information about Wiley products visit us at www.wiley.com.

Limit of Liability/Disclaimer of Warranty
While the publisher and authors have used their best efforts in preparing this work, they make no representations or warranties with respect to the accuracy or completeness of the contents of this work and specifically disclaim all warranties, including without limitation any implied warranties of merchantability or fitness for a particular purpose. No warranty may be created or extended by sales representatives, written sales materials, or promotional statements for this work. The fact that an organization, website, or product is referred to in this work as a citation and/or potential source of further information does not mean that the publisher and authors endorse the information or services the organization, website, or product may provide or recommendations it may make. This work is sold with the understanding that the publisher is not engaged in rendering professional services. The advice and strategies contained herein may not be suitable for your situation. You should consult with a specialist where appropriate. Neither the publisher nor authors shall be liable for any loss of profit or any other commercial damages, including but not limited to special, incidental, consequential, or other damages. Further, readers should be aware that websites listed in this work may have changed or disappeared between when this work was written and when it is read.

Library of Congress Cataloging-in-Publication Data

ISBN 978-1-119-82127-4

Cover image: Pixabay.Com
Cover design by Russell Richardson

Set in size of 11pt and Minion Pro by Manila Typesetting Company, Makati, Philippines

10 9 8 7 6 5 4 3 2 1

Contents

Preface

In the current digital era, artificial intelligence (AI) resembling human intelligence is enabling superior inventions for the advancement of the world. Broadening the scientific scope of AI has made it possible to change fundamentals and modulate everlasting facts in the wireless communication and networking domains. This breakthrough in AI miraculously preserves the inspired vision of communication technology.

Wireless communication and networking based on AI concepts and techniques are explored in this book, specifically focusing on the current research in the field by highlighting empirical results along with theoretical concepts. The possibility of applying AI mechanisms towards security aspects in the communication domain is also elaborated. Moreover, the application side of integrated technologies are also explored to enhance AI Revolution innovations, insights, intelligent predictions, cost optimization, inventory management, identification processes, classification mechanisms, cooperative spectrum sensing techniques, ad-hoc network architecture, and protocol and simulation-based environments.

This book allows both practitioners and researchers to share their opinions and recent research on the convergence of these technologies with those in academia and industry. The contributors have presented their technical evaluation and comparative analysis of existing technologies; and theoretical explanations and experimental case studies related to real-time scenarios are also included. Furthermore, this book will connect IT professionals, researchers, and academicians working on 5G communication and networking technologies.

The book is organized into 20 chapters that address AI principles and techniques used in wireless communication and networking. It outlines the benefits, functions, and future role of AI in wireless communication and networking. In addition, AI applications are addressed from a variety of aspects, including basic principles and prominent methodologies that offer researchers relevant instructions to follow in their research. The editing team and expert reviewers in various disciplines have thoroughly reviewed the information included.

- In Chapter 1, "Comprehensive and Self-Contained Introduction to Deep Reinforcement Learning," P. Anbalagan, S. Saravanan and R. Saminathan present a brief guide to the deep reinforcement learning process and its detailed applications and research directions in order to enhance the basics of reinforcement mechanisms.
- In Chapter 2, "Impact of AI in 5G Wireless Technologies and Communication Systems," A. Sivasundari and K. Ananthajothi present an in-depth overview of the implementation of AI to improve 5G wireless communication systems, discuss the role and difficulties faced, and highlight suggestions for future studies on integrating advanced AI into 5G wireless communications.
- In Chapter 3, "Artificial Intelligence Revolution in Logistics and Supply Chain Management," P.J. Satish Kumar, Ratna Kamala Petla, Elangovan K and P.G. Kuppusamy give a brief description of recent developments and some relevant impacts concerning logistics and supply chain related to AI.
- In Chapter 4, "An Empirical Study of Crop Yield Prediction Using Reinforcement Learning," M. P. Vaishnnave and R. Manivannan use reinforcement learning (RL) data technologies and high-performance computing to create new possibilities to activate, calculate, and recognize the agricultural crop forecast.
- In Chapter 5, "Cost Optimization for Inventory Management in Blockchain Under Cloud," C. Govindasamy, A. Antonidoss and A. Pandiaraj investigate some of the most prominent bases of blockchain for inventory management of blockchain and cost optimization methods for inventory management in cloud.
- In Chapter 6, "Review of Deep Learning Architectures Used for Identification and Classification of Plant Leaf Diseases," G. Gangadevi and C. Jayakumar describe the deep learning architectures for plant disease prediction and classification using standard techniques like artificial neural network (ANN), k-means classifier (K-means), recurrent neural network (RNN), k-nearest neighbor (K-NN) classifier, and support vector machine (SVM).

- In Chapter 7, "Generating Art and Music Using Deep Neural Networks," A. Pandiaraj, Lakshmana Prakash, R. Gopal and P. Rajesh Kanna develop a model using deep neural nets that can imagine like humans and generate art and music of their own. This model can also be used to increase cognitive efficiency in AGI (artificial general intelligence), thereby improving the agent's image classification and object localization.
- In Chapter 8, "Deep Learning Era for Future 6G Wireless Communications – Theory, Applications, and Challenges," S. K. B. Sangeetha, R. Dhaya, S. Gayathri, K. Kamala and S. Divya Keerthi encapsulate the background of 6G wireless communication with details on how deep learning has made a contribution to 6G wireless technology and also highlight future research directions for deep learning-driven wireless technology.
- In Chapter 9, "Robust Cooperative Spectrum Sensing Techniques for a Practical Framework Employing Cognitive Radios in 5G Networks," J. Banumathi, S.K B. Sangeetha and R. Dhaya discuss the use of cooperative spectrum sensing in cognitive radio systems to improve the efficiency of detecting primary users.
- In Chapter 10, "Natural Language Processing," S. Meera and B. Persis Urban Ivy elucidate natural language processing (NLP), which is a branch of computer science and artificial intelligence that studies how computers and humans communicate in natural language, with the aim of computers understanding language as well as humans do.
- In Chapter 11, "Class-Level Multi-Feature Semantic Similarity-Based Efficient Multimedia Big Data Retrieval," Sujatha D, Subramaniam M and A. Kathirvel present an efficient class-level multi-feature semantic similarity measure-based approach. The proposed method receives the input query and estimates class-level information similarity, class-level texture similarity, and class-level semantic similarity measures for different classes.
- In Chapter 12, "Supervised Learning Approaches for Underwater Scalar Sensory Data Modeling with Diurnal Changes," J. V. Anand, T. R. Ganesh Babu, R. Praveena and K. Vidhya describe an inter-depth variation profile in line with latitude and longitude in a particular area, calculate

attenuations by the temperature coefficient of real data sets, and attribute attenuation to a frequency-dependent loss.

- In Chapter 13, "Multi-Layer UAV Ad-Hoc Network Architecture, Protocol and Simulation," Kamlesh Lakhwani, Tejpreet Singh Orchu and Aruna discuss the use of flying ad hoc networks (FANETs) to provide communication among the UAVs. In FANET, the selection of a suitable mobility model is a critical task for researchers.

- In Chapter 14, "Artificial Intelligence in Logistics and Supply Chain," Jeyaraju Jayaprakash explains the source of activities in any white product manufacturing and service industry. This logistics and supply chain network will become more complex over the next few decades as a result of pandemic situations, natural disasters, increasing population, and other side entities developing smart strategies.

- In Chapter 15, "Hereditary Factor-Based Multi-Feature Algorithm for Early Diabetes Detection Using Machine Learning," S. Deepajothi, R. Juliana, Aruna S K and R. Thiagarajan indicate that the predominance of diabetes mellitus among the global population ultimately leads to blindness and death in some cases. The proposed model attempts to design and deliver an intelligent solution for predicting diabetes in the early stages and address the problem of late detection and diagnosis.

- In Chapter 16, "Adaptive and Intelligent Opportunistic Routing Using Enhanced Feedback Mechanism," V. Sharmila, Mandal K, Shankar Shalani and P. Ezhumalai discuss opportunistic routing of an intercepted packet to provide an effective wireless mesh network. Traditional opportunistic routing algorithms are being used to provide high-speed use batching of packets, which is a complex task. Therefore, an enhanced opportunistic feedback-based algorithm is proposed in this chapter in which individual packet forwarding uses a new route calculation in the proposed work that takes into consideration the cost of transmitting feedback and the capacity of the nodes to choose appropriate rates for monitoring operating conditions.

- In Chapter 17, "Enabling Artificial Intelligence and Cyber Security in Smart Manufacturing," R. Satheesh Kumar, G. Keerthana, L. Murali, S. Chidambaranathan, C.D. Premkumar and R. Mahaveerakannan propose an efficient green manufacturing approach in SM systems with the aid of AI and cyber security frameworks. The proposed work employs a dual-stage artificial neural network (ANN) to find the design configuration of SM systems in industries. Then, for maintaining data confidentiality while communicating, the data are encrypted using the 3DES approach.
- In Chapter 18, "Deep Learning in 5G Networks," G. Kavitha, P. Rupa Ezhil Arasi and G. Kalaimani discuss a 3D-CNN model combined with RNN model for analyzing and classifying the network traffic into three various classes, such as maximum, average and minimum traffic, which proves that the combined 3D-CNN and RNN model provides better classification of network traffic.
- In Chapter 19, "EIDR Umpiring Security Models for Wireless Sensor Networks," A. Kathirvel, S. Navaneethan and M. Subramaniam provide an overview of WSNs with their classification, as well as comparisons between different routing algorithms and the proposed EIDR (enhanced intrusion detection and response). Soundness of proposed EIDR is tested using QualNet 5.0.
- In Chapter 20, "Artificial Intelligence in Wireless Communication," Prashant Hemrajani, Vijaypal Singh Dhaka, Manoj Kumar Bohra and Amisha Kirti Gupta describe the applications of AI techniques in wireless communication technologies and networking, which can bring these changes through new research. Also, AI/ML techniques can improve the current state of network management, operations and automation. They can further support software-defined networking (SDN) and network function virtualization (NFV), which are considered important wireless communication technology components for the deployment of 5G and higher generation communication systems.

All of the contributors to this book deserve our heartfelt gratitude. With the fervent cooperation of the editorial director and production editor at Scrivener Publishing, we aspire to cross many more milestones to glory in the future academic year.

Prof. Dr. R. Kanthavel
Department of Computer Engineering,
King Khalid University
Abha, Saudi Arabia
Dr. K. Ananthajothi
Department of Computer Science and Engineering
Misrimal Navajee Munoth Jain Engineering College
Chennai, India
Dr. S. Balamurugan
Founder and Chairman, Albert Einstein Engineering and
Research Labs (AEER Labs)
Vice-Chairman, Renewable Energy Society of India, India
Dr. R. Karthik Ganesh
Department of Computer Science and Engineering
SCAD College of Engineering and Technology
Cheranmahadevi, India
January 2022

Comprehensive and Self-Contained Introduction to Deep Reinforcement Learning

P. Anbalagan*, S. Saravanan and R. Saminathan

Department of Computer Science and Engineering, Annamalai University, Annamalai Nagar, India

Abstract

Deep reinforcement learning is a type of machine learning and artificial intelligence in which smart robots, similar to the way people make good decisions, can learn from their actions. Implicit in this form of machine learning is that, depending on their behavior, an agent is rewarded or punished. Including unsupervised machine learning and supervised learning, reinforcement learning is yet another common type of artificial intelligence development. Deep reinforcement learning can lead to incredibly impressive results beyond normal reinforcement learning, due to the fact that it incorporates the core qualities of both deep learning and reinforcement learning. Since this is becoming a very broad and rapidly growing field, the entire application landscape will not be explored, but mainly based on comprehensive and self contained introduction to deep reinforcement learning. The goal of this chapter is twofold: (i) to provide a brief guide to the deep reinforcement learning process; (ii) to present detailed applications and research directions.

Keywords: Artificial intelligence, deep learning, machine learning, reinforcement learning

Corresponding author: anbalagansamy@gmail.com

R. Kanthavel, K. Ananthajothi, S. Balamurugan and R. Karthik Ganesh (eds.) *Artificial Intelligent Techniques for Wireless Communication and Networking*, (1–14) © 2022 Scrivener Publishing LLC

1.1   Introduction

Due to its effectiveness in solving complex sequential decision-making issues, Reinforcement Learning (RL) has become increasingly common over the past few years. Many of these accomplishments are due to the integration of deep learning techniques with RL. But, thanks to its ability to learn various levels of abstractions from data, deep RL has been effective in complex tasks with lower prior knowledge.For example, from visual perceptual inputs made up of thousands of pixels, a deep RL agent can successfully learn [14]. Deep RL also has potential for real-world areas such as medical, self-driving cars, finance and smart grids, to name a few. Nonetheless in implementing deep RL algorithms, many problems arise. The area of machine learning that deals with sequential decision-making is reinforcement learning (RL) [16, 20].

As an agent who has to make decisions in an atmosphere to maximize a given definition of accumulated rewards, the RL problem can be formalized. It will become apparent that this formalization extends to a wide range of tasks and captures many important characteristics of artificial intelligence, such as a sense of cause and effect, as well as a sense of doubt and non-determinism [5].

A main feature of RL is that good behavior is taught by an agent. This suggests that it incrementally modifies or acquires new habits and abilities. Another significant feature of RL is that it uses experience of trial and error (as opposed to for example, dynamic programming that *a priori* assumes maximum environmental knowledge). Therefore the RL agent does not need full environmental awareness or control; it just needs to be able to communicate with the environment and gather information. The knowledge is gained *a priori* in an offline environment, then it is used as a batch for learning (the offline setting is therefore also called batch RL) [3].

In comparison to the online world, this is where information becomes available in a linear order and is used to change the agent's actions gradually.

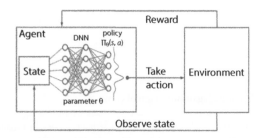

Figure 1.1 Reinforcement learning process.

The core learning algorithms are exactly the same in both situations, but the key difference is that the agent will affect how it gathers experience in an online environment. This is an important difficulty, primarily because while studying, the agent has to deal with the problem of exploration/exploitation. But learning in the online world can also be a benefit, as the agent can collect data directly about the most important part of the environment. For that purpose, RL approaches may provide the most algorithmically efficient solution in practice, even when the context is fully understood, compared to other dynamic programming methods that would have been inefficient due to this lack of precision [8].

Deep reinforcement learning contains aspects of neural networks and learning with reinforcement (Figure 1.1). Deep reinforcement learning is achieved using two different methods: deep Q-learning and policy specular highlights. Deep Q-learning techniques attempt to anticipate the rewards will accompany certain steps taken in a particular state, while policy gradient strategies seek to optimize the operational space, predicting the behavior themselves. Policy-based approaches of deep reinforcement learning are either stochastic in architecture. Certainly, probabilistic measures map states to policies, while probabilistic policies build probabilistic models for behavior [6].

The aim of this chapter is to provide the reader with accessible tailoring of basic deep reinforcement learning and to support research experts. The primary contribution made by this work is

1. Originated with a complete review study of comprehensive deep reinforcement learning concept and framework.
2. Provided detailed applications and challenges in deep reinforcement learning.

This chapter is clearly distinguished by the points mentioned above from other recent surveys. This gives the data as comprehensive as previous works. The chapter is organized as follows: Section 1.2 summarizes the complete description of reinforcement learning. The different applications and problems are explored in Section 1.3, accompanied by a conclusion in Section 1.4.

1.2   Comprehensive Study

1.2.1   Introduction

In most Artificial Intelligence (AI) subjects, we build mathematical structures to tackle problems. For RL, the Markov Decision Process (MDP) is the solution. It sounds complicated, but it provides a basic structure to model a complex problem. The world is observed and behavior performed by an individual (e.g. a human). Rewards are released, but they may be rare and delayed. The long-delayed incentives very often make it incredibly difficult to untangle the data and track what series of acts led to the rewards [11].

Markov decision process (MDP) Figure 1.2 is composed of:

State in MDP can be represented as raw images or we use sensors for robotic controls to calculate the joint angles, velocity, and pose of the end effector.

- A movement in a chess game or pushing a robotic arm or a joystick may be an event.
- The reward is very scarce for a GO match: 1 if we win or −1 if we lose. We get incentives more often. We score whenever we hit the sharks in the Atari Seaquest game (Figure 1.3).
- If it is less than one the discount factor discounts potential incentives. In the future, money raised also has a smaller

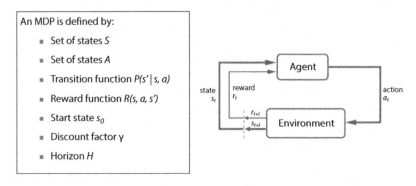

Figure 1.2 Markov process.

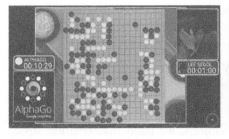

Figure 1.3 Raw images of State.

current value, and we will need it to further converge the solution for a strictly technical reason.

- We can indefinitely rollout behaviour or limit the experience to N steps in time. This is called the horizon.

System dynamics is the transformation function. After taking action, it predicts the next condition. When we address model-based RL later, it is called the model that plays a significant role. RL's ideas come from many areas of study, including the theory of power. In a particular setting, distinct notations can be used.It is possible to write the state as s or x, and the behavior as an or u. An action is the same as a control operation. We may increase the benefits or and the costs that are actually negative for each other [10].

1.2.2   Framework

Compared to other fields such as Deep Learning, where well-established frameworks such as Tensor Flow, PyTorch, or MXnet simplify the lives of DL practitioners, the practical implementations of Reinforcement Learning are relatively young. The advent of RL frameworks, however, has already started and we can select from many projects right now that greatly encourage the use of specialized RL techniques. Frameworks such as Tensor Flow or PyTorch have appeared in recent years to help transform pattern recognition into a product, making deep learning easier for practitioners to try and use [17].

In the Reinforcement Learning arena, a similar pattern is starting to play out. We are starting to see the resurgence of many open source libraries and tools to deal with this, both by helping to create new pieces (not by writing from scratch) and above all, by combining different algorithmic components of prebuild. As a consequence, by generating high abstractions of the core components of an RL algorithm, these Reinforcement Learning frameworks support engineers [7].

A significant number of simulations include Deep Reinforcement Learning algorithms, introducing another multiplicative dimension to the time load of Deep Learning itself. This is mainly needed by the architectures we have not yet seen in this sequence, such as, among others, the distributed actor-critic methods or behaviors of multi-agents. But even choosing the best model also involves tuning hyper parameters and searching between different settings of hyper parameters; it can be expensive. All this includes the need for supercomputers based on distributed systems of heterogeneous servers (with multi-core CPUs and hardware accelerators such as GPUs or TPUs) to provide high computing power [18].

1.2.3   Choice of the Learning Algorithm and Function Approximator Selection

In deep learning, the function approximator characterizes how the characteristics are handled to higher levels of abstraction (*a fortiori* can therefore give certain characteristics more or less weight). In the first levels of a deep neural network, for example, if there is an attention system, the mapping made up of those first layers can be used as a framework for selecting features. On the other hand, an asymptotic bias can occur if the function approximator used for the weighted sum and/or the rule and/or template is too basic. But on the other hand, there would be a significant error due to the limited size of the data (over fitting) when the feature approximator has weak generalization.

An especially better decision of a model-based or model-free method identified as a leading function approximator choice may infer that the state's y-coordinate is less essential than the x-coordinate, and generalize that to the rule. It is helpful to share a performant function approximator in either a model-free or a model-based approach depending on the mission. Therefore the option to focus more on one or the other method is also a key factor in improving generalization [13, 19].

One solution to eliminating non-informative characteristics is to compel the agent to acquire a set of symbolic rules tailored to the task and to think on a more extreme scale. This abstract level logic and increased generalization have the potential to activate cognitive high-level functions such as analogical reasoning and cognitive transition. For example, the feature area of environmental may integrate a relational learning system and thus extend the notion of contextual reinforcement learning.

1.2.3.1   Auxiliary Tasks

In the era of successful reinforcement learning, growing a deep reinforcement learning agent with allied tasks within a jointly learned representation would substantially increase sample academic success.

This is accomplished by causing genuine several pseudo-reward functions, such as immediate prediction of rewards (= 0), predicting pixel changes in the next measurement, or forecasting activation of some secret unit of the neural network of the agent.

The point is that learning similar tasks creates an inductive bias that causes a model to construct functions useful for the variety of tasks in the neural network. This formation of more essential characteristics, therefore, contributes to less over fitting. In deep RL, an abstract state can be constructed in such a way that it provides sufficient information to match the internal meaningful dynamics concurrently, as well as to estimate the estimated return of an optimal strategy. The CRAR agent shows how a lesser version of the task can be studied by explicitly observing both the design and prototype components via the description of the state, along with an estimated maximization penalty for entropy. In contrast, this approach would allow a model-free and model-based combination to be used directly, with preparation happening in a narrower conditional state space.

1.2.3.2   *Modifying the Objective Function*

In order to optimize the policy acquired by a deep RL algorithm, one can implement an objective function that diverts from the real victim. By doing so, a bias is typically added, although this can help with generalization in some situations. The main approaches to modify the objective function are

i) Reward shaping
For faster learning, incentive shaping is a heuristic to change the reward of the task to ease learning. Reward shaping incorporates prior practical experience by providing intermediate incentives for actions that lead to the desired outcome. This approach is also used in deep reinforcement training to strengthen the learning process in environments with sparse and delayed rewards.

ii) Tuning the discount factor
When the model available to the agent is predicted from data, the policy discovered using a short iterative horizon will probably be better than a policy discovered with the true horizon. On the one hand, since the objective function is revised, artificially decreasing the planning horizon contributes to a bias. If a long planning horizon is focused, there is a greater chance of over fitting (the discount factor is close to 1). This over fitting can be conceptually interpreted as related to the aggregation of errors in the transformations and rewards derived from data in relation to the real transformation and reward chances [4].

1.3   Deep Reinforcement Learning: Value-Based and Policy-Based Learning

1.3.1   Value-Based Method

Algorithms such as Deep-Q-Network (DQN) use Convolutional Neural Networks (CNNs) to help the agent select the best action [9].

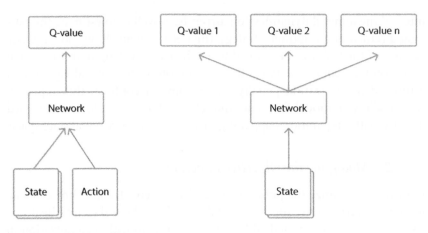

Figure 1.4 Value based learning.

While these formulas are very complicated, these are usually the fundamental steps (Figure 1.4):

1. Take the status picture, transform it to grayscale, and excessive parts are cropped.
2. Run the picture through a series of contortions and pooling in order to extract the important features that will help the agent make the decision.
3. Calculate each possible action's Q-Value.
4. To find the most accurate Q-Values, conduct backpropagation.

1.3.2 Policy-Based Method

In the modern world, the number of potential acts may be very high or unknown. For instance, a robot learning to move on open fields may have millions of potential actions within the space of a minute. In these conditions, estimating Q-values for each action is not practicable. Policy-based approaches learn the policy specific function, without computing a cost function for each action. An illustration of a policy-based algorithm is given by Policy Gradient (Figure 1.5).

Policy Gradient, simplified, works as follows:

1. Requires a condition and gets the probability of some action based on prior experience
2. Chooses the most possible action

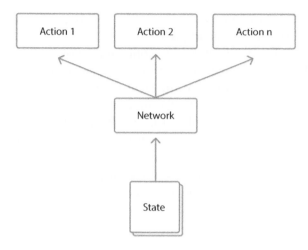

Figure 1.5 Policy based learning.

3. Reiterates before the end of the game and evaluates the total incentives
4. Using back propagation to change connection weights based on the incentives.

1.4 Applications and Challenges of Applying Reinforcement Learning to Real-World

1.4.1 Applications

The ability to tackle a wide range of Deep RL techniques has been demonstrated to a variety of issues which were previously unsolved. A few of the most renowned accomplishments are in the game of backgammon, beating previous computer programmes, achieving superhuman-level performance from the pixels in Atari games, mastering the game of Go and beating professional poker players in the Nolimit Texas Hold'em Heads Up Game: Libratus and Deep stack.

Such achievements in popular games are essential because in a variety of large and nuanced tasks that require operating with high-dimensional inputs, they explore the effectiveness of deep RL. Deep RL has also shown a great deal of potential for real-world applications such as robotics, self-driving vehicles, finance, intelligent grids, dialogue systems, etc. Deep RL systems are still in production environments, currently. How Facebook uses Deep RL, for instance, can be found for pushing notifications and for faster video loading with smart prefetching.

RL is also relevant to fields where one might assume that supervised learning alone, such as sequence prediction, is adequate. It has also been cast as an RL problem to build the right neural architecture for supervised learning tasks. Notice that evolutionary techniques can also be addressed for certain types of tasks. Finally, it should be remembered that deep RL has prospects in the areas of computer science in classical and basic algorithmic issues, such as the travelling salesman problem. This is an NP-complete issue and the ability to solve it with deep RL illustrates the potential effect it could have on many other NP-complete issues, given that it is possible to manipulate the structure of these problems [2, 12].

1.4.2   Challenges

Off-Line Learning
Training is also not possible directly online, but learning happens offline, using records from a previous iteration of the management system. Broadly speaking, we would like it to be the case that the new system version works better than the old one and that implies that we will need to perform off-policy assessment (predicting performance before running it on the actual system). There are a couple of approaches, including large sampling, for doing this. The introduction of the first RL version (the initial policy) is one special case to consider; there is also a minimum output requirement to be met before this is supposed to occur. The warm-start efficiency is therefore another important ability to be able to assess.

Learning From Limited Samples
There are no different training and assessment environments for many actual systems. All training knowledge comes from the real system, and during training, the agent does not have a separate exploration policy as its exploratory acts do not come for free. Given this greater exploration expense, and the fact that very little of the state space is likely to be explored by logs for learning from, policy learning needs to be data-efficient. Control frequencies may be 1 h or even multi-month time steps (opportunities to take action) and even longer incentive horizons. One easy way to measure a model's data efficiency is to look at the amount of data needed to meet a certain output threshold.

High-Dimensional State and Action Spaces
For several realistic real-world problems, there are wide and consistent state and action spaces, which can pose serious problems for traditional RL algorithms. One technique is to generate a vector of candidate action and then do a closest neighbor search to determine the nearest accessible real action.

Safety Constraints
Many control systems must function under security restrictions, even during phases of exploratory learning. Constrained MDPs (Markov Decision Processes) make it possible to define constraints on states and behavior. Budgeted MDPs enable the degree of constraint/performance trade-off to be explored rather than simply hard-wired by letting constraint levels be learned. Another solution is to add to the network a protection layer that prevents any breaches of safety.

Partial Observability
It is partly measurable for almost all real systems where we would like to incorporate reinforcement learning. For example, the efficiency of mechanical parts may deteriorate over time, 'identical' widgets may exhibit performance variations provided the same control inputs, or it may simply be unknown the condition of certain parts of the system (e.g. the mental state of users of a suggested system).

Two common strategies to dealing with partial observability, including input history, and modelling history using repeated networks in the model. In addition, Robust MDP formalisms provide clear mechanisms to ensure that sensor and action noise and delays are robust to agents. If a given deployment setting may have initially unknown but learnable noise sources, then techniques for device detection may be used to train a policy that can learn in which environment it operates.

Reward Functions
Device or product owners do not have a good image of what they want to refine in certain instances. The incentive function is always multidimensional and involves different sub-goals to be balanced. Another great insight here which reminds me of machine latency discussions) is that 'normal performance' (i.e. expectation) is always an inadequate measure, and for all task instances, the system needs to perform well. A common approach is to use a Conditional Value at Risk (CVaR) target to measure the full distribution of rewards across classes, which looks at a given percentile of the distribution of rewards rather than the predicted reward.

Explainability/Interpretability
Real systems are owned and controlled by humans who need to be informed about the actions of the controller and need insights into cases of failure. For this purpose, for real-world policies, policy clarity is critical. In order to obtain stakeholder buy-in, it is necessary to consider the longer-term purpose of the policy, particularly in cases where the policy can find another solution and unforeseen approach to managing a system.

Real-Time Inference
Policy inference has to occur within the system's control frequency. This could be in the order of milliseconds or shorter. This prevents us from using costly computational methods that do not follow the constraints (for example, certain types of model-based planning). Of course, systems with longer control intervals cause the opposite problem: in order to speed up data generation, we cannot run the task faster than in real time.

Delayed Rewards
Most real systems have interruptions in the state's sensation, the actuators, or the feedback on the reward. For instance, delays in the effects of a braking system, or delays between a recommendation system's choices and consequent user behaviors. There are a number of possible methods to deal with this, including memory-based agents that leverage a memory recovery system to allocate credit to distant past events that are helpful in forecasting [1, 15].

1.5   Conclusion

Deep Reinforcement Learning is the fusion of reinforcement learning (RL) and deep learning. This field of research has been able to solve a wide range of dynamic decision-making operations that were traditionally out of control for a computer. In applications such as medical, automation, smart grids, banking, and plenty more, deep RL thus brings up many new applications. We give an overview of the deep reinforcement learning (RL) paradigm and learning algorithm choices. We begin with deep learning and reinforcement learning histories, as well as the implementation of the Markov method. Next, we summarize some popular applications in various fields and, eventually, we end up addressing some possible challenges in the future growth of DRL.

References

1. Arulkumaran, K., Deisenroth, M., Brundage, M., Bharath, A., A Brief Survey of Deep Reinforcement Learning. *IEEE Signal Process. Mag.*, 34, 1–16, 2017, 10.1109/MSP .2017.2743240.

2. Botvinick, M., Wang, J., Dabney, W., Miller, K., Kurth-Nelson, Z., Deep Reinforcement Learning and its Neuroscientific Implications, *Neuron*, 107, 603–616. 2020.

3. Duryea, E., Ganger, M., Hu, W., Exploring Deep Reinforcement Learning with Multi Q-Learning. *Intell. Control Autom.*, 07, 129–144, 2016, 10.4236/ica.2016.74012.

4. Fenjiro, Y. and Benbrahim, H., Deep Reinforcement Learning Overview of the state of the Art. *J. Autom. Mob. Robot. Intell. Syst.*, 12, 20–39, 2018, 10.14313/JAMRIS_3-2018/15.

5. Francois, V., Henderson, P., Islam, R., Bellemare, M., Pineau, J., *An Introduction to Deep Reinforcement Learning*, Foundations and Trends in Machine Learning, Boston—Delft, 2018, 10.1561/2200000071.

6. Haj Ali, A., Ahmed, N., Willke, T., Gonzalez, J., Asanovic, K., Stoica, I., *A View on Deep Reinforcement Learning in System Optimization*, arXiv:1908.01275v3 Intel Labs, University of California, Berkeley, 2019.

7. Heidrich-Meisner, V., Lauer, M., Igel, C., Riedmiller, M., Reinforcement learning in a Nutshell. *ESANN'2007 Proceedings - European Symposium on Artificial Neural Networks*, Bruges (Belgium), 277–288, 2007.

8. Ivanov, S. and D'yakonov, A., Modern Deep Reinforcement Learning Algorithms, arXiv preprint arXiv:1906.10025, 1–56, 2019.

9. Le Pham, T., Layek, A., Vien, N., Chung, T.C., Deep reinforcement learning algorithms for steering an underactuated ship in: *2017 IEEE International Conference on Multisensor Fusion and Integration for Intelligent Systems (MFI 2017)*, 602–607, 2017, 10.1109/MFI.2017.8170388.

10. Li, M.-J., Li, A.-H., Huang, Y.-J., Chu, S.-I., Implementation of Deep Reinforcement Learning. *ICISS 2019: Proceedings of the 2019 2nd International Conference on Information Science and Systems*, pp. 232–236, 2019, 10.1145/3322645.3322693.

11. Liu, Q., Zhai, J.-W., Zhang, Z.-Z., Zhong, S., Zhou, Q., Zhang, P., Xu, J., A Survey on Deep Reinforcement Learning. *Jisuanji Xuebao/Chin. J. Comput.*, 41, 1–27, 2018, 10.11897/SP.J.1016 .2018. 00001.

12. Mnih, V., Kavukcuoglu, K., Silver, D., Rusu, A., Veness, J., Bellemare, M., Graves, A., Riedmiller, M., Fidjeland, A., Ostrovski, G., Petersen, S., Beattie, C., Sadik, A., Antonoglou, I., King, H., Kumaran, D., Wierstra, D., Legg, S., Hassabis, D., Human-level control through deep reinforcement learning. *Nature*, 518, 529–33, 2015, 10.1038/nature14236.

13. Mosavi, A., Ghamisi, P., Faghan, Y., Duan, P., Band, S., Comprehensive Review of Deep Reinforcement Learning Methods and Applications in Economics, *Mathematics*, 8, 1–42, 2020, 10.20944/preprints 202003.0309.v1.

14. Mousavi, S., Schukat, M., Howley, E., Deep Reinforcement Learning: An Overview, in: *Lecture Notes in Networks and Systems*, pp. 426–440, 2018, 10.1007/978-3-319-56991-8_32.

15. Nguyen, C., Dinh Thai, H., Gong, S., Niyato, D., Wang, P., Liang, Y.-C., Kim, D.I., Applications of Deep Reinforcement Learning in Communications and Networking: A Survey. *IEEE Commun. Surv. Tutorials*, 21, 4, 1–1, 2019, 10.1109/COMST.2019.2916583.

16. Sangeetha, S.K.B. and Ananthajothi, K., Machine Learning Tools for Digital Pathology—The Next Big Wave in Medical Science. *Solid State Technol.*, 63, 3732–3749, 2020.

17. Santhya, R., Latha, S., Balamurugan, S., Charanyaa, S., Further investigations on strategies developed for efficient discovery of matching dependencies. *Int. J. Innov. Res. Comput. Commun. Eng.* (An ISO 3297:2007 Certified Organization), 3, 18998–19004, 2014.

18. Tan, F. and Yan, P., *Deep Reinforcement Learning: From Q-Learning to Deep Q-Learning*, Springer, Cham, Guangzhou, China, pp. 475–483, 2017, 10.1007/978-3-319-70093-9_50.

19. Xiliang, C., Cao, L., Li, C.-X., Xu, Z.-X., Lai, J., Ensemble Network Architecture for Deep Reinforcement Learning. *Math. Probl. Eng.*, 2018, 1–6, 2018, 10.1155/2018/ 2129393.

20. Li, Y., *Deep Reinforcement Learning: An Overview*, arXiv:1701.07274v6, 2017.

2

Impact of AI in 5G Wireless Technologies and Communication Systems

A. Sivasundari* and K. Ananthajothi†

Department of Computer Science and Engineering, Misrimal Navajee Munoth Jain Engineering College, Chennai, India

Abstract

4G networks (with Internet Protocol or IP, telecommunications and reaction-based connectivity) have managed the network architecture. They have evolved and are now accessible in a multitude of ways, including advanced learning and deep learning. 5G is flexible and responsive and will establish the need for integrated real time decision-making. As the rollout has begun across the globe, recent technical and architectural developments in 5G networks have proved their value. In various fields of classification, recognition and automation, AI has already proved its efficacy with greater precision. The integration of artificial intelligence with internet-connected computers and superfast 5G wireless networks opens up possibilities around the globe and even in outer space. In this section, we offer an in-depth overview of the Artificial Intelligence implementation of 5G wireless communication systems. The focus of this research is in this context, to examine the application of AI and 5G in warehouse building and to discuss the role and difficulties faced, and to highlight suggestions for future studies on integrating Advanced AI in 5G wireless communications.

Keywords: Artificial intelligence, 5G, deep learning, machine learning, mobile networks, wireless communication

Corresponding author: siva.saibabu123@gmail.com
†*Corresponding author*: kanandjothime@gmail.com

R. Kanthavel, K. Ananthajothi, S. Balamurugan and R. Karthik Ganesh (eds.) Artificial Intelligent Techniques for Wireless Communication and Networking, (15–30) © 2022 Scrivener Publishing LLC

2.1   Introduction

Although 5G provides low latency and very high speed support capabilities (e.g., eMBB), a wide number of devices (e.g., mMTC), a heterogeneous mix of traffic types from a diverse and challenging suite of applications (e.g., URLLC), AI is complemented by observing from specific environments to provide independent reach of operation, turning 5G into a data-driven adaptive real-time network [13]. AI is used for 5G system modeling, automation of core network (e.g. provisioning, scheduling, prediction of faults, protection, fraud detection), distributed computing, reduction of operating costs, and improvement of both service quality and customer evolves on chatbots, recommendation systems, and strategies such as automated processes. In addition, AI is used across all layers, from the disaggregated radio access layer (5G RAN) to the distributed cloud layer (5G Edge/Core) to the integrated access backhaul to fine tune performance [5].

AI is used for the 5G distributed cloud layer to optimize device resource usage, autoscaling, identification of anomalies, predictive analytics, prescriptive policies, and so on. In addition, the 5G distributed cloud layer offers acceleration technologies to enable federated and distributed learning for AI workloads [19].

The growth of mobile 5G worldwide and its market overview are shown in Figure 2.1 and Figure 2.2. To support a multitude of emerging

in billions

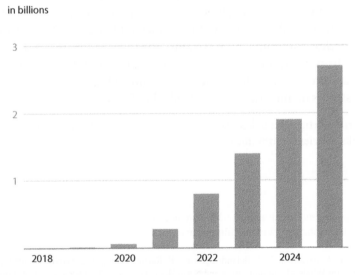

Figure 2.1 Growth of 5G Connections worldwide.

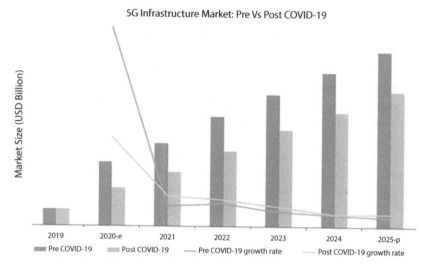

Figure 2.2 5G Market analysis.

technologies (e.g., AR/VR, Industrial IoT, autonomous vehicles, drones, Industry 4.0 projects, Smart Cities, Smart Ports), AI is also used for customer service management and business support systems. Several learning methods are used to train data models based on target use cases, such as supervised learning, unsupervised learning, reinforcement learning, federated learning, distributed learning, transfer learning, and deep learning based on algorithms such as Convolutional Neural Networks (CNNs), Recurrent Neural Networks (RNNs) [9].

AI needs a mixture of AI, localized AI, and end-to-end AI at the system stage. In individual network modules, device-level AI is used to solve self-contained problems where no data needs to be transferred onto the network. Where AI is extended to one network domain or cross-network domains, localized AI allows data to be passed on to the network, but is limited to a local network domain, such as at the RAN or fronthaul. End-to-end AI is where the whole network needs to be accessible to the network, and where it needs to gather data and information from various network domains in order to implement AI properly. Slice management and network service assurance can provide examples of end-to-end AI [4, 8].

5G and AI are some of the world's most groundbreaking innovations in hundreds of years. Although each sector is individually reshaping and allowing for unique ideas, 5G and AI integration will be truly revolutionary.

In reality this integration is central to our small sensor edge definition, which includes in-home computing, edge cloud and 5G, to create an integrated intelligent system and service networking tool. Substantial amounting data, be it via on-device AI or gradual edge cloud storage over moderate 5G, can be distributed close to its source. Online AI is important to process data closer to the source because it provides efficient and effective output such as security, consistency and reliability as well as support for knowledge in scale [22].

The topic has several introductions. They all serve a different purpose and offer a different perspective on these rapidly changing 5G communications. The goal of this review is to provide the reader with 5G usable artificial intelligence and to assist mobile users. The main contributions of this work are

1. Provided a complete groundwork of integrated services of 5G in AI and AI in 5G;
2. Provided a clear road map of artificial intelligence and 5G in the industrial space;
3. Described the role of artificial intelligence in the mobile networks along with research challenges.

This survey is clearly differentiated from other recent surveys by the above listed points. The paper is structured as follows: Along with this detailed introduction, the complete study of AI in 5G and 5G in AI are reviewed in Section 2.2. Section 2.3 discusses artificial intelligence and 5G in the industrial space. Section 2.4 briefly describes the roles of AI in mobile networks followed by a conclusion in Section 2.5.

2.2   Integrated Services of AI in 5G and 5G in AI

5G would be able and stronger than the conditions characteristic to host many more smart devices, particularly when about 41.6 billion Internets of Things smart devices are to be used by 2025. This is especially critical and many want a secure cloud access for efficient movement, such as driverless car systems and industrial sensors [12].

GSMA, the mobile network trading body, has identified wireless technology as providing three pillars of next-generation connectivity:

- enhanced mobile broadband (eMBB),
- ultra-reliable,

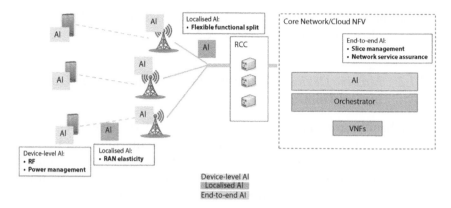

Figure 2.3 AI in next generation networks.

- low-latency communications (URLLC) and massive machine-type communications (mMTC).

Multiple devices based on high-speed and low-speed bandwide will be needed for the supporting equipment, both require online analytics in real-time. The large number of information generated requires the combination of 5G and Artificial Intelligence (AI) (Figure 2.3) [6].

2.2.1   5G Services in AI

AI can exist at every angle in the cloud environments, multi clouds, and mobile network of the potential. We also see significant suppliers of Technological innovations, such as NVIDIA, making significant contributions in 5G-based networks in connectivity, the Internet of Things (IoT) and other edge environments [14, 20].

2.2.1.1   Next-Generation Edge Convergence With AI Systems on Chip

5G is compatible with the wireless Long-Term Growth and Wi-Fi interfaces cellular networks. 5G can quickly extend through indoor and large areas when introduced in cross-technology access points. Ultimately, the implementation of technology will lead to radio spectrum convergence for these various radio channels and the development of single chip access points, which are easily accessible to seamless connectivity through various radio access technologies. For many mass device realms with neural network processing cycle, all this 5G interfaces will eventually turn into low-power low-cost chip systems (Figure 2.4).

2.2.1.2   Massive Device Concurrency Replenishing AI Data Lakes in Real Time

5G can handle up to one million competing boundary devices per square kilometer, which is larger than 4G networks in a magnitude order. The last scale would enable companies, in a shifting paradigm known as multi-access leading computing, to regularly obtain large amounts of data from cellphones, sensors, heating systems and other mobile devices. As 5G networks start to overwhelm water data structures with new telephone data globally, AI application analysts and data scientists can create more advanced analytical data.

2.2.1.3   Ultra-Fast, High-Volume Streaming for Low-Latency AI

5G connection times are substantially less as 4G, as small as 1 ms vs. the 50 ms 4G feature. As a result, 5G has far higher transmissions and processing rates than 4G, which is 20 Gb/s or 5–12 Mb/s for 4G. The stronger relation between the bandwidth of the system and the 5G power amplifier comes from the capacity to simultaneously transmit several data streams between the ground station and the borders. These fun working methods allow 5G to serve AI DevOps pipelines staff in low latency, from data intake, planning, modeling, training in real-time streaming scenarios. In addition, when coupled with its much lower latency, the faster download speeds of 5G will allow analysts to obtain, clean and evaluate much more information in a much shorter period of time.

2.2.2   AI Services in 5G

2.2.2.1   Distributed AI

AI is also a major aspect of the network that guarantees that AI and other software staffing levels can be accommodated with all their difficulty by 5G networks. New research shows that many providers of telecommunications are well on track to launch AI in order to operate 5G networks worldwide. 5G network will have to be self-regulating, self-sustaining, self-repairing and continuing self-optimizing in order to best support the next wave of decentralized AI applications. The key goal is to automate application-level

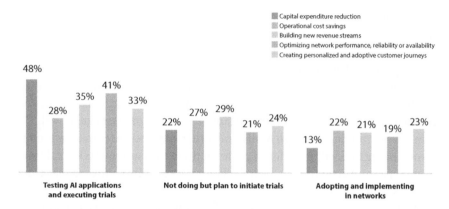

Figure 2.4 Service providers achieving benefits through AI.

net traffic, quality-of-service management, process development, analysis, and other associated processes more flexible, reliable, easily, and efficiently than conventional procedures. In addition, computer training and other AI frameworks may be implemented.

2.2.2.2 AI for IT Operations (AIOps)

To ensure that 5G provides much faster, safer and more RF-efficient connectivity than before, AIOps will be necessary. For the virtual machines in the network and multi-cloud management suites which tackle 5G networks and applications from one end to the next, AIOps technologies will have to be central. At least from the end-to-end through 5G ecosystems, AIOps drives consistent quality of service. AI-based controls can ensure continuous and accurate configuration of RF channels and other network infrastructures to support improvements in service quality, traffic patterns, and application tasks. They also encourage reliable alarm control, installation and healing and the optimization of the subscriber's interface.

2.2.2.3 Network Slicing

A 5G networking feature known as network slicing will be augmented by AIOps tooling. This allows many virtual networks to be run over one physical connection by 5G networks. AIOps tooling will allow proactive and dynamic supply of individual wireless service quality levels for many customer categories and edge device groups by using this virtualized resource allocation capacity. AIOps will also be required to increase dynamic 5G RF-channel allocation.

5G has smaller cells than 4G at each edge unit, reuses wavelengths more thoroughly, and must re-target "beam formed" base station phase-array millimeter-wave antennas continuously. In order to secure service quality, 5G base stations instantly predict as well as provide each user with the best wireless router. They do this because the problems associated with 5G mm waves moving through walls and other hard surface areas are constantly being tackled. In order to perform these measurements in real time over constantly evolving local wireless loops, a securely shuttered real-time analysis is necessary.

All this AI inside the 5G network, for example, would have a support system for data storage. We would expect to see regularly develop in 5G networks specialist data lakes, autoML applications, DevOps databases and other critical operational architectures to ensure that the best AI models are implemented in real time. This data/model governance will be introduced through cloud-to-edge architectures that fit into complex public/private federal environments typical of 5G [17, 21].

2.2.3   Evolution With AI in the 5G Era

2.2.3.1   Agile Network Construction

AI is extended to each level of 5G network creation in order to make network preparation more accurate and the implementation more successful. Various data points from major regions, the 5G industry, users and the advancement of today's technology are used for machine learning and incremental computing to rapidly and reliably construct plans for different scenarios. In the processes of survey, layout, overseeing, integration and adoption, innovations such as image processing, optical character recognition (OCR), speech recognition.

2.2.3.2   Intelligent Operations and Management

The co-existence of 2G, 3G, 4G and 5G networks, thereby providing customers a wide range of services, significantly affects the rate of communications between individuals and items. Subsequently, the amount of service requests and problems faced by operations and maintenance (O&M) personnel is also growing. According to data analysis over the past few years, network O&M problems are growing by 5% per annum.

2.2.3.3 Smart Operations

5G is ushering in a new age of communication. It will deliver enhanced resources, applications and unprecedented interactions to clients. It would also provide operators with a chance to leave the conventional pipe business model by enabling them to develop creative digital technologies, develop new business models, and encourage new industry alliances. An AI-based experience management platform with provider synergy will provide dynamic systems adjustment of customer experience and data plane. With its symmetric data service processes platform and intelligent engine, it helps operators efficiently and precisely attract new customers, facilitate user interaction, retain users and add profitability, transforming their conventional operations into smart activities [10, 15].

2.3 Artificial Intelligence and 5G in the Industrial Space

Artificial intelligence has reached many different business markets today. Compared to machine learning, it also occurs in factories and takes those experiences to the factory floor. An aluminum die-cast maker for transmission parts could previously identify 60% of the defects by manual checks in the automotive industry. By using computer vision and machine learning, at any given process stage, they are now getting close to 100% defect detection. The fourth industrial revolution, Industry 4.0, introduced a mixture of emerging innovations, such as machine learning and IoT smart devices [11].

By introducing condition monitoring systems and growing their analytics capabilities, many companies are already using IoT technologies to track resources in their warehouses and simplify their control rooms. One analysis found that within their set-ups, 35% of US manufacturers are already using smart sensor data. In processing, many data-intensive devices are also used in close vicinity. That's why the trick is networking with 5G. In an industry focused on data-intensive computer applications, the higher speeds and reduced power of 5G are needed for the efficient use of automated robots, wearable devices, and virtual reality (VR) headsets, discussing the future of industrial automation. AI, Machine Learning, Robot Process Automation (RPA), improved communication, are developing and adapting each of these technologies to fit various use cases and industrial requirements. To satisfy consumer needs and expectations, their abilities and ability are constantly evolving.

For a long time, the manufacturing sector has been grappling with legacy issues around quality management. Not only is it a costly, time-consuming and challenging operation, but it is one that is vulnerable to error. Before they lose concentration and precision, human beings can only do so much repetitive work. On the other hand, AI-powered quality control systems will keep working 24/7 without getting bored or tired. Their ability to repeat, rinse and repeat is what brings a much-needed advantage to the manufacturing sector to ensure continuous quality management [16].

Intelligent systems will radically change how the industry responds to these changes as quality management standards, enforcement criteria, and regulatory demands become more complicated and demanding. AI never sleeps, it can learn, it can adapt, and it can be managed within extremely precise limits to produce incredibly accurate results. It can be programmed, targeted, and precise. All the variables that play an increasingly important role in a company's long-term performance.

Although the technology is still in the early stages of its potential, it still provides a surprisingly powerful forum for the industry to develop integrated and effective solutions for quality control. Ultimately, as networking increases and systems are given increased capacity for linked communication and collaboration, process capability and effectiveness will be transformed by AI and automation [1].

The industrial sector is on the verge of a transformative shift with AI and 5G that will not only impact infrastructure, but cost, quality control, and growth. For industrial companies, motion control and tele-robotics will be a specific field of development as various companies will exploit the authority to influence real machineries through virtual objects via master control frameworks. Teleoperation is converted in Mind Commerce by digital twin technology, which corresponds to the mapping of the material realm to the virtual environment in which IoT networks the digital twin of a physical object can provide data about the product, such as its physiological body and disposition.

Various AI technologies and their use within the increasingly increasing enterprise and industrial data arena relative to analytics solutions. This analyzes new market models, leading businesses, and solutions. This discusses how to better use different forms of AI for problem solving. Also measured is the need for AI in IoT networks and systems. It offers unit growth and revenue forecasting for both metrics and IoT from 2019 to 2024 [3].

2.4   Future Research and Challenges of Artificial Intelligence in the Mobile Networks

There are many barriers to the implementation of 5G networks, and one way the market addresses those challenges is by integrating artificial intelligence into platforms. More than nearly half of decision-makers from 132 global cell phone carriers said they anticipate AI to be integrated into their 5G networks even by the end of 2020. The primary goal of AI integration is to minimize capital costs, enhance network capacity, and build new revenue streams.

By increasing network reliability and delivering personalized services, AI is already being used to boost customer support and build strong customer relationships, 55% of decision-makers said. Approximately 70% agree that using AI in network preparation is the best way to recover profits earned in converting networks to 5G. Approximately 64% of survey respondents would focus their AI efforts on network output management. Other fields in which cellular judgment intend to prioritize AI investments is handling SLAs, product mix, networks, and sales.

There are concerns associated with integrating AI into 5G networks, of course. Effective methods for capturing, organizing, and evaluating the massive amounts of data gathered by AI are necessary to develop. For that purpose, early AI adopters who find workable solutions will appear as the clear leading contenders as 5G networks become interconnected [18].

5G raises new challenges for mobile telecom service providers, although the technology solves some complexities by integrating artificial intelligence (AI) capability into the infrastructure.

Key Findings

- The key priority of AI's networks now is on reducing capital investment, enhancing network capacity and creating new sales streams.
- In order to enhance customer support and increase customer loyalty, AI would be crucial.
- In their systems, AI will help development communications service providers (CSPs) move to 5G to rebound.
- New data problems are created by implementing AI, even as it solves network complications.

2.4.1   Research Directions

2.4.1.1   AI Is Being Adopted Into Mobile Networks by Communication Service Provider Now

The value of incorporating AI in their networks is now being harvested by service providers from around the world. Over half (53%) service providers predict that AI will be completely incorporated into their networks by the end of 2020. At the end of this year some already expect to see AI launched with an additional 19% estimate of duration of three to five years.

2.4.1.2   AI and Customer Experience

In the next three years, 68% of service providers have stressed the enhancement of customer service as an overall business goal, while 55% have agreed that AI has already a positive impact in this sector. AI is expected to further improve customer experience in many areas, including enhancing network efficiency and delivering customized goods.

2.4.1.3   Recouping the Network Investments That 5G Demands

The key goals that service providers aim to achieve through artificial intelligence are to reduce operating risk and to maintain returns on network investment. Around 70% believe that their network preparation will make the greatest return from digital transformation, while 64% expect to concentrate their IT efforts on network effectiveness management.

2.4.1.4   Data Challenges Presented by Artificial Intelligence Adoption

Network providers accept that efficient processes are required to capture, structure and review massive quantities of data that AI has the ability to collect. A key aspect of the study is the obvious first-mover advantage for early investors at AI, who find today's and potential obstacles and opportunities. We believe that knowledge can provide the mobile communications industry with exciting opportunities as it can be used to develop a more personal consumer approach while reducing the cost of building and running networks.

2.4.1.5   Network Intelligence and Automation

Network intelligence and automation are crucial to the growth of 5G, IoT and industrial digitalization. With 5G-enabled technology growing, operators will need to increase their network capacity. But with extra power, there is additional complexity.

Consumers are now seeing upwards of 1 Gbps per second over the air as 5G networks are lit up in urban cores and devices begin to enter the market. In addition to better mobile broadband, 5G facilitates the Internet of Things on an unthinkable scale, up to 1 million devices per square kilometer until recently. And as we transition from 3GPP Release 15 to Release 16, changes to enable ultra-reliable low latency communications applications such as precision robotics and remote industrial control in virtually every sector of the economy will drive transformation. In the future, operators are exploring AI today for a variety of use cases that generate value for both the service provider and the consumer. The use of AI in mobile networks is not an aspirational endeavor set for a nebulous period. In reality, 53% of carriers plan to be using AI on their networks by the end of next year, according to recently published research focused on conversations with executives at 132 mobile operators around the world [7].

2.4.2   Challenges to a 5G-Powered AI Network

The 5G rollout is only starting, but the industry hasn't really discussed what 5G can do with machine learning, understandably. There are some barriers to introducing 5G on a scale so that everybody can use it [2].

2.4.2.1   Dealing With Interference

To start with when they move through physical artifacts, a 5G signal is more vulnerable to interference. To combat this at closer intervals than the 4G network towers we're used to seeing now, 5G networks will be operated by smaller stations distributed around locations.

2.4.2.2   Dealing With Latency

Another barrier to 5G networks running AI software depends on where the AI software can be run. In terms of computing power and low latency requirements, these systems are very challenging, so they're not stable without them. A 5G network, too it completely needs low latency, otherwise it's not beneficial. If the information the AI needs is stored far away from the AI program in a cloud system, and with a 5G network powering it, there would still be too much delay for the work of the AI to be as useful as it should be.

In basic terms, with the distance and congestion of network networks, latency increases. Latency could become a critical issue, depending on the device using the 5G network. Autonomous vehicles, for example, would not operate with high latency systems because they need to identify objects in real time, such as pedestrians. Delays in response times of microseconds may have catastrophic effects for both passengers and others outside the vehicle.

2.4.2.3   Solving Latency

Using edge computing systems inside the network will be a solution to this problem, because it can bring the data and/or computing power required by the AI closer to the AI that does the job. The 5G network will make all this happen more easily, helping the AI to do its job effectively as well. AI software will help make the entire network more predictive, routing traffic as required to the appropriate device or machine, so that whatever data is on it is completely configured to manage it [3].

2.5   Conclusion

5G technology is going to revitalize the cellular infrastructure for internet service providers with mm wavelength frequency support. Wireless AI is still in its early stages and is expected to build smarter wireless networks in the coming years. Network topology, architecture and propagation models, along with user mobility and use patterns in 5G, will be complex. AI can play a critical role in helping telecom operators to deploy, operate and sustain 5G networks with the proliferation of IoT devices. In 5G networks, AI will produce more information and facilitate a move from network management to systems integration. AI can be used to address multiple use cases in order to assist wireless operators move from a human management model to self-driven automated management that transforms network operations and maintenance processes. An in-depth study of the integration with Artificial Intelligence of 5G wireless communication systems is therefore being reviewed.

References

1. https://www.ericsson.com/en/networks/offerings/network-services/ai-report
2. https://www.qualcomm.com/news/onq/2020/02/04/5gai-ingredients-fueling-tomorrows-tech-innovations

3. https://www.thalesgroup.com/en/markets/digital-identity-and-security/ mobile/magazine/using-artificial-intelligence-shape-5g

4. Aljumaily, M., *AI in 5G and Beyond Networks*, Presentation, https:// www.researchgate.net/publication/342787463_AI_in_5G_and_Beyond_ Networks , 2020.

5. Arjoune, Y. and Faruque, S., Artificial Intelligence for 5G Wireless Systems: Opportunities, Challenges, and Future Research Direction. Semantic Scholar, https://doi.org/10.1109/CCWC47524.2020.9031117, 1023–1028, 2020.

6. Bajaj, A., Tamanna, Sangwan, O., SMART 5G: Artificial Intelligence Empowered 5G Networks, Conference: 2nd National Seminar on "Design of 5G Mobile Networks Using Soft Computing Techniques", Guru Jambheshwar University of Science and Technology, Hisar, Haryana, March 2019.

7. Ge, X., Thompson, J., Li, Y., Liu, X., Zhang, W., Chen, T., Applications of Artificial Intelligence in Wireless Communications. *IEEE Commun. Mag.*, 57, 12–13, 2019.

8. Goyal, D., Balamurugan, S., Peng, S.-L., Verma, O.P., *Design and Analysis of Security Protocol for Communication*, John Wiley & Sons, Inc., Bridgewater, NJ, 2020.

9. Haider, N., Baig, M.Z., Imran, M., Artificial Intelligence and Machine Learning in 5G Network Security: Opportunities, advantages, and future research trends, 2020.

10. Javaid, N., Sher, A., Nasir, H., Guizani, N., Intelligence in IoT-Based 5G Networks: Opportunities and Challenges. *IEEE Commun. Mag.*, 56, 94–100, 2018.

11. Kilinc, C., Sun, C., Marina, M., *5G Development: Automation and the Role of Artificial Intelligence*, Wiley online Library, https://onlinelibrary.wiley.com/ doi/10.1002/9781119471509.w5GRef128, 2020.

12. Li, R., Zhifeng, Z., Zhou, X., Ding, G., Chen, Y., Zhongyao, W., Zhang, H., Intelligent 5G: When Cellular Networks Meet Artificial Intelligence. *IEEE Wireless Commun.*, 2–10, 2017. Published in: https://ieeexplore.ieee.org/xpl/ RecentIssue.jsp?punumber=7742 IEEE Wireless Communications (Volume: 24, https://ieeexplore.ieee.org/xpl/tocresult.jsp?isnumber=8088405 (Issue: 5, October 2017).

13. Morocho-Cayamcela, M.E. and Lim, W., Artificial Intelligence in 5G Technology: A Survey. Conference, 860–865, Oct. 2018.

14. Pérez-Romero, J., Sallent, O., Ferrus, R., Agusti, R., Artificial Intelligence-based 5G network capacity planning and operation, Semantic Scholar, https://doi.org/10.1109/ISWCS.2015.7454338 246–250, 2015.

15. Ranjani, V. and Sangeetha, S.K.B., Wireless data transmission in ZigBee using indegree and throughput optimization. *International Conference on Information Communication and Embedded Systems (ICICES2014)*, Chennai, India, pp. 1–5, 2014.

16. Shafin, R., Liu, L., Chandrasekhar, V., Chen, H., Reed, J., Zhang, J., Artificial Intelligence-Enabled Cellular Networks: A Critical Path to Beyond-5G and 6G. *IEEE Wireless Commun.*, 1–6, 2020. Published in: https://ieeexplore.ieee.org/xpl/RecentIssue.jsp?punumber=7742 IEEE Wireless Communications (Volume: 27, https://ieeexplore.ieee.org/xpl/tocresult.jsp?isnumber=9085248 (Issue: 2, April 2020)

17. Soldani, D. and Illingworth, S., *5G AI-Enabled Automation*, Wiley online Library https://onlinelibrary.wiley.com/doi/abs/10.1002/9781119471509.w5G Ref225, 2020.

18. Varga, P., Peto, J., Franko, A. *et al.*, 5G support for Industrial IoT Applications—Challenges, Solutions, and Research gaps. *Sensors (Basel)*, 20, 3, 828, 2020.

19. Wang, S., Wang, C.-X., Hong, X., McLaughlin, S., Artificial Intelligence to Manage Network Traffic of 5G Wireless Networks. *IEEE Network*, 32, 58–64, 2018.

20. Wang, C.-X., Di Renzo, M., Stanczak, S., Wang, S., Larsson, E., Artificial Intelligence Enabled Wireless Networking for 5G and Beyond: Recent Advances and Future Challenges. *IEEE Wireless Commun.*, 27, 16–23, 2020.

21. Xiaohu, Y., Zhang, C., Tan, X., Jin, S., Wu, H., *AI for 5G: Research Directions and Paradigms*, Springer Link, Science China Information Sciences, 62, 21301, 2019.

22. Yao, M., Sohul, M., Marojevic, V., Reed, J., Artificial Intelligence Defined 5G Radio Access Networks. *IEEE Commun. Mag.*, Science China Information Sciences, http://scis.scichina.com/en/2019/021301.pdf, 57, 14–20, 2019.

3

Artificial Intelligence Revolution in Logistics and Supply Chain Management

P.J. Sathish Kumar[1]*, Ratna Kamala Petla[2], K. Elangovan[2] and P.G. Kuppusamy[2]

[1]Dept. of CSE, Panimalar Engineering College, Chennai, India
[2]Dept. of ECE, Siddharth Institute of Engineering & Technology (Autonomous), Puttur, India

Abstract

With Artificial Intelligence (AI) and Machine Learning (ML), which will further intensify the discrepancy between winners and losers, the logistics and supplies chain business are already changing their face. By removing deep-rooted short-comings and complexities, artificial intelligence and machine learning provide creativity with insights into all the logistics and supply chain fields that people cannot easily copy on a scale. In the sense of more accurate capacity management, better efficiency, high quality, lower cost and better quality, artificial intelligent systems aim at achieving the efficient optimization expertise necessary in the logistics and supply chains while at the same time promoting safety. We present a brief description of recent developments and some relevant impacts in logistics and supply chain related to artificial intelligence. Since this is becoming a very large and rapidly growing field, we will not explore the entire application landscape, but concentrate primarily on logistics and supply chain related to artificial intelligence. Our goal is threefold: (i) to provide a complete theory behind logistics and supply chain in terms of impacts and trends; (ii) In order to have a future for the company to improve the logistics and the supply chain–automation exploitation.

Keywords: Artificial intelligence, logistics, machine learning, proactive systems, self learning, supply chain

---

*Corresponding author: sathishjraman@gmail.com

R. Kanthavel, K. Ananthajothi, S. Balamurugan and R. Karthik Ganesh (eds.) *Artificial Intelligent Techniques for Wireless Communication and Networking*, (31–46) © 2022 Scrivener Publishing LLC

3.1   Introduction

The COVID-19 outbreak, the economic effects of which will continue for months, has severely affected a significant number of global supply chains. Coronaviruses could halve global growth, according to the Organization for Economic Cooperation and Development (OECD), with many industries facing a major drop across-the-board. The country's quickest economy and other domestic supply chains are declining as the coronavirus is spreading in other Asian countries [19]. As a result, safety precautions aimed at preventing the further spread of the disease, including immigration bans and huge quarantines, have only contributed to the further deterioration and destruction of global supply chains for food retail and medical supplies and the locking of enterprise resource planning [14, 18].

According to the recent International Data Corporation (IDC) digital economy model, more than 50% of the global nominal gross domestic product should be generated by digitally transformed companies prior to 2023. In 2025, Gartner predicted that growth of AI by 2021 would amount to $2.9 billion in market value and will bring in a development time of $6.2 billion to staff by 2011 and will have implemented AI capabilities in at least 90% of new business applications. But many do not fully understand what this is and how it can help improve activities, including the nominal growth, service and risk mitigation, with all their ardour and enthusiasm [1].

In the past ten years, artificial intelligence (AI) ran each day without understanding something, from high-tech laboratories to anything people use. AI serves all sectors, including the supply chain and logistics, in contrast to powering various applications and other digital materials. In reality, many companies have already taken advantage of AI acquisitions. According to the study, artificial intelligence is one of the key areas where businesses, supplier chain and services generate AI investment revenue [9]. With data in supply chains and logistics rising every day, there is an urgent need for innovative processing technology. That is why many businesses, such as machine education, in-depth education and natural linguistic processing, embrace AI-based computer technologies. These strategies facilitate efficient processing of large quantities of data for advanced analysis, the development of a function or event based on the results of the analysis, describing it and performing many other complex parts [18].

An increasing data volume is not the only factor that leads to IA growth. The trend is in fact driven by a number of other main factors, such as computer power and speed, algorithmic advances, and increased access to AI data. The quick production of computers permits companies to use AI in their work, which requires significant developments in power and process performance.

One such innovation was, for example, the development of GPUs that expanded the conventional functions of CPUs. An increasing data volume is not the only factor that leads to IA growth. In fact, the pattern depends on many other significant aspects, including machine strength and speed, computational progress and enhanced access to huge data by the AI system. AI requires large quantities to generate and use multiple data rapidly in the supply chain and logistics companies to show its strength. In recent decades, several new forms of data have arisen and are providing comprehensive machine learning algorithms with a significant amount of juice, which have been used for the best use. In recent years, the data have improved and have allowed for patterns to be detected and connections considered hard to discover by people and conventional technology. Smart algorithms, for example, can provide useful statistics, such as the number of trucks available for distribution in advance, so that consumers can understand the cost and estimated time frames for possible deliveries [2].

Figure 3.1 depicts the AI in the supply chain and logistics market and Figure 3.2 illustrates the growth rate ranking of AI in logistics and supply

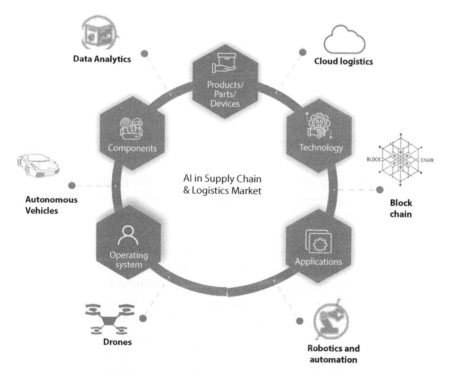

Figure 3.1 AI in supply chain and logistics market.

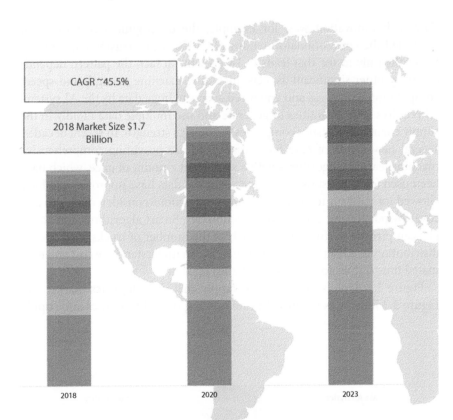

Figure 3.2 Growth rate ranking of AI in logistics and supply chain market ecosystem.

chain markets. With other markets like AI, very few markets have inter-connectivity. Our Interconnectivity module concentrates in depth on the main nodes of heterogeneous markets. Some of our main research areas are data analytics, cloud logistics, blockchain, drones and autonomous vehicle markets. Globally, artificial intelligence is rising at a rapid rate in the logistics and supply chain, so one-third of U.S. employees will need to move positions by 2030 due to the increased use of robotics [12, 16].

Although Amazon is leading the way, other companies are researching and developing robotic-based systems to accelerate operations, including carriers such as FedEx and DHL. One estimate shows that the EU logistics sector will achieve cost savings of between EUR 100 and 300 billion in terms of 10–30% increase in productivity in the European industry. The Chinese company Alibaba invested $248 billion in Asia–Pacific transactions, which are higher than the investment in the supply chain and logistics of Amazon and eBay. China is on a course to overtake the United States as the world's technology leader [5].

The purpose of this review is to provide the reader with available artificial intelligence being tailored for supply chain and logistics. The main contribution of this work is

1. Drawn up with a full foundation of artificial intelligence in the logistics and supply chain.
2. Provided a clear road map theory and impacts of how artificial intelligence has been implemented in supply chain and logistics.

This survey is clearly differentiated from other recent surveys by the above listed points. This gives the details as detailed as previous works. The paper is designed in the following manner: With the complete context analysis on artificial intelligence in the supply chain and logistics during the implementation, Section 3.2 deals with the varying effects and features of AI on the supply chain and logistics.

3.2 Theory—AI in Logistics and Supply Chain Market

3.2.1 AI Impacts

There is already high artificial intelligence and it is still growing. Anything from self-driving vehicles to social media is characterized by the rapid advancement of technology or even by the degree to which machines function as human beings. While business applications, such as IT and machine learning (ML), are still in the new growth stages, they continue to drive business developments. McKinsey & Company expects businesses to benefit from an economic impact of 1.3–2 dollars each year from the use of AI in their supply chains. By 2030 the AI could benefit the global economy nearly $15.7 billion, according to Pricewaterhouse Coopers [6].

Companies' knowledge of the challenges raised by the operation of a global logistics network is an important explanation why AI is being implemented in the supply chain. AI helps businesses to better and more flexibly decide and forecast issues, properly implemented. AI-enabled proactive systems increase service efficiency, achieving customer expectations for shipments that are on-time and undamaged. By automating compliance processing, they further improve efficiency. This results in lower prices and less problems in the logistics network. However, AI's nearly endless skill is most exciting [11].

When combined with related technology, including ML, the Internet of Things (IoT) and predictive analysis, algorithms become more powerful. Additional data entry enables companies to see their global logistics networks more clearly. This is an essential degree of transparency as it recognizes that the way we think about the management of the supply chain and logistics is changed. Companies incur losses on request of stock lags. AI will increase the number of vehicles and will guide them into areas where high demand is anticipated by traders. AI will speed up network production and success with predictive supply to help merchants become more proactive. This lowers running costs [10].

Customer service is being redefined by chatbots. Bots can manage 80% of all consumer engagements, according to Accenture. The partnership between clients and logistics providers can be personalized by AI. A recent example of customer support from DHL is its partnership with Amazon. By triggering the 'competence' of the DHL Parcel with the Alexa App, Alexa customers may order to connect to Amazon Echo or Echo Dot Smart Laundries. Echo clients should contact DHL directly for support from their customer service team in the event of interaction challenges. Intelligent warehouses had more success. A smart warehouse is a fully integrated system in which robotics or software is used for the largest number of workers. This approach simplifies repetitive procedures and reduces the cost of operations. Alibaba and Amazon have already automatically revamped their shops. Amazon has recently created machines automating customer orders for boxing tasks [15].

Genetic algorithms are increased distribution times and cost savings. In the logistics industry, every mile and minute counts. For optimum distribution paths, companies may use a genetic algorithm path planer. UPS uses Orion, a GPS program that allows drivers to deliver on an efficient basis. Routes may be designed and configured in compliance with traffic conditions and other variables. Orion was helping UPS save almost $50 million annually. The new competition standards in supply chain management will be set in the near future by AI. The globally connected logistics companies are handling data in this organized, clever and productive game, conduct business and serve customers, develop quickly and develop new standards [20].

3.2.2   Revolutionizing Global Market

Artificial intelligence is moving ahead in industrial logistics and supply chain management. These fields should undergo a more drastic transformation according to some managers from the transport industry. Continued progress is said to be able to disrupt and accelerate innovation in certain industries in the field of technologies such as artificial intelligence, computer education and related emerging technology. Artificial intelligence comes with computer systems to collect huge amounts of knowledge obtained from logistics and supply chain. Some methods can be used and tested for outcomes that can cause complex tasks and processes.

Investment decisions in artificial intelligence have already benefited several businesses. Approximately 15% have begun using AI, while 31% anticipate it will be in operation in 2019, according to Adobe. Medical research, innovative products, supply chain management and customer support can be the areas in which revenues can be produced. Artificial intelligence is now changing the lives of consumers. In businesses, it is also gaining momentum. Everyone knows that in technology, healthcare and finance, AI is propagating magic [17].

Nonetheless, we did not consider the only organization, which most benefits from the AI logistics and supply chain management. The entire process between the storage and the delivery of goods is controlled by logistics and supply chain management. The process can appear to be quick, but a person working on the field only understands the long logistics and supply chain management processes. There are data hedges throughout the process and many people work to keep it in line with the requirements of customers [3].

3.2.3   Role of AI

The supply chain was used for a while by Artificial Intelligence (AI), but companies need to use their skillful capacities more urgently. A study from Gartner shows that computer technology will possibly double in the next couple of years—while the exploration has only finally started to collect more and more data. With the assistance of AI, something in the logistics chain is difficult to understand. The system will analyze and save the data using formulas to respond, intervene and work accordingly. AI also has the potential to evaluate and learn from past data to enable organizations to use predictive analytics for better recommendations.

Rising automation for instance is one of AI's logistics opportunities. AI-driven, empty factories can be restored, but also forecast when they are running low. Even though not inherently trustworthy. In effect, Carousel is the leading supplier of customer logistics and predicts smart forecasting systems and real worth capabilities as one of the highest growing fields, where the use of artificial intelligence is a significant contributor to efficient data processing, both from real time data gleaned in store stocks and from full visibility [4].

3.2.4   AI Trends in Logistics

In the AI and logistics industry, there are currently two trends: Anticipatory Logistics and Self-Learning Systems [17].

3.2.4.1   Anticipatory Logistics

Predictive logistics are based on massive data-driven learning analytics. This helps logistics specialists to boost their productivity and quality by anticipating the demand of their customers before ordering. A lack of patience for long delivery times is the principal influencer of anticipatory logistics. Customers still want to balance their experience of online shopping with the ease of quick delivery. In this region, all parties involved in the supply line profit from anticipatory logistics by predicting demand, enabling companies to invest their money before demand shoots up.

AI expects consumer demand to grow for the new model, which will then boost the manufacturer's production of that particular model. In the field of risk control, forward-looking strategies even operate well. AI tools predict safety features and potential risks closely linked to the management forecasts of infrastructure. The automotive and transport system utilizes AI technology to repair vehicles and facilities. Predictive maintenance in this case is based on the sensor data obtained from smart machines and vehicles.

In order to evaluate infrastructure conditions and other properties, KONUX, a Munich based IIoT company combines smart sensor systems with an AI based analysis, allowing preventive modeling. One way is to track and examine switches by rail operators. The computer controls the mechanical wear and detects anomalies in time. This avoids the failure of the railway switch.

3.2.4.2   Self-Learning Systems

Machine learning uses massive computer power to classify feature vectors that people never see and develop to become smarter and more accurate in real time with new data. Machine learning and self-learning are very common concepts in industries such as automated pattern recognition, e-discovery and sensor data processing. While machine learning in the logistics sector has been particularly sluggish, other insightful companies have systems for self-learning.

Machine learning uses data from various systems and data sets. The system brings together all data in the logistics context inside the carrier network. The strength of machine learning is the integration of information through different systems and data sets. In order to improve the accuracy of shippers' forecasts of demand, predictive patterns in supply chains, seasonal calendars and daily tracks in lines, we are able to integrate all the information we have inside our carrier network with external sources of data, such as GPS, historical price rates and FMCSA.

When they get more data over time, self-learning logistics systems enhance their algorithms. The device operates by identifying data patterns, analyzing them, and issuing specific reports or behavior. Handwritten text is decoded by common use cases for machine learning and logistics. These self-learning logistics are also commonly used by the post office, as are major shipping companies such as UPS and FedEx.

We use educational approaches in the logistics industry to make faster and better decisions, helping suppliers to boost cost saving, classification, routing and tracking processes for the carriers. Machine learning will assist you to solve an issue that you don't realize has thousands of disparate data points gathered and evaluated. Analytics focused on master learning and self-development will recognize complex attributes such as the environment or traffic over time in order to detect patterns that people may not see.

Intelligent warehouses are a newer advancement of self-learning systems. These systems detect trends and events repeatedly, analyze data over time, connect data to entities, such as deliveries and clients, and initiate pre-pack instructions. Another popular example is AI and robotics which check inventory levels to rearrange and restore as needed. Self-learning over time helps the machine to refine its algorithms for even more detailed responses.

3.2.5   AI Trends in Supply Chain

AI-driven tools are very useful in inventory management with their ability to handle bulk data. These smart systems can easily understand and interpret vast datasets and provide expert service on forecasts of supply and demand. These AI systems can also anticipate and evaluate different consumer tastes with intelligent algorithms and forecast seasonal demand. This development of AI contributes to forecasting future market demand patterns and reduces the cost of overcrowding inventories.

A successful warehouse is one essential part of the distribution chain, and automation helps to recover a warehouse product in a reasonable period and ensures that the customer moves smoothly. AI systems can deal with many warehouse problems quicker and more effectively than any human being can, simplifying complicated procedures and speeding up work. In addition, automation projects powered by AI would greatly reduce the need for and the cost of warehouse jobs, as well as saving valuable time.

AI-base automated tools can provide smarter preparation as well as improved warehouse management that can improve worker and product safety. AI may also assess the perceived seriousness and warn producers of potential threats on the workplace. The system will record and initialize storage requirements along with sufficient input and careful maintenance. This allows producers to respond quickly and decisively so that warehouses are secure and comply with safety requirements.

Automated smart systems will operate from customer service to the factory for a longer time free of errors minimizing the amount of errors at the workplace and accidents. Robots in warehouses have higher speed and precision and higher performance. AI systems can help to reduce manual reliance so that the whole process is simpler, safer and smarter. This allows the customer to perform promptly, according to the undertaking. Automated systems speed up conventional storage processes, removing operational bottlenecks and minimizing effort to meet supply chain distribution goals [7, 8, 12, 13, 15, 21].

3.3 Factors to Propel Business Into the Future Harnessing Automation

3.3.1 Logistics

3.3.1.1 Predictive Capabilities

With AI power, business performance in the areas of route optimization and predictive demand is growing. Businesses will become more proactive with a method that can help planning capability and accurate demand forecasting. If they are confident that the customer is aware of what they want to see, they can easily move vehicles to areas of greater demand and thus reduce running costs. The data helps companies to make the most of their money and to make the best possible use of it, which is made possible by artificial intelligence.

3.3.1.2 Robotics

While robotics is regarded as a future-oriented technological phenomenon, the supply chain is still used. They are used for monitoring, locating and moving inventories in warehouses. These robots are provided with deep learning algorithms, which allow robots to decide independently about the various warehouse processes.

3.3.1.3 Big Data

Big data is easier than ever for logistics companies to boost their potential efficiencies and forecast accurate prospects. In addition to artificial intelligence, this improves the different facets of the supply chain, such as supply chain transparency and track optimization. In the logistics industry the production of clean data is a significant step forward for AI and cannot be introduced without such practical numbers. Since data comes from different sources, measuring output is not easy. Such data cannot be improved at the source level and algorithms are used for data assessment, data quality enhancement, and identification of problems in transparency that can be used for business purposes.

3.3.1.4 Computer Vision

When you transport freight around the world, it is always good to have a pair of eyes and when it comes to advanced technology, this can be easier. Now you can see things differently using computer vision based on artificial logistics intelligence.

3.3.1.5 Autonomous Vehicles

Autonomous vehicles are the next huge concern that the supply chain delivers artificial intelligence. A self-driving vehicle would take some time, but the logistics sector used elevated driving to improve productivity and security. Sub-assisted braking, lane assistance, and transportation autopilot are bound to evolve dramatically in industry. Better driving systems will bring in lower fuel consumption and will rely on assembling several trucks to provide training. Computers regulate and connect such systems. Computers regulate such systems. Such a configuration would greatly save fuel for the trucks.

3.3.2   Supply Chain

3.3.2.1   Bolstering Planning & Scheduling Activities

Supply chain managers typically fail to create an end-to-end process for preparing competitive supply network accounting, particularly in the face of globalization, shifting product portfolios, higher complexity and constant client uncertainty. This task is much more difficult in the absence of full visibility in current product ranges because of unexpected injuries, plant stoppages and transport issues. Multiple goods, replacement parts and essential components are a typical smart supply chain system which is responsible for reliable performance. These goods or components can be identified with many features that take on a number of values in various supply chain industries. This will lead to a large number of product settings and implementations.

3.3.2.2   Intelligent Decision-Making

The app for supply chain management AI-lead amplifies crucial decisions with cognitive forecasts and feedback. In the supply chain, this will help improve overall production. It also has the largest benefit in terms of time, expense and revenue with possible effects across various scenarios. Even as relative circumstances change, it continuously builds on these recommendations by continually learning over time.

3.3.2.3   End-End Visibility

For the manufacturers to achieve optimum visibility of the whole supply value chain, with a minimum effort, the dynamic supply chains network currently exists. A single virtualized data layer offers an integrated cognitive AI-driven platform to reveal cause and effect, reduce bottleneck activities, and select process improvements. Instead of historical data that is outdated, all of this uses real time data.

3.3.2.4   Actionable Analytical Insights

Today, many institutions lack critical intelligence to drive fast decisions with pace and agility that exceed expectations. Cognitive automation with the power of AI is able to see patterns and calculate tradeoffs on a much better scale than traditional systems with vast quantities of distributed knowledge.

3.3.2.5   Inventory and Demand Management

The management of optimal stock prices to prevent 'stock-out problems' is a major problem faced by supply chain companies. At the same time, surplus inventory contributes to high expenditure costs, which do not contribute to the production of contract revenue. By enhancing the product art and storage costs the right balance is established here. AI & ML concepts are highly detailed predictions based on potential demand and used for consumer transactions. When used. For instance, the decline and end of life of a product on a distribution channel are easy to predict correctly along with the creation of the launch of a new product on the market.

3.3.2.6   Boosting Operational Efficiencies

As well as the wealth of differentiated data system silos in most businesses, IoT-enabled physical sensors across supply chains now provide a golden mine of knowledge for tracking and manipulating supply chain planning processes as well. Analysis of this golden pot manually using billions of sensors and software will result in massive waste of operating resources and delayed production cycles. Intelligent AI-driven analytics have tremendous value in the supply chain and logistics. As supply chain components become the principal nodes for placing data and algorithms for driving machines, innovative efficiencies can be achieved.

AI systems are typically cloud based and need a constant server bandwidth. Often operators need specialized hardware to achieve this AI capability, and a significant initial investment is required for several supply chain partners in this intelligence hardware. The problem here is that most AI and cloud-based systems are very flexible and need to be more successful in the real opening users/systems stage. Since every AI system is unique and distinct, it has to be addressed in detail with its supply chain partners. As any other approach to digital technology, training is another factor that takes considerable time and money commitment. Business efficiency will be impacted because supply chain suppliers will need to work with AI supplier to create a training solution which is cost-effective and effective during the integration procedure.

3.4   Conclusion

More and more sectors and realms of our lives are being conquered by artificial intelligence and machine learning, and logistics is no exception.

In the supply chain sector, AI and logistics machine learning can be an excellent aid. Using them, systems can be streamlined, errors that humans can create or miss can be avoided, potential possibilities and problems can be anticipated. In terms of global supply chain and logistics, Artificial Intelligence is becoming highly explosive. Many logistics officials agree that a significant transition is likely to occur in these regions. It can interrupt the ongoing development of advanced and digital technologies such as machine learning, artificial intelligence, processing of natural languages (NLP), etc. and encourage progress in these sectors. Therefore, this study provides a complete theory behind logistics and supply chain in terms of impacts and trends and describes briefly about how logistics and supply chain can propel the business into the future—harnessing automation.

References

1. https://www.europeanbusinessreview.com/artificial-intelligence-ai-in-supply-chain-planning-the-future-is-here-now/
2. https://supplychainbeyond.com/6-ways-ai-is-impacting-the-supply-chain/
3. https://www.tristatetechnology.com/blog/how-ai-can-transform-the-logistics-and-supply-chain-management-industry/
4. Abdullayeva, A., Impact of artificial intelligence on agricultural, healthcare and logistics industries. *Ann. Spiru Haret Univ. Econom. Ser.*, 19, 167–175, 2019.
5. Baryannis, G., Validi, S., Dani, S., Antoniou, G., Supply Chain Risk Management and Artificial Intelligence: State of the Art and Future Research Directions. *Int. J. Prod. Res.*, 57, 2179–2202, 2018.
6. Devi, N. and Paul, V.M.T., Artificial Intelligence: Pertinence in Supply Chain and Logistics Management. *Xi'an Jianzhu Keji Daxue Xuebao/J. Xi'an Univ. Archit. Technol.*, 12, 701–709, 2020.
7. Gunasekaran, A. and Ngai, E., Expert systems and artificial intelligence in the 21st century logistics and supply chain management. *Expert Syst. Appl.*, 41, 1–4, 2014.
8. Hellingrath, B. and Lechtenberg, S., *Applications of Artificial Intelligence in Supply Chain Management and Logistics: Focusing Onto Recognition for Supply Chain Execution: Bridging the Gap Between Information Systems Research and Practice*, Springer, 2019. https://citations.springernature.com/item?doi=10.1007/978-3-030-06234-7_27
9. Kar, U., Dash, R., McMurtrey, M., Rebman, C., Application of Artificial Intelligence in Automation of Supply Chain Management. *J. Strategic Innov. Sustainability*, 14, 43–53, 2019.
10. Kowalski, M., Zelewski, Bergenrodt, D., Klüpfel, H., Application of New Techniques of Artificial Intelligence in Logistics, pp. 323–328, European simulation and modelling conference, 2012.

11. Klumpp, M., Automation and artificial intelligence in business logistics systems: Human reactions and collaboration requirements. *Int. J. Logist.*, 21, 224–242, 2017, https://doi.org/10.1080/13675567.2017.1384451
12. Klumpp, M., *Artificial Intelligence Applications*, Springer, 2019.
13. Makkar, S., Naga Rama Devi, G., Solanki, V., Applications of Machine Learning Techniques in Supply Chain Optimization, in: *ICICCT 2019 – System Reliability, Quality Control, Safety, Maintenance and Management*, pp. 861–869, Springer, 2020.
14. Min, H., Artificial intelligence in supply chain management: Theory and applications. *Int. J. Logist.-Res. Appl.*, 13, 13–39, 2010.
15. Ruamsook, K. and Tracey, S., Jr, C., *Supply Chain Management in the Age of AI Revolution*, 2019.
16. Shanmugam, B., Palaniswami, V.-R., Venkatesh, R.S., Strategies for Privacy Preserving Publishing of Functionally Dependent Sensitive Data: A State-of-the-Art Survey. *Aust. J. Basic Appl. Sci.*, 8, 5, 353–365, 2014.
17. Thamer, H., Börold, A., Benggolo, A., Freitag, M., Artificial intelligence in warehouse automation for flexible material handling, in: *9th International Scientific Symposium on Logistics in Magdeburg (June 13-14, 2018)*, pp. 143–149, BVL, Bremen, 2018.
18. Thành Long, N., Artificial Intelligent (AI) and the Future of supply chain, Opulence, 2, 1, 1–44, 2018.
19. Toorajipour, R., Sohrabpour, V., Nazarpour, A., Oghazi, P., Fischl, M., Artificial intelligence in supply chain management: A systematic literature review. *J. Bus. Res.*, 122, 502–517, 2020.
20. Xing, B., Gao, W.-J., Battle, K., Marwala, T., Nelwamondo, F., Artificial Intelligence in Reverse Supply Chain Management: The State of the Art, 2010. https://arxiv.org/abs/1012.4046
21. Zhang, Y., The application of artificial intelligence in logistics and express delivery. *J. Phys.: Conf. Ser.*, 1325, 012085, 2019.

An Empirical Study of Crop Yield Prediction Using Reinforcement Learning

M. P. Vaishnnave[1]* and R. Manivannan[2]

[1]Dept of IT, University College of Engineering Villupuram, Villpuram, India
[2]Dept of CSE, Meenakshi Ramaswamy Engineering College, Ariyalur, India

Abstract

In the world economy, agriculture plays a vital role. Stresses on the agriculture system will increase as the human population continues to expand. With the advancement of modern research fields, agritechnology and accurate farming, which are also referred to as digital agriculture, employ data-intensive approaches to stimulate agricultural production, minimizing its environmental impact. Reinforcement Learning (RL) has grown with large data technologies and high-performance computing to build new possibilities to activate, calculate and recognize. In the agricultural crop forecast, we will present a comprehensive review. There are also several related papers which highlight the main features of popular RL models.

Keywords: Agriculture, crop prediction, deep learning, machine learning, reinforcement learning

4.1 Introduction

The science of training machines is commonly used, and not for anything to learn and create models for future predictions. In the global economy, farming plays a crucial role. As the human population continues to develop, recognizing global crop yields is central to addressing the challenges of food security and reducing the impacts of climate change. A significant agricultural issue is crop yield prediction. Agricultural yield varies based

---

*Corresponding author: vaishnnave03@gmail.com

R. Kanthavel, K. Ananthajothi, S. Balamurugan and R. Karthik Ganesh (eds.) *Artificial Intelligent Techniques for Wireless Communication and Networking*, (47–58) © 2022 Scrivener Publishing LLC

on climatic conditions, pesticides (rain, temperature, etc.). For making decisions associated with agricultural risk management and future forecasts, accurate information on crop yield history is critical [2].

In order to maintain precise import and export evaluations, politicians rely on sound forecasts to improve national food security. In order to create good varieties, crop companies must anticipate the achievement of new hybrids in different conditions. A return forecast is also used to inform the farmers' operational and financial decisions. However, because of multiple significant variables, the prediction of crop production is very difficult [12].

More specifically, reinforcement learning methods, including multiple regressions, random forest, association rule, and convolutional neural networks, have been introduced for crop yield prediction. The performance (crop yield) as an inferred function of the input variables (genes and environmental elements), which could be a strongly anti and complex function, is a crucial aspect of machine learning models. In addition, reinforcement learning is analogous to an umbrella that has different methods and methodologies that are meaningful. We will see the use of artificial and deep neural networks through studying the most popular models in agriculture [7].

Crop yield is a massively complicated characteristic determined by a number of factors, including genotype, climate and interactions. Current yield prediction requires a basic understanding of the working relationship between yields and immersive factors and requires both thorough datasets and powerful algorithms to expose such a relationship. But the prediction of crop yields is extremely difficult because of many complex factors. For example, high-dimensional marker data, which contains thousands to millions of manufacturers for each plant, usually represents genotype information. It is essential to quantify the effects of genetic marks, which may be linked to several forecast and field business strategies.

Deep learning assesses results from various raw data arrangements. In deep learning, for example, a probable strategy can be developed by integrating a decade of elderly data and providing insight into crop productivity under various climatic conditions in advanced automation and incremental artificial intellectual technology called deep reinforcement learning. Smart decision-making in various fields is profound, such as a comprehensive convergence of reinforcement approaches to neural networking, the management of energy, robotics, healthcare, intelligent grid, cognitive science, computer vision, natural language processing, emotional analysis, etc. This model has helped to overcome a number of complex decisions which had previously been beyond the limitations of the machine. This is a persuasive model for smart agricultural frameworks growth [1, 10].

A deep successor infrastructure, a multi-agent deepened learning, and a deep Q-network are standard models for deep improvement learning. RL implementations in the crop field have been sub-categories that include yield prediction, disease identifications, crop weed detection efficiency and organism recognition. One of the key issues in agriculture precision, yield predicting, yield estimate, matching crop offer with demand and crop management to boost productivity, is highly important [9].

The present works are organised as follows: in Section 4.2, the RL terminology, description, learning tasks in agriculture are first defined. Section 4.3 explains the effect of enhancement learning on farming and crop management applications. Finally, Section 4.4 concludes the benefits of incorporating RL in crown forecasts as well as potential aspirations in the sector.

4.2 An Overview of Reinforcement Learning in Agriculture

4.2.1 Reinforcement Terminology and Definitions

Reinforcement Learning (RL) is a method of machine learning software that provides an agent to learn from his/her own events and behaviors in an immersive experience thru the trial and error. Although supervised and enhanced learning uses input/output mapping, improved education uses incentives and sanction as metrics of positive and negative behaviour, as compared to supervised formation, when an agent has received feedback to carry out a task [5]. Reinforcement learning is the training in a wide

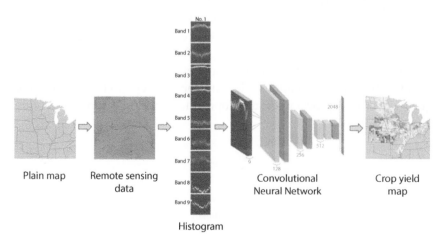

Figure 4.1 General neural network framework for crop yield analysis [7].

range of machine-learning models. In uncertain, conceivably complex conditions, the agent is able to achieve a target. The most accurate method to imply the naivety of the method by search power and multiple tests is perhaps strengthening.

- Environment: physical world of the agent
- State: Agent's present situation
- Reward: Environmental feedback
- Policy: Method for mapping the state of agents to actions
- Value: Future prize an agent receives through action in a specific state.

In comparison to unsupervised learning, improving learning is distinct in terms of aspirations. Since the goal is to recognize similitudes and varying data points in unexpected learning, the objective is to find an appropriate behavioural model to optimize the agent's cumulative overall benefit [4]. Figure 4.1 illustrates the basic principle of a reinforcement learning model.

4.2.2   Review on Agricultural Reinforcement Learning

In a way good farming includes making complicated decisions based on the interrelationships of a multitude of factors, including requirements of crops, soil quality, climate change, and more. Farming techniques have historically been added to the current sector or its part at best. Agricultural enhancement learning enables farmers to handle plants and animals almost separately, thereby significantly improving their farmers' choices' efficiency. On a specific day, successful harvesting results in the identification of the most effective acres and crops (Figure 4.2).

Today's technology for yield prediction does not base policy solely on historical data, but also utilizes software for computer vision correlated with smart weather analysis to meet the ever-growing demand for agriculture. RL has a tremendous effect on the efficacy of classification and quality of crops, agrochemical development, identification and prevention of diseases [8].

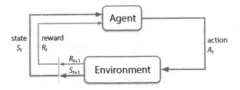

Figure 4.2 Reinforcement learning [5].

Even knowledgeable farmers have a difficult time separating two very similar plants because they are differentiated in many cases by only small differences in color or form. Image processing greatly increases the precision and speed of the identification of animals, which also saves time and money for farmers. By evaluating the leaf vein map containing the decisive detail, RL algorithms can precisely detect a specific plant type. A very resource-intensive and time-consuming method is breeding for the desired characteristics in crops, which drives much value in the agricultural economy, however. Presently, the world's smartest people are researching different RL applications in normative plant breeding and AI experts to make their choices more educated (Figure 4.3).

Agrochemical goods reached the mass market decades ago and revolutionized farming. Eventually, different chemical products, including pesticides, antioxidants, and antimicrobials, made it possible for farmers to fight the havoc of harmful insects and bacteria. However there is a negative effect on the atmosphere and human health by reducing crop losses with the aid of these chemicals. These chemicals can be made much less toxic and more environmentally friendly by RL.

The wide range of soil features, including humidity, temperature, and levels of nitrogen, play a significant role in the well-being of crops.

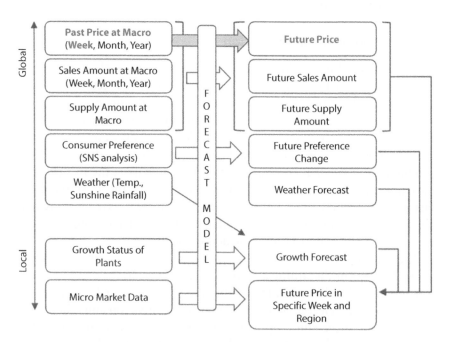

Figure 4.3 Time series forecast of agricultural reinforcement learning [8].

Conventionally, farmers distribute equal quantities per square meter of pesticides. Such a wasteful use of energy not only greatly affects the financial planning of growers, but also tampers with flora and fauna, lowering the amount of species of pollinators. The levels of soil erosion and medical problems in specific cultivations in confluence with software for image analysis can be analyzed using RL tools. The information gathered is then used to evaluate the specific regions in the field, improve agricultural to use pesticides concisely where necessary. Worldwide, such customization of care can have a significant impact on the environment.

There are major obstacles on the road to the wide adoption of reinforcement learning, despite agriculture being a rather data-centric industry. The first complexity layer lies in the location-based variation of circumstances. Although the AI hysteria is obviously over, the technology is still nascent. The importance of smart automation, however, is commonly recognized across several vertical components. Perhaps more significantly, RL is set to become an accomplice of more efficient use of natural resources behind the scenes and an immense contributor to a better world.

4.3 Reinforcement Learning Startups for Crop Prediction

4.3.1 Need for Crop Prediction

Assessing agricultural yield before harvesting is a crucial subject in agriculture, because variations in crop yield from year to year affect international industry, food supply, and world market prices. Predicting agricultural yield before harvesting is an important issue. Also, early crop yield prediction provides policy planners with valuable knowledge. For the effective designs of land use and economic policy, appropriate prediction of crop productivity is needed. Forecasts of crop productivity at the in-field level have improved in recent times. Climate conditions are the most important factor in crop productivity. If the weather-based forecast is made more reliable, it is possible to warn farmers well in advance so that the big losses can be mitigated and support economic development.

The forecast would also help farmers make choices, such as selecting alternate crops or discarding a crop at an early stage in the event of a critical situation. Furthermore, forecasting crop yield will make it easier for farmers to have a clearer view of seasonal crop cultivation and scheduling. Therefore for successful crop management and expected outcomes, it is important to simulate and predict the crop yield before cultivation. Since there is a non-linear relationship between crop yield and crop variables, reinforcement learning techniques may be useful for predictions of yield.

4.3.2   Reinforcement Learning Impacts on Agriculture

Agri Information Management System
Many environmental factors such as temperature, groundwater sources, and soil health, depend on agricultural productivity. Also in neighboring fields or often, in various areas of the same field, these cause yield variations. By integrating remote sensing with RL, precision agriculture aims to minimize this uncertainty. In order to provide farmers with transparent and timely services, the Agricultural Information Management System (AIMS) was initiated. The system provides farmers with online facilities to implement different schemes and services.

Livestock Monitoring
In the poultry industry, animal health depends on the care of specific chickens on a farm. It mitigates such ethical issues, improves wellbeing in the group, and enhances yield. An uphill challenge, however, is round-the-clock manual supervision of all chicken. Appealing solutions are reinforcement learning algorithms that analyse camera feeds to track all birds. In ability to forecast the performance of chicken from previous results and historical data, the framework uses reinforcement learning networks and predictive analytics, while also allowing better breeding plans to enhance poultry efficiency.

Climate Recipes
Distinctions in their growth and yield are caused by variability between different plants of the same crop. Growing them minimizes this variability in regulated environments. For large tracts of land, however it is not a feasible solution. The constraints of space and uncertainty respectively are tackled by vertical farming and environment recipes. A climate recipe is a collection of atmospheric conditions that allow the plants to produce the desired result. The reinforcement learning-based monitoring system enables growers in controlled growth environments to build inexpensive climate recipes.

Intelligent Spot Spraying System
In agriculture, farmers use herbicides to eliminate weed growth. Their unregulated use, however, has a major impact on the environment and contributes to the growth of herbicide-resistance among weeds. Solutions

that replace more accurate use of carpet spraying of herbicides minimize costs and alleviate unintended effects resulting from their overuse. In the 1990s a great deal of pioneering work was done in that area at the Silsoe Research Institute in Great Britain. The study examined the use of GPS for mapping species of weeds that generally grow in clumps or patches. Spot spraying is no more a distant ambition for research than a reality for individual weeds. Commercial systems for conventional sprayers and future generation of autonomous weed control robots are now also available.

Image-Based Anomaly Detection
A lot of crops annually are destroyed by plant diseases such as blight and gall. In leaves, signs of such diseases are often first detected as spots or lesions. The large variety of leaves, though, makes general techniques for detection impractical. Reinforcement learning algorithms solve this obstacle and by scanning leaves, detect crop diseases. The algorithms identify early-stage diseases and therefore reduce the expense of using pesticides. Compared to high-position work such as roping, automatic drone blade inspection requires less work and a dramatic reduction of inspection time. The images recorded are also useful for different purposes in the long term. But it still depends on the visual inspection of the images by trained experts to determine whether the image shows evidence of damage.

4.3.3   Deep Q Networks for Crop Prediction

Deep Q-networks are advanced learning agents using Deep Neural Networks (DNN) to map state-to-state relations and Q–Q table-like behavior. The DNNs like Convolution Neural Networks (CNN), Recurrent Neural Network (RNN) and Sparse Auto-Encoder may specifically train the abstract representation of the raw data of the sensor. A DQN agent communicates with the environment, similar to the Q-Learning agent task, through a collection of observations, behavior and incentives. Strengthened learning is a widely-designed method of learning, for example in fields like operations analysis, game theory, multifunctional systems and signal processing [6].

In order to assess the crop output in the regions concerned, this controlled learning crop yield predicting method has to include crop yield data and associated costs. The overall benefit for the learning effectiveness of yield prediction agents is estimated by the RL methods. This gives agents unstable feedback to adapt their results together with supervised learning techniques. In other words, the inputs would not allow the agents to identify which samples are not adequately studied during the learning process.

This forces the agent to be more productive by showing the profound contrasts between crop yield characteristics [3].

The ROPS is focused on input parameters that turn the supervised study process into a reinforced learning process, to recognize the DRL-based ROP [11]. The condition can be calculated as an output prediction game. Each game includes a few parametric changes and thresholds which promote crop development and a collection of samples and labels is included in each variation. The parameter values of the Crop Return are determined by acting to receive the awards at playback.

Deep learning models are widely used for the extraction of signed cultivation features. Although these methods might solve the problem of the yield prediction, the following insufficiencies exist: The performance of such models depends heavily on the quality of the extracted properties and is unable to create a direct non-linear or linear modeling between raw data and crop output value. Deep enhanced learning guides and stimulates the previously mentioned shortcomings. Combining intelligence of enhanced education and deep learning, which can map raw information on crop prediction values, creates a comprehensive crop yield prediction framework. Deep Recurrent Q-Network model, the in-depth study algorithm used to estimate crop yields for recurrent neural networks by the Q-Learning algorithm (Figure 4.4) and (Figure 4.5). The data parameters are used to supply the sequentially stacked Recurrent Neural network layers. The Q-learning network constructs an ecosystem based on the input criteria for crop yield prediction.

A linear layer maps output Q values from the Recurrent Neural Network. A parametric integration with the threshold helps to predict crop yield includes the reinforcement learning agent. Finally, for the measures carried out, the agent gets an added value by minimizing the error and optimizing its forecast accuracy. In order to create new chances for identifier, evaluating and recognizing broad data procedures for the agricultural frameworks, deepening education has developed in addition to enormous increase of data and improved persistence measures. Certain key factors in structuring the deep enhancement training models need to be analyzed:

- Comprehension of patterns and basic structures from the limited sample area.
- To consistently take dynamic measures, the framework needs to be performed appropriately.

Deep Q-network is a state-of-the-art learning device that uses a Deep Neural Network (DNN) to map links between states and actions similar to a Q-Table. DNNs such as the Convolution Neural Network (CNN),

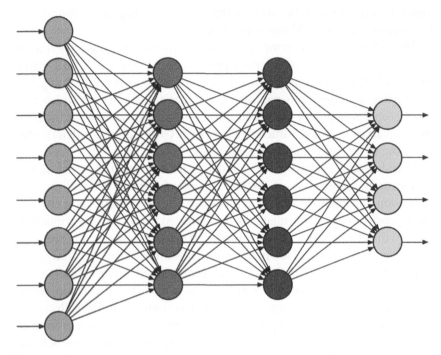

Figure 4.4 Deep Q Networks in RL [13].

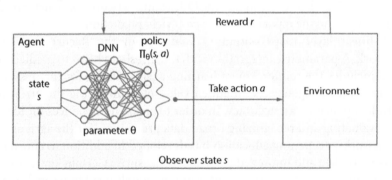

Figure 4.5 Deep Q Network for crop prediction [11].

Recurrent Neural Network (RNN), and sparse automotive encoder can directly learn the abstract representations of raw data from the sensors. With actual improvements like Q-learning, it can be discriminated against and analyzed to predict crop yield because of the limited ability of such methods to describe the countries. The proposed method is used to predict crop output through the recurring neural network DNN, inspired by DQN, by various parameters of environmental and soil water. The repetitive neural network, DNN, is used in the proposed process to predict crop production using different environmental and soil water parameters, inspired by DQN's concept of high data processing.

An important part of the model development process is model accuracy evaluation. It identifies the optimal model in future timestamps for data representation and model performance. Precision refers to the prediction ratio predicted by the model precisely. Accuracy re-sets the closeness to the current or true value of the forecast value. One of the major drawbacks is the fact that the approach process is limited to a slow and inefficient bottom-up process. In the assessed error measures the DR QN reported the smallest possible error and nearly maintained the original data distribution.

4.4 Conclusion

Analysis of all of the above points concludes that one of the most important subjects for precision agriculture is yield prediction, yield estimation and the matching of crop demand supply and crop management to increase productivity. The prediction of yields is one of the key and most common subjects in precision agriculture, as it explains yield mapping and projections, crop demand matching supply and crop management. The cutting-edge approaches have greatly surpassed the fundamental historic data-driven forecasts. The application of computational vision technology involves on-the-go data and comprehensive multidimensional crop analysis, climate and economic conditions in order to take advantage of farmer and population returns. Price of products shall be increased and waste will be reduced by precise identification and classifying crop quality characteristics. Compared with experts from the human field, machines can reveal and recognize new qualities that have an overall role in crop quality using seemingly unrelated information and inter-connections.

In both outdoor and greenhouse environments, the most used method for pest and disease control is to spray pesticides evenly over the crop area. In order to succeed, this approach calls for vast amounts of pesticides and results in high environmental and financial costs. The RL is used in general precise agriculture management, which focuses on the input of agrochemicals, time, place and plants affected. Weeds are the main threat to crop production, apart from pests. The biggest challenge in fighting weeds is that crops are difficult to detect and discriminate against. Computer vision and RL algorithms can improve cost-effective weed detection and discrimination, without environmental challenges. This will drive robots in the future to kill weeds, reducing the need for herbicides.

References

1. Balamurugan, S., Divyabharathi, N., Jayashruthi, K., Bowiya, M., Shermy, R.P., Shanker, R., Internet of agriculture: Applying IoT to improve food and farming technology. *Int. Res. J. Eng. Technol. (IRJET)*, 3, 10, 713–719, 2016.
2. Chaudhary, K. and Kausar, F., Prediction of Crop Yield Using Machine Learning. *Int. J. Eng. Appl. Sci. Technol.*, 04, 153–156, 2020, 10.33564/IJEAST.2020.v04i09.019.
3. Champaneri, M., Chachpara, D., Chandvidkar, C., Rathod, M., Crop Yield Prediction Using Machine Learning. *Int. J. Sci. Res. (IJSR)*, 9, 4, 645–648, 2020.
4. Chlingaryan, A., Sukkarieh, S., Whelan, B., Machine learning approaches for crop yield prediction and nitrogen status estimation in precision agriculture: A review. *Comput. Electron. Agric.*, 151, 61–69, 2018, 10.1016/j.compag.2018.05.012.
5. Crane-Droesch, A., Machine learning methods for crop yield prediction and climate change impact assessment in agriculture. *Environ. Res. Lett.*, 12, 1–39, 2018, 10.1088/1748-9326/aae159.
6. Elavarasan, D. and Vincent, P.M.D., Crop Yield Prediction Using Deep Reinforcement Learning Model for Sustainable Agrarian Applications. *IEEE Access*, 8, 86886–86901, 2020, 10.1109/ACCESS.2020.2992480.
7. Fegade, T. and Pawar, B., 2019, Crop Prediction Using Artificial Neural Network and Support Vector Machine. *Data Manage. Analytics Innov.*, 311–324, 10.1007/978-981-13-9364-8_23.
8. Klompenburg, T., Kassahun, A., Catal, C., Crop yield prediction using machine learning: A systematic literature review. *Comput. Electron. Agric.*, 177, 105709, 10.1016/ j.compag.2020.105709, 2020.
9. Mahendra, N., Crop Prediction using Machine Learning Approaches. *Int. J. Eng. Tech. Res.*, 9, 08, 23–26, 2020, 10.17577/ IJERT V 9IS080029.
10. Sanjudharan, M.S.M., Dharrsan, V., Immanuel, C., Crop Yield Prediction Using Machine Learning. *Adalya J.*, 9, 4, 98–102, 2020, 10.37896/aj9.4/012.
11. Selvanayagam, T., Palendrarajah, P., Manogarathash, M., Gamage, A., Kasthurirathna, D., Agro-Genius: Crop Prediction Using Machine Learning, 4, 10, 243–249, 2019.
12. Sriram, K., A Survey on Crop Prediction using Machine Learning Approach. *Int. J. Res. Appl. Sci. Eng. Technol.*, 7, 3231–3234, 2019, 10.22214/ijraset.2019.4542.
13. Vaishnnave, M.P., Suganya Devi, K., Ganeshkumar, P., Automatic method for classification of groundnut diseases using deep convolutional neural network. *Soft Comput.*, 24, 21, 16347–16360, 2020.

5

Cost Optimization for Inventory Management in Blockchain and Cloud

C. Govindasamy[1*], A. Antonidoss[1†] and A. Pandiaraj[2‡]

[1]Department of Computer Science and Engineering, Hindustan Institute of Technology & Science, Chennai, India
[2]Department of Information Science and Engineering, Bannari Amman Institute of Technology, Sathyamangalam, India

Abstract

Excess stocks, poor service reliability, poor performance metrics, lack of stock, inadequate knowledge of trends in market and difficulty interpreting. In other words, all the problems of stock management and all the obstacles which limit the organization's competitiveness. It should be correctly, efficiently and accurately managed, because inventory is probably one of the most critical parts of any enterprise. So, blockchain is a distributed ledger that can be used in inventory management that stores digital documents or event records in a way that makes them tamper-resistant. While blockchain was not initially developed to improve and optimize inventory control for warehouses, the system is adept at each of these tasks. With such transparency, producers are better able to handle product sources, traceability, future recalls and peri-records. Warehouse inventory management can forecast demand effectively with blockchain and thus always have the appropriate quality and amount of inventory needed to meet expected demand. Blockchain Inventory management provides a live, commercial version of an energy exchange solution that will expose substantial cost savings for many areas. This chapter explores some of the most prominent bases of blockchain for inventory management for blockchain and cost optimization methods for inventory management in cloud.

*Corresponding author: cgovindcs@gmail.com
†Corresponding author: aro.antoni@gmail.com
‡Corresponding author: pandiaraja@bitsathy.ac.in

R. Kanthavel, K. Ananthajothi, S. Balamurugan and R. Karthik Ganesh (eds.) Artificial Intelligent Techniques for Wireless Communication and Networking, (59–74) © 2022 Scrivener Publishing LLC

Keywords: Blockchain, cloud computing, cost optimization, inventory management, warehouse

5.1   Introduction

Inventory is an unused resource that has value and is available. Men, resources, materials, plant acquisition, spares and others may be stocked to meet potential demand. It is also possible to describe inventory as a stock of products kept for potential use or sale. As it better serves our contextual interpretation, we embrace the above as a formal description of inventory [8]. To ensure the uninterrupted supply of materials and the maintenance of optimum stock, inventory management is essential. Different organizational styles have different criteria for inventory. Manufacturers, hospitals, financial institutions, colleges and a number of others are among these organizations. Their stock is bought in the form of raw materials or finished products [6].

To maintain effective controls over unused or used materials, there are a range of monitoring methods used over time. These control measures include ABC (Always Better Control) analysis, VED (Vital Critical Desirable) analysis, FSN (Fast, Slow Moving and Non-Moving) analysis, SDE (Scarce, Difficult, Easy) and HML (High, Medium, Low) analysis for the rating of the value of consumption and stock units [9]. The primary purpose of inventory management is to reconcile the contradictory economics of not having to keep too much inventory. Thus, money must be tied up and expenses incurred, such as stock, spoilage, pilferage and obsolescence. Where and where necessary (quality and quantity wise), the incentive to make products or commodities available becomes imperative in order to avoid the expense of not fulfilling those requirements [21].

The role of inventory as a hedge against uncertainty has been recognized for a long time. More specifically, however, the disadvantages of retaining inventory have been widely acknowledged, particularly with regard to the adverse impact this can have on the supply chain's resilience. According to conventional inventory management theory, economic complexity has also tended to result in prolonged supply lead times, leading to increased inventory levels to offer the same quality of service. In lean supply chain thinking, inventory is considered one of the earliest "wastes" and is thus regarded as something that should be reduced as much as possible [7].

Similarly, inventory is managed in agile supply chains at a few stages, with goods moving rapidly through supply chains so that companies can respond quickly to changes in customer demand. There have been distinct supply chain formulae based on these concepts and most stress the need for inventory reduction under each of the categories. There are two significant costs associated with inventory when solving the cost dilemma that is fundamental to inventory management: cost of procurement and cost of shipping [19].

The annual cost of procurement varies according to the number of orders. This means that if the item is procured often in small lots, the procurement cost would be high. The annual cost of procurement is directly proportional to the quantity of inventory. If the quantity ordered per order is minimal, the inventory carrying cost decreases. The two expenses are diametrically opposed to each other. One that strikes a balance between the two costs of opposition is the right quantity to be ordered. This sum is classified as Economic Order Quantity (EOQ). If a company does not have a strong inventory system, with any kind of precision, it would not be able to predict demands, and this might cause them to run out of stock every so often [13].

In Figure 5.1 for both supply chain and inventory distribution, blockchain is basically a game changer as it offers improved security, enhanced accountability and untraceability, which is actually seriously lacking in inventory management systems. That said, it is still uncertain if the system is primarily implemented or not, and there is insufficient case for realistic use of a blockchain, however correct, one thing is very evident; it is a groundbreaking

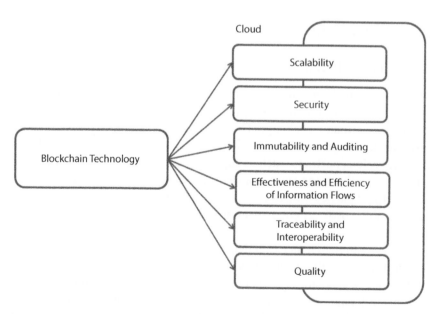

Figure 5.1 Blockchain based inventory management in cloud.

phenomenon, which has recently become the region's topic [20]. Many supply chain organizations face difficulties in delegating the right to buy products on their behalf to other entities. However, blockchains make this complicated process incredibly easy because their digital ledger is continually updated. In blockchain inventory management, blockchain technology has the ability to have many cost-saving advantages [4].

The purpose of this review is to provide the reader with available cost optimization methods of blockchain inventory management. The main contribution of this work is

1. Section 5.1 originated with a complete groundwork of inventory management and importance of block chain in inventory management.
2. Section 5.2 provided a clear road map of current problems faced by inventory management and how blockchain is applied for proactive inventory management.
3. Section 5.3 describes the list of cost optimization methods for blockchain inventory management in cloud.

This survey is clearly differentiated from other recent surveys by the above listed points.

5.2   Blockchain: The Future of Inventory Management

5.2.1   Issues Faced in Inventory Management

The current stock management is based on the approach of supply-and-demand. In controlling their supply chain network with this strategy, companies face a major challenge. Down the supply chain, there is a lack of visibility that hinders customer demand assessment. Such supply chains include various partners, such as suppliers, distribution centers, and retail partners. For the management of transactions and the movement of goods, each of these parties utilizes their own methods and systems. This method is incredibly costly, as enterprises are still a step behind the needs of the consumer [5].

There is often a chance of a delay in meeting the demands of the consumer, leading to financial losses. Companies will face difficulties if they understock or overstock goods while predicting consumer trends. Even if any misunderstanding or mistake happens in the supply chain system, a lot of time and human capital are lost. Manipulation of data and unethical practices followed by staff is also a serious problem faced by businesses. In a unified, fixed, transparent, and decentralized record, Blockchain helps link all the parties involved. It helps minimize inconsistencies and helps businesses stay ahead of the curve [14].

5.2.2   Inventory Management Scenario

Inventory management is an essential part of reactive manufacturing process and regeneration for most consumer packaged goods manufacturers. They witness an increase in rivalry and a rising demands. An item is sold and more items are manufactured in the online shops and centers for brick and mortar stocks. Highlights the risks of measuring and meeting swinging demand, many are reluctant to continue to live on this reactive model [17].

In Figure 5.2 a reactive model creates supply and demand disparities that can take a number of forms.

- One item may have been famous, although by the time a company is ready to recover, businesses may have gone over to the next big thing already. The network's surplus inventory contributes to costly maintenance costs for businesses.
- We still have to wonder what the surplus inventory is all about. Are we marketing massive markdowns? Should we move them to shops, suppliers or other secondary outlets for surplus supplies?
- A business can subproject demand and not produce sufficient goods. They must rush to have enough resupply as

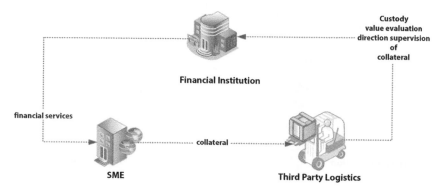

Figure 5.2 Inventory financing scenario.

disappointed customers are eventually struggling to get out of stock because of lack of sales.

The reason businesses are forced to conform to a reactive design is the disconnection between their supply chains upstream and downstream. After all, the majority deal with a dynamic, massive structure involving a variety of vendors, factories, retail outlets and suppliers, each using its own transaction management procedures and transporting goods. The full data silos indicate that producers do not expect demand at the consumption level so that quality standards cannot be prepared [10, 16].

There is now another method, which links various parties with a shared, always record of all interactions in the value chain. It is a revolutionary, modern solution which has shaken many market circles already: the blockchain.

5.2.3   A Primer on Blockchain Technology

Blockchain was created in 2009 by Satoshi Nakamoto, Bitcoin's founder. He planned to create a digital public directory to monitor the Bitcoins exchange. Any transfer is stored in cryptographic "blocks" which is the name of the technology. In Figure 5.3 any transaction is transparent to all network entities and no one can change a record without the permission of others. This level of transparency encourages trust, transparency and collaboration among all Blockchain-related people. The information is often

Figure 5.3 Blockchain example.

released in real-time and helps make key business decisions, which is why it is increasingly common in various industries [23].

A movie studio, for instance, may use Blockchain to regulate proprietary content delivery and rights in entertainment. Both sales and licensing deals may be tracked and processed, ensuring that content is lawfully used and piracy is prevented. In healthcare, system enables for the proper store and exchange of medical records. Blockchain is able to digitize and store patient data in a centralized web, accessible by licensed providers only, in place for putting patient information in compartmentalized data or physical file cabinets at risk of loss or theft [22].

5.2.4 Blockchain for Proactive Inventory Management

How can Blockchain deal with the problems of a fragmented supply chain and boost inventory management? Blockchain designs CPG brands and manufacturers, from suppliers and manufacturing plants to fulfillment centers and retail partners, to connect each party in the supply chain to an extensive and enduring history of any transaction. This degree of transparency and durability can be of benefit to producers who have a product source, traceability, reminder and even lose life products [18].

Blockchain allows each group participating in the supply chain to communicate with the others. It helps improve coordination across the supply chain between parties and leads to less mistakes. As the data is accessible in real time, Blockchain helps to streamline the process and ensure a hassle-free and reliable framework. Blockchain is a shared ledger that offers full protection and accountability for all supply chain transactions. The transaction records are maintained and available inside the network to everyone. Without the consent of every person concerned, the data once registered cannot be altered, and every transaction and change on a blockchain is traceable. This helps to minimize employee theft and to allow for a traceable time-saving process if there is some instance of fraud. By implementing blockchain technology, companies can more reliably forecast consumer demand. As a consequence, rather than merely responding to stock-outs, the inventory management team will proactively prepare for restocking. Blockchain will assist businesses to modify their current inventory management strategy. Blockchain and other emerging technologies will transform inventory management and help businesses shift their strategy from reactive to proactive [11].

It is the lynchpin of a Blockchain-based system that the data flows smoothly between entities on real time. This gives manufacturers an immediate view of consumer demand, which they have never been able to do before. This helps them to anticipate demand more accurately and prepare for development and re-deployment proactively than respond simply to inventories. They are able to optimize sales and profitability in that sweet spot, thereby reducing the risk of lost revenues and carrier costs. This means that the goods and amount of inventory remain correct for demand with minimal excess.

Blockchain adoption in operations management is, as per the 2018 MHI Annual Market Survey, just 5% but is forecast to rise to 54% in the next five years. The intended adoption is fair because Blockchain offers suppliers a way to start inventory implementation and drive sales from source to shelf with maximum openness and efficient data flows. The businesses who want to join now are able to receive the incentives sooner than later [12].

5.3 Cost Optimization for Blockchain Inventory Management in Cloud

5.3.1 Optimizing Blockchain Inventory Management

Optimizing the stock of blockchains means using blockchains to find the optimal balance. Optimized inventory for product spares preserves an inventory level that, while increasing performance and decreasing inventory costs, subsequently removes out-of-stock circumstances.

Companies need a strategy that supports the specific management criteria of inventory in the cloud to achieve key business benefits, including:

- High criticality
- Long lead time
- High price
- Generally infrequent and highly variable usage
- Low data quality.

The integrated blockchain inventory involves data points periodically obtained and inventory creation on the basis of some real-time steps. Inventory managers with an effective tool for managing their business goals and making their teams significantly effective create a decision support system that incorporate best management strategies [15].

By leveraging technological technologies, automated procedures, and inventory management industry standards to maximize spares and supplies, asset-intensive companies will reliably achieve results like these:

- 15–25% reduction in funds invested in safety inventories
- 5–20% decrease in excess and obsolete stock write-offs
- 10–25% for improved availability and productivity, fewer stock-outs
- 10–25% drop in administrative costs for inventory replenishment
- 33–66% less resource time spent on inventory management.

5.3.2 Best Practices of Blockchain Inventory Cost Optimization in Cloud

The traditional processes concentrate on the design and optimization of expert inventories. Success factors are crucial to achieving substantial inventory reductions and significant fundamental benefits that are key components to maximizing inventory [1, 2].

5.3.2.1 Criticality Analysis

For each stock item, generate a recommended criticality (business impact code) by analyzing:

- Service (where used and fitted).
- classifications of goods
- Practical considerations in the "real world" or "workarounds"
- vendor
- Cost.

5.3.2.2 Demand Forecasting

The implementation of specialized hardware can be supposed to boost demand for such inventory pieces. Request forecasting resources should include:

- Identification of appropriate architectures for forecasting
- Automatic optimization selection for every single stock object
- Usage of forecasts and quantitative assignments necessary to satisfy various spares, such as slow movement and drop demand
- Methods for the processing and retrieval of irregular data

- The ability to distinguish routine operations from unplanned production and project requirement
- Effects used for making forecasts using knowledge of future expectations or patterns in the economy

5.3.2.3   Lead Time Forecasting

A crucial factor in the determination of optimum safety stocks is predicted lead time, which helps to achieve these capabilities:

- Normal forecast time for sales orders and receipts
- Methods of scanning and scraping to remove irregular data
- Call lead times as necessary and measure the lead time gap to determine the expected service level.

5.3.2.4   Issue Size Forecasting

In the calculation of stock levels, the number of units usually required for a request (the problem size) is also a crucial factor.

- The capacity to use the background of problems to estimate an average sample mean
- To remove abnormal data, adequate filtering and clipping techniques
- Capabilities to override the problem size of forecasts as needed
- Calculation and utilization of the problem gap in the planned level of service.

5.3.2.5   Economic Modeling

"For what-if" modeling of inventory trade-off decisions, economic modelling capabilities should allow:

- Stock holding expenses for various kinds of products
- Complete costs of resupply for various buying methods
- Costs in facilitating or immediate freight
- Stock-out prices, depending on containment and stock-out length
- Comparison of current and optimized performance for metrics such as sales revenue, operational efficiency and more.

5.3.2.6   Optimization of Reordering Parameters

The main determinants of the corporate value are the inventory management parameters for the output schedules (minimum and total quantities (MIN/MAX) used by the ERP materials control system. Periodically optimized rearrangement parameters should reflect the adjustments. Highlights of the optimization case:

- Options to automatic the higher and lower demand for suitable algorithms
- A choice alternative to a policy of fixed quality of service, with an efficient cost model that considered inventory, repair, expedition and inventory costs
- Instead of another group of artefacts, one at a time
- The ability to design if reached equilibrium are measured against the real inventory output
- Real world constraints are taken into account including the average bin size, storage capacity, and more.

5.3.2.7   Exception Management

A management by exception approach ensures that for complex systems inventories, inventory review time has been spent on high value or problem objects. Exception Control features include:

- User software with the required warning thresholds for identification of a number of exception terms
- The ability to use exemptions to browse, sort and process
- Mechanisms for excluding reordering parameter adjustments for products with exception words.

5.3.2.8   Inventory Segmentation

Inventory segmentation offers an inventory management mechanism that recognizes that different item profiles require a range of different management techniques:

- The stock divisions are based on features such as use or retention, movement rate and more

- Use policy statements or business regulations, such as manual tracking of unique goods or exams or possibly obsolete objects, to control each inventory segment.

5.3.2.9   Spares Risk Assessment

Some inventories will have a high share, which is critical, will have little or no planned use and will require substantial capital expenditure. These things require specific techniques:

- Danger modeling, one or two sets, of the effects of keeping zero
- Calculated the ability to understand sensitivity from medium- and stock-out costs
- The ability to model or override all packing decisions.

5.3.2.10   Spares Pooling

By pooling or exchanging high-value, infrequent products (insurance spares) across several locations, substantial reductions in total security stock investment are possible. In order to promote such arrangements, businesses should:

- Find related sequence similarity for sharing
- Set the optimum amount of collected spare parts to maintain
- Determine the safest place to store the spares.

5.3.2.11   Knowledge Capture

A significant business method in preventing errors and re-investigation is the capture of organizational information related to inventory items; the solution for inventory optimization should:

- Capture comments and inventory object commentary
- Offer decisions with an audit trail
- Ensuring consistent quality for input variables and identification codes
- Include notifications when feedbacks are due.

5.3.2.12   Reporting Inventory

Inventory monitoring is important in order to allow improvements in enhancing inventory to be tracked. Information should be included:

- A series of predetermined inventory management analyses
- The capability to instantly capture a wide range of stock pre-defined
- The ability to customize users' reports and statistics

Competitive advantage needs a positive attitude about innovation and technology for today's asset-intensive firms. Businesses are left to deal with manual procedures, regular ERP framework features, and ad hoc databases or spreadsheets without technological solutions and best practices. These manual methods to production are prone to errors and difficult to handle on a daily basis. Realizing and preserving inventory management is feasible and sustainable with the right tools and the right help.

5.4 Cost Reduction Strategies in Blockchain Inventory Management in Cloud

5.4.1 Reduce Useless Inventory

It might not sound like this, but it would cost long-term money to get a surplus inventory that did not sell. The warehouse will be best used, instead of having valuable space taken up by bad sales products, by holding stocks that are well sold. An obsolete stock surplus may indicate major problems, such as planning lack, accuracy of the product, and poor forecasting. One of the best things they can do for the organization is identifying worthless inventory. Reducing costs, bundling or simply reducing losses and completely removing them minimizes the sum of expired stocks.

5.4.2 Let Experts Manage Inventory (VMI)

While loads of trivial inventory are lying, if it is becoming too difficult to handle the inventory, find out that the resources are diminishing. They deal with this problem for too long, instead of concentrating on other aspects of the business. A Vendor Controlled Inventory (VMI) is a safer way to prevent that, where the vendor is responsible for the inventory of the customer. After VMI implementation, the producer is able to adjust time after a cash production when the order point is reached.

5.4.3 Develop Relationships With Suppliers

Inadequate coordination is the most common problems in stock management anywhere on the road. The maintenance of a good provider partner would dramatically boost the performance of the business by minimizing overall costs, ensuring timely delivery and prompt notification of interrupts. Creating a successful relationship with providers means prioritizing companies and striving to maintain businesses a little harder.

5.4.4   Install Industrial Vending Machines

Inventory management's most common issues are due to a lack of touch. The continuing strong supplier relationship would significantly boost the company's performance by minimizing total costs, timely delivery and notification of disruptions. Establishing a strong relationship with suppliers guarantees customer appreciation and the business is a little more difficult to maintain.

5.4.5   Order Smaller, More Frequently

More daily orders will help keep the company in outdated inventory as low as possible. As long as a commodity is in stock, its depletion is higher. To reduce future hazards and dangers, keeping inventories as small as possible for the shortest possible time. Any risks that can be reduced by smaller orders can save a great deal of stress and money.

The method the organization uses to manage monitoring and organizing inventory is an inventory monitor. This technique starts with the goods sold by the retailer hitting the warehouse and finishes with the purchase and service of the goods. Other factors, like too much or too little inventory, may have a big impact on the company's budget and productivity. A disrupted warehouse can also cause uncertainty and reduce customer sales and loyalty [3].

5.5   Conclusion

In order to revolutionize supply chain operations, blockchain technology is intended. Around the same time, in response to environmental issues, legislative and regulatory initiatives push businesses to change their supply chains. The objective of this study is therefore to provide a basis for blockchain inventory management for monitoring supply chain performance and cost optimization strategies in a synchronized fashion, producing a better outcome for the supply chain.

References

1. https://www.mbtmag.com/best-practices/article/13246333/blockchain-the-future-of-inventory-management-available-now
2. https://www.sccgltd.com/featured-articles/can-blockchain-reduce-supply-chain-complexity-and-costs/
3. https://www.dxpe.com/cost-reduction-strategies-inventory-management/
4. Awwad, M., Kalluru, S.R., Kazhana Airpulli, V., Zambre, M.S., Marathe, A., Jain, P., Blockchain Technology for Efficient Management of Supply Chain, 2018.
5. Boone, C., Craighead, C., Hanna, J., Critical Challenges of Inventory Management in Service Parts Supply: A Delphi study. *J. Oper. Manage. Res.*, 1, 31–39, 2008.
6. Boschi, A., Borin, R., Raimundo, J., Batocchio, A., An exploration of blockchain technology in supply chain management, pp. 27–28, 2018.
7. Casino, F., Dasaklis, T., Patsakis, C., Enhanced Vendor-managed Inventory through Blockchain, 2019, 10.1109/SEEDA-CECNSM.2019.8908481.
8. Chang, J., Katehakis, M., Melamed, B., Shi, J., Blockchain Design for Supply Chain Management. *SSRN Electron. J.*, 2018. Available at http://dx.doi.org/10.2139/ssrn.3295440
9. Cole, R., Stevenson, M., Aitken, J., Blockchain technology: Implications for operations and supply chain management. *Supply Chain Manag.: Int. J.*, 24, 4, 469–483, 2019.
10. Deepika, K., Naveen Prasad, N., Balamurugan, S., Charanyaa, S., Evolution of Cloud Computing: A State-of-the-Art Survey. *Int. J. Innov. Res. Comput. Commun. Eng.*, 3, 1, 2015.
11. Goyat, R., Rai, M., Kumar, G., Saha, R., Implications of Blockchain Technology in Supply Chain Management. *J. Sys. Manage. Sci.*, 9, 3, 92–103, 2019.
12. Hoek, R., Exploring blockchain implementation in the supply chain: Learning from pioneers and RFID research. *Int. J. Oper. Prod. Manage.*, 39 829–859 (6/7/8), 2019.
13. Nedeltcheva, G. and Spassov, K., Blockchain-Based Supply Chain Management, in: *APDSI 2019 - 24th annual conference of the Asia Pacific Decision Sciences InstituteAt*, Brisbane, Australia, 2019.
14. Patil, H. and Divekar, R., Inventory Management Challenges for B2C E-commerce Retailers. *Proc. Econ. Financ.*, 11, 561–571, 2014.
15. Perboli, G., Musso, S., Rosano, M., Blockchain in Logistics and Supply Chain: A Lean Approach for Designing Real-World Use Cases. *IEEE Access*, 6, 1–1, 62018–62028, 2018.
16. Plinere, D. and Borisov, A., Case Study on Inventory Management Improvement. *Inf. Technol. Manage. Sci.*, 18, 2015, 10.1515/itms-2015-0014.

17. Sheakh, T., A Study of Inventory Management System Case Study. *J. Dyn. Control Syst.*, 10, 1176–1190, 2018.

18. Song, J.M., Sung, J., Park, T., Applications of Blockchain to Improve Supply Chain Traceability. *Proc. Comput. Sci.*, 162, 119–122, 2019.

19. Tijan, E., Aksentijevic, S., Ivanić, K., Jardas, M., Blockchain Technology Implementation in Logistics. *Sustainability*, 11, 1185, 2019.

20. Tribis, Y., El Bouchti, A., Bouayad, H., Supply Chain Management based on Blockchain: A Systematic Mapping Study. *MATEC Web of Conferences*, vol. 200, 00020, 2018.

21. Wu, H., Cao, J., Yang, Y., Tung, C., Jiang, S., Tang, B., Liu, Y., Wang, X., Deng, Y., *Data Management in Supply Chain Using Blockchain: Challenges and a Case Study*, pp. 1–8, 2019.

22. Yaga, D., Mell, P., Roby, N., Scarfone, K., *Blockchain Technology Overview*, National Institute of Standards and Technology, 68, 2019.

23. Zheng, Z., Xie, S., Dai, H.-N., Chen, X., Wang, H., An Overview of Blockchain Technology: Architecture, Consensus, and Future Trends, in: *2017 IEEE International Congress on Big Data (BigData Congress*, IEEE, 2017, 10.1109/BigData Congress.2017.85.

6

Review of Deep Learning Architectures Used for Identification and Classification of Plant Leaf Diseases

G. Gangadevi[1*] and C. Jayakumar[2]

[1]Department of Information Technology, Meenakshi College of Engineering Chennai, Tamil Nadu, India
[2]Department of Computer Science, Sri Venkateswara College of Engineering Chennai, Sriperumbudur, Tamil Nadu, India

Abstract

The plant leaf disease detection and classification are a very significant help for raising the quality and quantity of the food product. There are many plant diseases that are not found in the right time to protect the plant. But nowadays, the researchers are really focusing on the predicting and classifying plenty of plant diseases through deep learning techniques. So the strategy of the recent works involves training the model with huge number of dataset and predicting the disease and also classifying it. There are lot of models are in queue which are all outperforming in both the task of the disease. The stages of the models are filtering, feature extracting, characterize them on the diverse premise. There are numerous techniques for plant disease prediction and classification are using standard techniques like Artificial Neural Network (ANN), k-means Classifier (K-means), Recurrent Neural Network (RNN), K Nearest Neighbor (K-NN) classifier and Support Vector Machine (SVM).

Keywords: K-means, SVM, K-NN, ANN, fuzzy, feature extraction, RNN

6.1 Introduction

Plant disease is one of the significant factors which have a high impact on the production food. The location and clustering of plant sicknesses are directly

---

Corresponding author: ganga2007mtech@gmail.com

R. Kanthavel, K. Ananthajothi, S. Balamurugan and R. Karthik Ganesh (eds.) Artificial Intelligent Techniques for Wireless Communication and Networking, (75–90) © 2022 Scrivener Publishing LLC

involved in plant profitability and financial development [1]. This procedure is based on Artificial Intelligence (AI) Computer Vision (CV), Machine Learning (ML), and innovations that have been accomplished in engaging, exact and opportune recognizable proof of the plant leaves diseases. We have considered 15 papers with various plant leaf databases for our comparison, for our search review papers were discussed in extraction techniques and feature, used for classification techniques which are based on plant leaf that has been worked for best accuracy.

6.2   Literature Review

Marvan Adan Jasim [2] proposed a convolutional neural network for finding out disease in plants by leaf diseases in plant using deep learning methods. They have taken the dataset of 20,636 images with 15 different classes for example, Pepper bell Bacterial spot, Tomato Yellow Leaf_Curl Virus, Tomato Septoria leaf spot. So, the researchers have done their effort to find affected leaves of the sample taken and used CNN LeNet Neural network system which can apply and help to detect the diseases. The researcher Kawasaki suggested a CNN model which is used to find a variant in the samples and defective cucumbers in the pictures of given leaves in the two main viruses. The proposed system consists of several steps which identify a plant leaf disease system. The CNN has 10 filter layers followed by a 3×3 convolution layer and batch proceeding then Relu. Also alternative layers which have max pooling have been designed. Later, part of the layer's filter sizes was extended to a 20.64-like that pattern. This experiment is taken in the Lab with 4 GB processor and CPU. Then he extracts the overall dataset of 2,056 images to 15 different classes. It is then resized to 128×128 resolution, as this gives the accuracy by training progress and validation. The researcher decided to develop different kinds of samples and gets the accuracy for training (98.29%) and for testing (98.029%) and overall accuracy (94.95%).

Sardogan *et al.* [3] proposed CNN with LVQ algorithm to detect and classify plant leaf disease which affects the crop quality. It detects a disease using raw images aided with deep sense of artificial intelligence. Learning Vector Quantization was used for classification which is an adaptive model which contains three layers like an initial input, followed by Kohonen (competition) and then finally an output layer. The learning phase of the model happens in the middle layer. It has four layers for mathematical operation that reduce the output size, Recognition and classification and training the data classification. LVQ has "winner takes all" strategy where the weight of the winning reference which is near to the input gets repeatedly updated. The winner takes all strategy works using Euclidean distance calculation. Upon taking 100 tests from a tomato leaf, it provides 20 images of each class with an accuracy average of 86% and only some leaves are classified incorrectly for every class.

Arsenovic [4] focused on the interconnection between the plant and climate which affect the plant growth then tried to solve the problem through a Conventional Neural Networks (CNN) system to rate and notice the sheath disease in practice methods. The author proposed the appearance used Piece Swarm intelligence. The author has taken the images from the Internet and stored them in the dataset collection. The usual methods preowned for picture processing are by chroma investigation. Some distinct perspective are suggested by the networks namely Artificial Neural Networks (ANNs). This system is only done to understand the tea leaf diseases. After all the regulates the frameworks of system general exactness is 96%. By using these routines the plant illness can be secured for use for later generation.

Adem *et al.* [5] proposed the faster R-convolution neural network system for spotting diseases in leaf of *Cercospora beticola* Sacc automatically. To achieve this they used the subset of machine learning—deep learning because it comes up with a high range of accuracy and performance. They have taken images from different datasets. In this paper standard architecture AlexNet and GoogleNet models were used for developing a classifier around 54,306 images and for large scale image recognition a VGG16 model was used in 4,980 images among them 90% using this model. Here at the training phase they got high accuracy by capturing images. For Training and testing models around 155 images for Detection purposes were used. In this work author gave a 95.48% efficiency for spotting diseases in leaf.

Francis and Daisy *et al.* [6] proposed the basic Convolutional Neural Network system. They used deep learning because it is much popular due to its high level performance and accuracy. They used a machine learning model which is controlled by CPU or graphics processing unit. CNN performs various layers and they designed each phase for prediction. They used a filter (k) which are 3×3, 5×5, and 7×7. Overfitting the model, they proposed a classification using CNN. In this research paper, dataset is captured by camera which it contains 3,663 images. So that they concluded, with high accuracy with min size, and complexity, testing accuracy is 74% and model accuracy is 87%. The visual understanding of disease can be used in mobile or any other application.

Ferentinos [7] proposed the research study about plant diseases detection and finding it using photographs of normal and infected plants, using deep learning concepts and network types. The research of models was held with 87,846 photographs, with 25 specific plants in a set of discrete classes. A handful of models were kept under processing to reach a level of success of 99.53% for detecting the corresponding pair of plants and their diseases with 0.47% error. To differentiate the type of image into a single GUI was 2 ms which makes it practical into mobile apps for farmers. Its high potential makes it broader in plant species and their diseases and more vigorous in red cultivation condition.

Iqbal *et al.* [8] proposed that the advanced technique for mechanical disease observed by using picture pretreat plans. The illness marks remain split via executing the Rim noticing and Vermin methods and also k-Mean gathering techniques were used. Then they have talk about recognition and categorizing of lime disease using SVM and Neural Network. The appearance characteristics are the better prominently used for view of infection of the picture using SVM Neural Network.

According to the proposal of Hossain [9] a K-nearest neighbor classifier IS used for classifying and detecting diseases in leaf. They used machine learning technique for the models accuracy and efficiency to make decisions to achieve high rate of accuracy. Here dataset contains around 237 images and also consists of five classes. In this paper they took 200 images for the training purpose and THE remaining 37 were for testing purpose. To assess the trained classifier they use ROC and confusion matrix to obtain the model performance. GLCM feature was also used in this research for image analysis. Finally KNN has good efficiency and has an accuracy of 96.76%.

Kumari [10] proposed a leaf disease detection using Neutral Network tool to identify the normal and diseased cotton and tomato leaf. The author also proposed obtaining the image, image segments into clusters, Extraction of Feature, then classified them later. Using the feature of collecting images from database, image acquisition is segmented into small clusters by using k-means clustering algorithm which differentiates defected part region and healthy leaf region. Feature extraction occurs to find out the correct feature using clusters which are segmented. Cotton and Tomato plants features are extracted for diseases identification [11]. ANN classifications were used in terms of accuracy. In this study researchers found four different diseases: septoria leaf spot, bacterial leaf spot, leaf mold and target spot. Its average accuracy is 92.5%.

Bandala *et al.* [12] have proposed detection of particular disease in Tomato (i.e. Diamante Max) using Deep Learning methods. Their deep learning system works well for both normal and affected dataset and they have constructed a transfer learning of pre trained AlexNet for recognition of image. The transferred network implemented with five convolution layers, then max-pooling layers, followed dropout layers, and finally three fully connected layers. The dataset consists of 4,923 images of leaves of tomato plant which are supervised with four labels. The efforts are focused specifically for AlexNet architecture focusing on "Large Scale Visual Recognition Challenge" (LSVRC). Based on the efforts of this work of 36 samples, the accuracy of the system ranges from 91.6 to 92.6%. The CNN is built complexly to ensure the accuracy of the system for the tomato leaf disease.

Sharif *et al.* [13] proposed classification and detection of citrus plant leaf disease enchanced feature selection and segmentation weight. The image processing technique was used for detection and classification. There are two hybrid methods like detection of lesion spot and classification of citrus diseases. Segmentation method is performed by enhancing input images. They used two types of dataset for detection and classification of citrus diseases like anthracnose, blackspot, etc. The proposed techniques outperform the existing method and produce an accuracy of 97% in classification, and an accuracy of 89% in Merged dataset and for their own dataset the accuracy rate is 90.4%.

Indumathi *et al.* [14] proposed a system that detects the leaf disease using the image processing method using smart IOT architecture. The process starts with Image acquisition, Classification Detection of disease, Image preprocessing, segmentation, Feature Extraction and Clustering based on that fertilize suggestion is given. The proposed system takes the I/P as infected image and RGB colors of the given I/P is represented as bar graph. Then identified pixels are clustered randomly. Then the 13 features are calculated by (i.e.) Contrast, Smoothness, Entropy, Std Deviation, Energy mean and Homogeneity. Then Calculated value is dt for the given leaf which is compared with normal image so that provides the prediction of disease and suggestion for the fertilizer that can be given for the crop.

Sharma *et al.* [15] propose the artificial intelligence method of detecting the leaf disease of plant and classify them and also provide quick and easy remedies to rid and cure the disease. There are four phases they have done: Image Collection, Image Processing, Segmentation, Selection of Classifiers, Analyzing results. The Images are collected using Git Hub, kaggle data sets of 20,000 in numbers. They were 19 different Classes available. The diseases like early blight, late blight, leaf scorch bacterial blight black rot and many more like Grape, Potato, Apple, Strawberry, Corn. The noise free data is considered which is through Gaussian Blur RGB to HSV transformation for color intensity then segmentation is done to remove the leaf from noise environment with the support of K-means clustering of two cluster centers. Then selection of classifier is done using CNN layer which has convolution layer for the IMG size 64 * 64 * 3 which is fed into convolution layer which gives 64 * 64 * 10 O/P there are five convolution Layers that build the kernel size 3 * 3. The man Pooling layer is used with the size of 3 * 3. Then activation layer ReLu is used in complete layers to derive last layer. Also they have used Softmax. Then fully connected layer which have two dense layers of 1,024& 1q units. They got 98% accuracy for the considered data set.

Agarwala *et al.* [16] proposed a system that provides an CNN based system for Tomato Leaf disease detection which has triple convolution layer, triple Max Pooling layer & double fully connected layer. The output was related to pre-trained model VGG 16 Inception V3 and Mobile Net. The classification and detection accuracy were varied from 75 to 100%. They have achieved 91.2% of average accuracy for nine diseases and one healthy class. The diseases they have considered are Target spot, Early blight Septoria leaf Spot Spider mites (two Spotted spider mite). Overall IMG Considered are 10,000 and 1,000 IMG were healthy and 1,000 were diseased category of Tomato Plant. Some IMG were augmented for generating new image. The image size is 25 * 256 and total storage space needed for the system is 1.5 MB.

Jasim *et al.* [17] proposed to classifying and discovering the disease in plant leaf. To achieve this they used the subset of machine learning technique namely "deep learning" because it comes up with high range of accuracy and performance and also to maintain layers they took CNN algorithm. By this we can categorize plant disease. The "PLANT VILLAGE" DATASET is a website that contains around 20,636 images of plants and its diseases where these images involve 15 classes. For better outcome pictures were improvised into 128 × 128 resolution, and saved in jpg forms. For Training and testing purposes 70% of data was used for each separately. Ultimately they got 98.29% for Training and 98.029% for testing.

Kumar *et al.* [18] constructed rectified model for the delayed detection of diseases in coffee crops. Most crops in India are affected badly. To help the farmers to achieve high production. CNNs (Convolutional Neural Networks) in image recognition and image processing prove its efficiency of training time and accuracy using method of Transfer Learning. With the use of Data Augmentation technique a huge 97.61% rate of accuracy could be attained. CNN has found various coffee diseases and categorizes them into five normal, affected Leaf with Cercospora spots, Phoma, Coffee Leaf Rust (CLR), and Leaf Miner. The detection of the diseases in coffee crops helps to increases the coffee production of India. For earlier detection of the diseases could impact the production of coffee various parameters using plantation time, hotness, humidity and location weather [19].

An advanced system can be made using trained data set for further updation of the proposed system.

Kosamkar *et al.* [20] put forward the structure which works on image preprocessing using digitization, CNN based feature extraction and classification of disease and suggesting pesticide using Tensor Flow. Major procedure is followed using deep learning based Java Web Services android application. Also we have followed CNN with multiple layers of 5, 4 and 3 trained for multiples of five epoch cycles, The model as a user interface with JWS for communication between these structure. The outcome shows the graphs of excessive precision attained for 5-layered model with 95.05% for 15 epochs and 90% for 20 epochs.

Yadhav *et al.* [21] introduced a technique to find the disease of the leaves and disease which affect plants and surrounding area by using CNN model and also they suggest using fertilizer to prevent damage. The CNN is implemented by Raspberry pi kit. The authors proposed a technique to find the damage by clustering algorithm, using a database by system Architecture where the models use the many layers to classify the image clustering. The mathematical function role is achieved by CNN and optimization is achieved by function. The system detects the disease present in leaf and the camera. It shoots the leaves image to classify the disease and also they do the graph for training and validation accuracy for each layer from 1 and 2 and dense layer and loss graph for training and validation loss. The maximum accuracy is compared with activation function for sensitivity and specificity. Activation function is compared with prediction the accuracy of CNN model is 95% and speed of CNN is increased by 83%. The maximum sensitivity and specificity is 81%.

As per Madhulatha and Ramadevi's [22] proposal the increased number of plant diseases will cause the reduced quality of agricultural products and affect their production. To recognize the plant diseases we can use many technologies like machine learning, Artificial intelligence, and Digital Image Processing. But in this paper they had done the research using CNN to improve segmenting of images and classifying it with great accuracy. In CNN model they use different architectures like LeNet, AlexNet, etc. They use these to identify the different diseases of tomato, apple leaves, soya beans, etc. They did their research on different datasets which contain billions of images both diseased as well as healthy plant leaf images. These images should be processed by separating the diseased leaves from good ones where we can compare, detect and identify the plant diseases. Here we can only use the colored images which produce the higher accuracy of the images comparatively to the greyscale images. It has been concluded that Convolutional Neural Network (CNN) will be a greater method to recognize the different plant diseases.

Shubham [23] states that nearly 45% of the planet supply produce are lost to illness and plague cankers. As stated and observed, the elevated amount of smallholder self-murders and that is the crucial causes for here for the negligence of supplies. To solve these issues we used the pair of picture categorizing like Generative Adversarial Networks (GANs) to increase the bounded integer of neighborhood pictures accessible. The categorizing is carried out by a Convolutional Neutral Network (CNN) representation located in pocket pc software. The pair of CNN construction imitations Inception v3 and MobileNets came to be studied. The Inception v3 is representation was pre-taught on the ImageNet data collection of rehabilitation to effort metadata of herb illness. This representation reaches an exactness of 89%. The MobileNets contain many layers in the construction, the Mobilenets representation pre-owned for herb illness noticing had been pre-taught in picnet data collection, where this representation reached by 93%. Additionally effort on better cell refinement for the pocket pc software is as well as a mandatory zone of additional analysis.

Gangadevi [24] in his work introduced the idea is based on finding the infected area in the plant disease image using the region of interest. The work suggests that selection search mechanism for finding the important part of the disease affected plant using RCNN method. The boundary box regression done used the function $c_k(L) = w_k^T \Phi3(L)$. The activation layer includes Tanh function for strongly negative results.

6.3   Proposed Idea

The CNN supports any type of data such as audio, video, image, etc. The combination of CNN layers which could dense in architecture helps to understand the scenario of the disease and it could provide better results. There are plenty of pretrained architectures available: Alex Net, Google Net, VGG (Visual Geometry Group) Leach and they were used for particular problem domain. The classifiers which are non-parametric in nature are neural network. There are many classifiers which are back propagation, CPC (Counter Propagation Classifier) MLP (Multilayer Perceptron). Some classifiers are good at classification accuracy and some classifiers are good at Simplicity and some are good at robustness. Leaves disease prediction using Back Propagation Classifier of multilevel iteration [25] are able to identify the brown spots of rice. Counter propagation classifiers are able to identify leaf disease faster and with quicker response Figure 6.1.

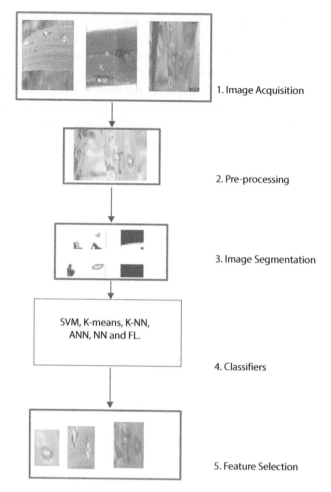

1. Image Acquisition

2. Pre-processing

3. Image Segmentation

SVM, K-means, K-NN,
ANN, NN and FL.

4. Classifiers

5. Feature Selection

Figure 6.1 Plant disease identification and localization.

The various popular model architectures available are AlexNet, GoogLeNet, VGGNet, ResNet, etc. The VGGNet is prominently used as a feature extraction algorithm in many research papers. VGGNet acts as an effective model for single-shot Detectors used for object detection techniques in image processing Technique. ResNet helps in the vanishing gradient problem to a minimum level The large number of layers in deep learning models needs to have low error rate for which does not propagate back so, Vanishing gradients can change in low rate. LSTM models can associate the sequential information between the caption and the image. The development of the any deep learning model and its learning rate do not need huge time because the data set is well developed and perfectly labeled. The inference is that the ResNet with VGGNet or Resnet with LSTM Models or Resnet with Yolo might perform well with high accuracy rate. The proposed idea suggests that the ResNet could work with Yolo to overperform the other combinations. The prediction of the disease with Yolo is used with the grid cell and every grid cell is used for detection and classification of disease of bounding box. The size of the grid cell depends on the affected area.

Figure 6.2 shows the layer present in the convolution block present in the proposed model which consists of convolution layer, batch

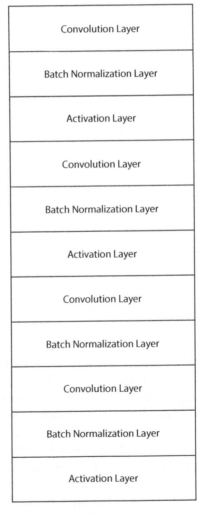

Figure 6.2 Convolution block of proposed system.

normalization and activation layer. The Convolution neural network apply filters to image for feature mapping which has been used for the detection of features in the input. The Batch Normalization used for batching the size of input has to get processed to next layer. The activation Layer helps to find the result which could fire the neuron or not. The CNN and RNN can be also enhanced by combining the network of CNN and RNN using LSTM for efficient crop management [26].

The ResNet performs in "vanishing gradient" problem and also can handle thousands of layers easily along with that yolo supports the CNN to learn easily. The diseased places are concentrated with grid cell (with different attributes). The idea makes the grid learn only in the area which is in grid instead of background data (Figure 6.3 and Figure 6.4).

(a)   **(b)**

(c)

Figure 6.3 (a) Leaf which has brown spot. (b) Leaf blast with background noise. (c) Bacterial blight disease with background noise.

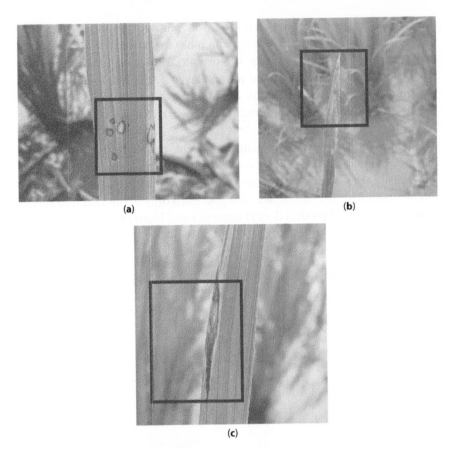

Figure 6.4 (a) Leaf which has identified brown spot using Yolo. (b) Identified leaf blast without noise. (c) Yolo identifies bacterial blight disease.

6.4   Reference Gap

Architecture	Plant type	No of diseases	Performance analysis accuracy
CNN	Tea leaf	1	96.3%
CNN with LVQ	Tomatoes	2	86%
CNN with OPS	Pepper	2	94.95%
CNN	Potatoes	2	91.69%
LENET	Cucumber	1	86.7%

(Continued)

(*Continued*)

Architecture	Plant type	No of diseases	Performance analysis accuracy
CNN	Citrus	2	90.4%
SVM	Lemon	3	91%
KNN	Species	5	96.76%
ANN	Cotton	4	92.5%
R-CNN	Sugar beet	1	95.48

6.5   Conclusion

The review of CNN-based research disease on leaf was performed that explains the particular affected area and it focuses on overall precision/accuracy achieved. CNN outperforms high precision in the problems solving where they have been used for scoring better precision than other image-processing techniques in classification and detection of disease on leaf. The objective of this survey is to encourage researchers to explore with CNN and DL, and applying them to solve various involving classification or prediction of disease in agricultural area. The convolutional neural network (CNN) strategy is the most emerging technique of predicting the plant diseases using the classification of a test model. So, the researchers have to hybrid the architectures to come out with the new architecture which highly outperforms in their own way.

References

1. Chouhan, S.S., Kaul, A., Singh, U.P., Jain, S., Bacterial foraging optimization based radial basis function neural network (BRBFNN) for identification and classification of plant leaf diseases: An automatic approach towards plant pathology. *IEEE Access*, 6, 8852–8863, 2018.
2. Jasim, M.A. and Al-Tuwaijari, J.M., Plant Leaf Diseases Detection and Classification Using Image Processing and Deep Learning Techniques. *2020 International Conference on Computer Science and Software Engineering (CSASE)*, IEEE Access.
3. Sardogan, M., Tuncer, A., Ozen, Y., Plant Leaf Disease Detection and Classification based on CNN with LVQ Algorithm. *2018 International Conference on Computer Science and Engineering (UBMK)*, IEEE Access, pp. 128–131.

4. Sladojevic, S., Arsenovic, M., Anderla, A., Culibrk, D., Stefanovic, D., Deep Neural Networks Based Recognition of Plant Diseases by Leaf Image Classification. *2016 Computational Intelligence and Neuro Science*, Hindawi Access.

5. Ozguven, M.M. and Adem, K., Automatic detection and classification of leaf spot disease in sugar beet using deep learning algorithms. *Phys. A: Stat. Mech. Appl.*, Elsevier, 535(C), 2019, https://ideas.repec.org/s/eee/phsmap.html.

6. Francis, M. and Deisy, C., Disease Detection And Classification In Agricultural Plants Using Convolutional Neural Network—A Visual Understanding. *2019 6th International Conference on Signal processing and Integrated Networks (SPIN)*, IEEE Access Psgrd, pp. 232–257.

7. Ferentinos, K.P., Deep Learning Models for Plant Disease Detection and Diagnosis, Department of Agriculture Engineering Ethens, Greece. Science Direct Access. *Comput. Electron. Acr.*, 145, 311–318, 2018, https://www.cabdirect.org/cabdirect/search/?q=do%3a%22Computers+and+Electronics+in+Agriculture%22.

8. Iqbal, Z., Khan, M.A., Sharif, M., Shah, J.H., Rahman, M.H.U., Javed, K., An automated detection and classification of citrus plant diseases using image processing techniques. Scilit net access Department of Electronics and Agriculture. *Elsevier BV Comput. Electron. Agri.*, 153, 12–32, https://doi.org/10.1016/j.compag.2018.07.032.

9. Hossain, E., Hussain, M.F., Rahaman, M.A., A Color and Texture Based Approach for the Detection and Classification of Plant Leaf Disease Using KNN Classifier, in: *2019 International Conference on Electrical, Computer and Communication Engineering (ECCE)*, pp. 1–6, 2019.

10. Usha Kumari, C., Jeevan Prasad, S., Mounika, G., Leaf Disease Detection: Feature Extraction with K-means clustering and Classification with ANN. *IEEE Access*, 1, 6, 1095–1098, June 2014.

11. Ananthajothi, K. and Subramaniam, M., CLDC: Efficient Classification of Medical Data Using Class Level Disease Convergence Divergence Measure. *Int. J. Innov. Technol. Exploring Eng. (IJITEE)*, 2019.

12. de Luna, R.G., Dadios, E.P., Bandala, A.A., Automated Image Capturing System for Deep Learning-based Tomato Plant Leaf Disease Detection and Recognition. *2018 IEEE Region 10 Conference*, pp. 1414–1419.

13. Sharif, M., Khan, M.A., Iqbal, Z., Azam, M.F., Irkan Ulah Lali, M., Javed, M.Y., Detection and Classification of Citrus diseases in agriculture based on Optimized Weighted Segmentation and Feature Selection. Department of Electronics and Communication Engineering. *IEEE Access*, 150, 220–234, 2018.

14. Indumathi, R., Saagari, N., Thejeswavi, V., Swarnareka, R., Leaf Disease Detection And Fertilizer Suggestion. *2019 International Conference of System Computation Automation and Networking IEEE International Conference on System, Computation, Automation and Networking (ICSCAN)*.

15. Sharma, P., Hans, P., Gupta, S.C., Classification of Plant Leaf Diseases Using Machine Learning And Image Preprocessing Techniques. *IEEE 2020 International Conference on Cloud Computing, Data Science & Engineering-Confluence.*
16. Agarwal, M., Singh, A., Arjaria, S., Sinhad, A., Guptaa, S., ToLeD: Tomato Leaf Disease Detection using Convolution Neural Network. *International Conference on Computational Intelligence and Data Science (ICCIDS 2019).*
17. Jasim, M.A. and Al-Tuwaijari, J.M., Plant Leaf Diseases Detection and Classification Using Image Processing and Deep Learning Techniques. *2020 International Conference on Computer Science and Software Engineering (CSASE), IEEE UTC, Duhok, Kurdistan Region—Iraq.*
18. Kumar, M., Gupta, O., Madhav, P., Disease Detection in Coffee Plants Using Convolutional Neural Network. *Proceedings of the Fifth International Conference on Communication and Electronics Systems (ICCES 2020) IEEE Conference.*
19. Ananthajothi, K. and Subramaniam, M., Efficient Classification of Medical data and Disease Prediction using Multi Attribute Disease Probability Measure. *Appl. Math. Inf. Sci.*, 13, 5, 783–789, 2019.
20. Kosamkar, P.K. and Kulkarni Krushna Mantri, V.Y., Leaf Disease Detection and Recommendation of Pesticides using Convolution Neural Network. *International Conference on Computing Communication Control and Automation (ICCUBEA), IEEE, 2018.*
21. Yegneshwar Yadhav, S., Senthilkumar, T., Jayanthy, S., Judeson Antony Kovilpillai, J., Plant Disease Detection and Classification using CNN Model with Optimized Activation Function. *Proceedings of the International Conference on Electronics and Sustainable Communication Systems (ICESC 2020), IEEE Xplore.*
22. Madhulatha, G. and Ramadevi, O., Recognition of Plant Diseases using Convolutional Neural Network. *Proceedings of the Fourth International Conference on I-SMAC (IoT in Social, Mobile, Analytics and Cloud) (I-SMAC), IEEE Xplore, 2020.*
23. Shubham, R.G., Nandita, N., Ponkshe, Y.S., Plant Disease Detection Using CNNs and GANs as an Augmentative Approach. *2018 IEEE International Conference on Innovative Research and Development (ICIRD).*
24. Gangadevi, V., Subhashini, R., Anitha, G., Ajitha, S.M., MenakaGandhi, J., An Android Application For Pest Detection and Classification Using Regional Convolution Neural Network. *Int. J. Adv. Sci. Technol.*, 29, 10s, 7469–7475, 2020, Retrieved from http://sersc.org/journals/index.php/IJAST/article/view/23731.
25. Ananthajothi, K. and Subramaniam, M., Multi level incremental influence measure based classification of medical data for improved classification. *Clust. Comput.*, 22, 15073–15080, 2019, https://doi.org/10.1007/s10586-018-2498-z.

26. Gangadevi, G. and Jayakumar, C., An Efficient Crop Field Management Using Bi Directional LSTM Neural Network (August 5, 2019). *International Conference on Recent Trends in Computing, Communication and Networking Technologies (ICRTCCNT"19)*, October 18–19, 2019, Kings Engineering College, Chennai, Tamilnadu, India. *Proceedings of International Conference on Recent Trends in Computing, Communication & Networking Technologies (ICRTCCNT)*, 2019, https://ssrn.com/abstract=3432218 or http://dx.doi.org/10.2139/ssrn.3432218.

7

Generating Art and Music Using Deep Neural Networks

A. Pandiaraj*, S. Lakshmana Prakash†, R. Gopal‡ and P. Rajesh Kanna§

Bannari Amman Institute of Technology, Sathyamangalam, Erode, Tamil Nadu, India

Abstract

The aim of this project is to develop a model using deep neural nets which can imagine like humans, and generate Art and Music of its own. AI systems are known for their lack of creativity and imagination. We intend to falsify this statement. This model can be used for increasing cognitive efficiency in AGI (Artificial General Intelligence) thereby improving the agent's image classification and object localization. Music is a very humane thing, and by making the AI systems learn to generate music, we are one step closer in solving intelligence.

Keywords: Artificial intelligence, machine learning, deep neural network

7.1 Introduction

Artificial intelligence is expected to be the definite future of the computers. There have been a lot of advances on how machines learn and think to perform simple tasks which require some common sense. We started off in this direction with the idea of automating repeated tasks. For instance, the task can be as simple as sending bulk emails. We don't have to write the same email every time to send it to multiple people today. That's a simple task which doesn't require any thinking and can be clearly instructed. But what if we wished to send two different kinds of email to multiple people

Corresponding author: pandiaraja@bitsathy.ac.in
†*Corresponding author:* lakshmanaprakashs@bitsathy.ac.in
‡*Corresponding author:* gopalr@bitsathy.ac.in
§*Corresponding author:* mailmeatrajeshkanna@gmail.com

R. Kanthavel, K. Ananthajothi, S. Balamurugan and R. Karthik Ganesh (eds.) Artificial Intelligent Techniques for Wireless Communication and Networking, (91–104) © 2022 Scrivener Publishing LLC

from the same list. A decade ago the simple solution would have been to split the list and send it to them using bulk email service. But what if the list contains millions of email ids. Practically, it will take a lot of resources and time to split the list. With the introduction of AI, one can simply feed in the data and the emails to send, and the computer will do the thinking. The computer today, has the ability to split the list on its own and take the action as instructed further. Today, the computer can perform a number of intellectual tasks. It can do all the jobs from data filling to reporting to teaching and even engineering except one. The only thing which AI machines are unable to do today is to imagine.

7.1.1   Traditional Approach

Traditionally we relied on artistic personalities like Picasso to paint something creative and beautiful every time. These artists are often pressured to bring out something creative and unique every time they take the paintbrush in their hand. They end up being under heavy pressure. On the other hand, even the consumer has to pay a hefty amount for their creativity. The same is the case for music. This has what led this big music industry of today's world. No doubt these people have been very creative. But today's creativity seems to be limited.

7.1.2   Modern Computing Approach

Generating music and art has been favored a lot by the modern computing instruments. There have been a lot of software and specialized hardware to make the work of these artists simpler. For instance, with the use of the instrument called seaboard the music composers are capable of creating some new sound which is very pleasing and also unique. Similarly, with the use of the electrical drawing boards, the arts are able to splash some new tone of colors in the drawing area, which would have been difficult to make or find otherwise. Also, it enables them to reuse the same drawing boards, so they never run out of paper sheets. Now the technology also allows the artists to absorb the color from the real world, just by scanning it with the e-drawing pen.

7.2   Related Works

Magenta may be a project dedicated to music and art generation with machine intelligence [1]. It is a search project exploring the role of machine learning within the process of making art and music. Primarily this involves developing new deep learning and reinforcement learning algorithms for generating songs, images, drawings, and other materials. But it is also a search in building smart tools and interfaces that allow artists and musicians to increase their processes using these models. Magenta was started by some researchers and engineers from the Google Brain team but many others have contributed significantly to the project. It uses Tensor Flow.

Deepjazz was built by Ji-Sung Kim from Princeton University, Department of computing [2]. It uses Keras & Theano, two deep learning libraries, to get jazz music. Specifically, it builds a two-layer LSTM, learning from the given MIDI file. It uses deep learning, the AI tech that powers Google's AlphaGo and IBM's Watson, to form music. Deepjazz has been featured within the Guardian, Aeon Magazine, Inverse, Data Skeptic and therefore the front page of HackerNews. It has led to the foremost popular "AI" artist on SoundCloud with 172,000+ listens. Currently, Deepjazz is getting used as reference material for the course "Interactive Intelligent Devices" at the University of Perugia.

7.2.1   Feeling Investigation on Social Media

Web-based media is an online stage which assists with communicating and offers individual assessments among various parts of life. Web-based media constructs social associations with others who share comparative individual or vocation interests, exercises, foundations or genuine associations. A large portion of the market-based organizations assess the items or administrations dependent on buyer's perspective so as to improve their presentation and fulfill their requirements. Verbal, related knowledge of item or administration helps in ad libbing the organizations market [4, 5].

This examination depicts a slant investigation of more than 1,000 Facebook posts about broadcasts which brings about the significance of Facebook as a stage for web-based showcasing. The objective is consistently to know "who" is talking about "what", "when" and in "what sense". The conclusion mining and estimation investigation are significant for deciding suppositions on brands and purchasers' prerequisites. This examination assesses unpredictability of public perspectives, quick access of text.

A neural organization based generally approach for opinion characterization inside the blogosphere [5]—Long Sheng fowl variety [6]. Sites have become a partner degree indispensable to a piece of on-line culture. Nowadays everyone peruses web journals whether it's related with one's work or point based generally. So the most arrangement of this investigation is perceiving the inclination condition of the bloggers that licenses firms to ad lib their item quality. to achieve the objective etymology direction lists and AI ways are utilized. In any event, assuming the phonetics direction file doesn't perform brilliantly, anyway rapidly restores the outcome. Exactness of the framework is best characterized by AI anyway needing training time. This investigation extended a neural organization that utilizes phonetics direction as contribution to work out the feelings of the bloggers. The test results show that the extended methodology beats antiquated methodologies just as option neural organizations and various different phonetics direction records.

7.3   System Architecture

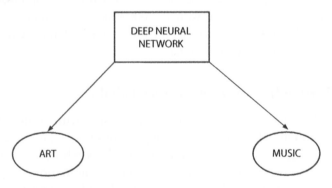

Figure 7.1 System architecture.

Figure 7.1 shows the overall outline of the project. The main module can be divided into two major modules namely the art module and the music module. It will be a desktop application which can also run by executing the python file using the command prompt. We can use the local servers like XAMPP and WAMP to run the file on the local host. This can be done to run the file through a web interface. Running the file through the web interface will allow the real-time system to be run from anywhere remotely. Before launching the application, we must ensure that the system has the apt version of the python.

The initial step is to make sure that the input files are named properly and also are kept in the appropriate folder. The python files kick-start the whole system. It will then the intake the input(s) and processes it. In case of the LSTM algorithm, we will even be able to listen to the music while it's being generated once the model decides the few initial matches [21].

7.3.1   Art Module

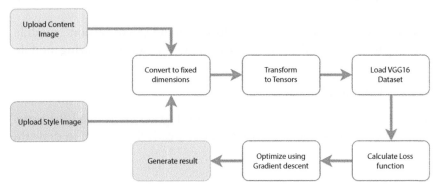

Figure 7.2 Art module.

Figures 7.2 and 7.3 show the art module makes the first major part of our System. This module is solely responsible for getting the input, processing it and then generating the output. We then magnify the details of this module into various stages or modules.

1. Upload content Image
2. Upload style Image
3. Convert to fixed Dimension
4. Transform to Tensors
5. Load VGG16 Data set
6. Calculate Loss Function
7. Optimize Using Gradient descent
8. Generate result.

7.3.2   Music Module

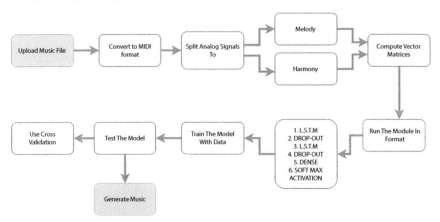

Figure 7.3 Music module.

7.4   System Development

An art system consists of upload module, conversion module, Transformation module, Loading Data set module and optimizing module.

7.4.1   Upload Module

This is the first module in the Art system. Figures 7.4 (a) and (b) represent the Content image and Style image respectively. We aim to draw the

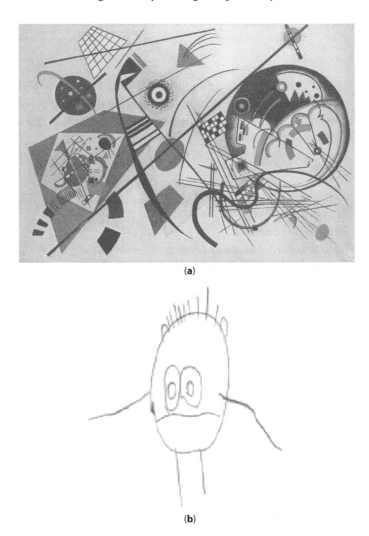

(a)

(b)

Figure 7.4 (a) Content image (b) Style image.

content image in the style of the style image. The Style image is the sample style of the renowned artist and was obtained from the Google Images under the reusable license. In this input module we add a content image and a style image.

7.4.2   Conversion Module

In this second module we will resize the images. This is done so that the model can identify and compare the images correctly. We will convert both the input images into a fixed 512 × 512 dimension.

7.4.3   Transformation Module

In this third module we will convert all the images into tensors. Tensors are equivalent to multidimensional array. Converting all the images into tensors, it can be divided into various parts like vector, matrix, and tensor (Figure 7.5).

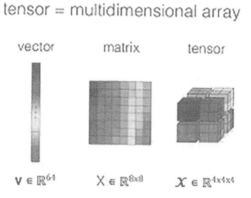

Figure 7.5 Transformation module.

7.4.4   Loading Dataset Module

In this forth module we will load the dataset. We will be loading VGG16 dataset (Figure 7.6).

(a)

ConvNet Configuration					
A	A-LRN	B	C	D	E
11 weight layers	11 weight layers	13 weight layers	16 weight layers	16 weight layers	19 weight layers
input (224 × 224 RGB image)					
conv3-64	conv3-64 **LRN**	conv3-64 **conv3-64**	conv3-64 conv3-64	conv3-64 conv3-64	conv3-64 conv3-64
maxpool					
conv3-128	conv3-128	conv3-128 **conv3-128**	conv3-128 conv3-128	conv3-128 conv3-128	conv3-128 conv3-128
maxpool					
conv3-256 conv3-256	conv3-256 conv3-256	conv3-256 conv3-256	conv3-256 conv3-256 **conv1-256**	conv3-256 conv3-256 **conv3-256**	conv3-256 conv3-256 conv3-256 **conv3-256**
maxpool					
conv3-512 conv3-512	conv3-512 conv3-512	conv3-512 conv3-512	conv3-512 conv3-512 **conv1-512**	conv3-512 conv3-512 **conv3-512**	conv3-512 conv3-512 conv3-512 **conv3-512**
maxpool					
conv3-512 conv3-512	conv3-512 conv3-512	conv3-512 conv3-512	conv3-512 conv3-512 **conv1-512**	conv3-512 conv3-512 **conv3-512**	conv3-512 conv3-512 conv3-512 **conv3-512**
maxpool					
FC-4096					
FC-4096					
FC-1000					
soft-max					

(b)

Figure 7.6 (a) VGG16 data set image. (b) VGG16 architecture.

7.4.5   Optimizing Module

In this module we calculate the loss function and then optimize the image using gradient descent.

7.4.5.1   Calculating Loss Function

The crux of the paper we're trying to reproduce is that the style transfer problem can be posed as an optimization problem, where the loss function we want to minimize can be decomposed into three distinct parts: the content loss, the style loss and the total variation loss Figures 7.7 (a) and (b).

Lcontent(c,x) & Lstyle(s,x)

We then define the squared-error loss between the two feature representations.

$$\mathcal{L}_{\text{content}}\left(\vec{p}, \vec{x}, l\right) = \frac{1}{2}\sum_{i,j}\left(F_{ij}^{l} - P_{ij}^{l}\right)^{2}.$$

(a)

$$\frac{\partial \mathcal{L}_{\text{content}}}{\partial F_{ij}^{l}} = \begin{cases} \left(F^{l} - P^{l}\right)_{ij} & \text{if } F_{ij}^{l} > 0 \\ 0 & \text{if } F_{ij}^{l} < 0, \end{cases}$$

(b)

Figure 7.7 (a) L content squared-error loss function. (b) Derivative of loss with respect to activations.

The derivative of this loss with respect to the activation in layer l equals
All five modules to be follow music system. This music system will work LSTM Algorithm. This algorithm will use only music file.

7.5   Algorithm-LSTM

Long Short-Term Memory (LSTM) algorithm is run twice over the music file.

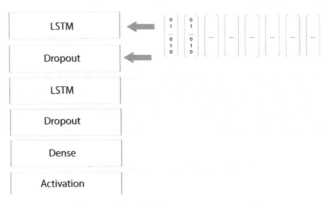

As stated we will run the LSTM algorithm twice on the music chunk in the RNN. The LSTM will cross mix and match the small portion of the tune; in the second iteration the matches will be more accurate. The LSTM will remember only the better part and will leave out the wastage. This saves us memory as well as the processing time. The working of LSTM with RNN is depicted in Figure 7.8.

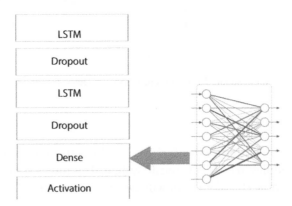

Figure 7.8 Working of LSTM with RNN.

7.6   Result

We will analyze the system according to the dataset that we have taken. Data required for experimentation is collected for testing. We used the pre-trained VGG16 Dataset for out art prototype. This dataset is named as Train Dataset. Another dataset called Test Dataset is created and the images of those 40 persons with different expressions are stored in it.

7.6.1 Sample Input and Output

Figures 7.9 (a) and (b) show sample input and sample output.

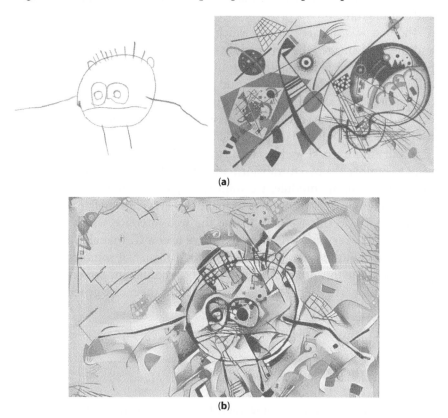

(a)

(b)

Figure 7.9 (a) Sample input. (b) Sample output.

7.7 Conclusions

This system which uses RNN and CNN was used to generate the music and art enables any user to perform creative work using the system model. Our project was divided into two parts. The initial plan was to create the art section only but, the later motivation and interest to explore it more lead to the development of the music segment. The system model takes in the sample input and produces the output based on the input given. For instance, the style image will help one determine the type of drawing they expect to draw. Giving jazz music as input will result in jazz type music. However, it was noted that none of them either art or music cannot be classified as one of the types. So, the system was segregated into two major parts namely Art Module and the Music Module. Once it was possible to generate the music and art, our main focus was to optimize the processing and training time.

The first was the art module which takes two inputs, a content image and the style image. The art module is based on the convolution neural networks. It then produces the output image. Its output can be accessed through the output folder. The second part is the music module. It accepts one input, which can be the music in popular formats. The music module is based on the recurrence neural networks. It then produces the output music and stores it in the output folder.

In our future work, we plan to further optimize the system model. We want to remove the MIDI transformation to further reduce the processing time. In case of art module, we want to implement multiple styles on a single content image. Our aim is to make this service available to anyone, anywhere. To do this we plan to use the web-interface which can store the files in the server. Also, we want to give user a UI that allows them to upload the input files and obtain output in a matter of minutes. We also plan to separate this project into completely two different projects namely, the project for art generation and the project for the music generation.

References

1. Huang, A. and Wu, R., *Deep learning for Music*, Stanford University, Stanford, CA, United States, 2015.
2. Analyzing Six Deep Learning Tools For Music Generation, by Frank, The Asimov Institute, Utrecht, Netherlands.
3. Jayant, N.K. and Borra, S., Attendance Management System Using Hybrid Face Recognition Techniques. *2016 Conference on Advances in Signal Processing (CASP)*.
4. Mao, H.H., Shin, T., Cottrell, G.W., *DeepJ: Style-Specific Music Generation*, Ithaca, NY, United States, arXiv: 1801.00887v1 [cs.SD], 3 Jan 2018.
5. Neri, F., Aliprandi, C., Capeci, F., Montserrat Cuadros, T., Sentiment Analysis on Social Media. *International Conference on Advances in Social Networks Analysis and Mining*, pp. 951–958, 2012.
6. Chen, L.S., Liu, C.H., Chiu, H.-J., A neural network-based approach for sentiment classification in the blogosphere. *J. Informetr.*, 5, 313–322, 2011.

7. Kaushik, A. and Naithani, S., A Study on Sentiment Analysis: Methods and Tools. *Int. J. Sci. Res.*, 4, 287–291, 2015.
8. Das, S. and Chen, M., Yahoo! for Amazon: Extracting market sentiment from stock message boards, in: *Asia Pacific Finance Association*, 2012.
9. Gokulakrishnan, B., Priyanthan, P., Ragavan, T., Prasanth, N., Opinion Mining and sentiment Analysis on a Twitter Data Stream. *The International Conference on Advances in ICT for Emerging Regions*, pp. 182–188.
10. Bhatt, A. *et al.*, Amazon Review Classification and Sentiment Analysis. *Int. J. Comput. Sci. Inf. Technol.*, 6, 6, 5107–5110, 2015.
11. Kumar, N., Nagalla, R., Marwah, T., Singh, M., Sentiment dynamics in Social media news channels. *Online Soc. Netw. Media*, 18, 42–54, December 2018.
12. Binu, D. and Kariyappa, B.S., RideNN: A New Rider Optimization Algorithm Based Neural Network for Fault Diagnosis in Analog circuits. *IEEE Trans. Instrum. Meas.*, IEEE, 68, 1, 2–26. 2018.
13. Lee, H.G., Noh, K.Y., Ryu, K.H., Mining Bio Signal Data: Coronary Artery Disease Diagnosis using Linear and Nonlinear Features of HRV. *Proceedings of International Conference on Emerging Technologies in Knowledge Discovery and Data Mining*, pp. 56–66, 2007.
14. Palaniappan, S. and Awang, R., Intelligent Heart Disease Prediction System using Data Mining Techniques. *Int. J. Comput. Sci. Netw. Secur.*, 8, 8, 1–6, 2008.
15. Guru, N., Dahiya, A., Rajpal, N., Decision Support System for Heart Disease Diagnosis using Neural Network. *Delhi Bus. Rev.*, 8, 1, 1–6, 2007.
16. Le Duff, F., Munteanb, C., Cuggiaa, M., Mabob, P., Predicting Survival Causes After Out of Hospital Cardiac Arrest using Data Mining Method. *Stud. Health Technol. Inform.*, 107, 2, 1256–1259, 2004.
17. Parthiban, L. and Subramanian, R., Intelligent Heart Disease Prediction System using CANFIS and Genetic Algorithm. *Int. J. Biol. Biomed. Med. Sci.*, 3, 3, 1–8, 2008.
18. Noh, K., Lee, H.G., Shon, H.-S., Lee, B.J., Ryu, K.H., Associative Classification Approach for Diagnosing Cardiovascular Disease, in: *Intelligent Computing in Signal Processing and Pattern Recognition*, vol. 345, pp. 721–727, 2006.
19. Frawley, W.J. and Piatetsky-Shapiro, G., Knowledge Discovery in Databases: An Overview. *AI Mag.*, 13, 3, 57–70, 1996.
20. Ordonez, C., Improving Heart Disease Prediction using Constrained Association Rules. *Technical Seminar Presentation*, University of Tokyo, 2004.
21. Pandiaraj, A., Sentiment analysis on newspaper article reviews: Contribution towards improved rider optimization-based hybrid classifier. *Kybernetes*, Vol. ahead-of-print No. ahead-of-print. https://doi.org/10.1108/K-08-2020-0512.

8

Deep Learning Era for Future 6G Wireless Communications—Theory, Applications, and Challenges

S.K.B. Sangeetha[1]* and R. Dhaya[2]

[1]School of Computing, SRM Institute of Technology, Vadapalani Campus, Chennai, India
[2]Dept. of CS, King Khalid University-Sarat Abidha Campus, Abha, KSA

Abstract

Over hundreds of years have passed since wireless communication technology was first introduced. The developers have made remarkable strides since 1880, including setting up an LTE network. Industry experts, from Verizon to Qualcomm, together with various experts, have a range of ideas about how to accelerate the evolution of wireless communication into — and even beyond — the 21st century. The wireless network technology requires smooth connectivity, easy accessibility, and safe connections at worldwide supply. 5G wireless technology is designed to provide higher data peak speeds, very reduced latency, increased reliability, massive network bandwidth, improved availability, plus an enhanced UI6G. Mobile users with a higher speed, superb coverage and no latency can broaden their existing mobile ecosystems into new worlds. 6 G will impact all sectors to increase the safety of transport, distributed health, agricultural accuracy, digitised logistics and more. Therefore, efforts on 6 G networks from both industry and academia have already been put into the study. Recently deep learning has been used as a new paradigm for designing and optimizing high-intelligence 6 G networks. With the realistic account of all challenges and opportunities of wireless technology from engineering perspectives, requires a complete study of available methods. In this chapter, huge potential efforts are made to study the background of 6G wireless communication with the detail of how deep learning made a contribution to 6G

*Corresponding author: skbsangeetha@gmail.com

R. Kanthavel, K. Ananthajothi, S. Balamurugan and R. Karthik Ganesh (eds.) *Artificial Intelligent Techniques for Wireless Communication and Networking*, (105–120) © 2022 Scrivener Publishing LLC

wireless technology. In the end, this chapter also highlights future research directions for deep learning-driven wireless technology.

Keywords: Deep learning, 6G, wireless communication, artificial intelligence, challenges

8.1   Introduction

Since the turn of the millennium, the wireless industry has drastically advanced. Today's wireless operation ecosystem is focused on the secure link of 4G from voice-only 2G platforms and web-enabled 3G. Wireless network infrastructure of the fifth generation, generally known as 5G, is now being carried out in cities across the globe. By 2024, an estimated 1.5 billion mobile subscribers with a production of 40% of the existing global industry will be using 5G broadband networks. GSMA Intelligence analysis suggests how global traffic will expand rapidly across different providers. But as with any technological product, as the technology matures, customers can expect both positive and negative ones. Before it enters mass acceptance, 5G still has a way to go. As a consequence of a higher capacity, the networks are required to serve cell phones, not only as existing mobile networks, but also as particular internet service providers for desktops and tablets and to compete with existing ISPs such as the Internet of Things (IoT) and the machine to the area. The new networks requiring 5G enabled wireless devices cannot be operated by 4G mobile phones. Towns and regions are, however, rushing to build the infrastructure needed to reach the next technological revolution. About 25 nations have deployed 5G cellular networks since the late 2018. Notable milestones include South Korea, which in April 2019 became the first nation worldwide to release 5G wireless technology. Switzerland, officially at 225 and counting, has the largest number of 5G network installations [10].

The list is endless: 5G will, very simply, not only extend broadband internet services but also permit new technology and use of cases from the embedded IoT to the self-supporting cars, intelligent buildings and intelligent factories [5]. Highband 5G uses 25–39 GHz frequencies, close to the base of the millimeter wave band, but higher frequencies may in long term be used. It frequently reaches download speeds similar to cable Internet in the gigabit per second (Gbit/s). Millimeter waves, however, have a smaller range (mmWave or mmW) that require many small cells. Some components like walls and windows are difficult to pass through. Due to their higher costs, these cells should only be deployed in highly urbanized areas and areas where crowds of people gather, like sporting venues and convention centers. Highly anticipated innovations like artificial intelligence (AI), virtual reality, low connectivity, extremely high data rates and quality are needed by the Internet of Everything (IoE) for the transmission and reception as shown in Figure 8.1, which cannot be fulfilled by conventional ubiquitous mobile ultra-broadband and ultra-high data capacity of current 5G. There is no doubt, however, that 6G is taking shape. In different technological blogs and workshop panel discussions, visionaries from industries and universities have shared some immediate impressions on 6G. AI-enabled technologies were used for the purpose of network intelligence, closed-loop automation and smart wireless networking for 6G networks.

AI techniques which can be used in 6G networks to perform intelligently, exploring knowledge, advanced learning, organizing structure and complicated decisions, with strong analytical skills, learner skills, optimising skills and intelligent perception capabilities. In 6G, we intend to see Artificial Intelligence (AI) at the edges of the network in action with distributed preparation, which is still an open issue at the moment [13].

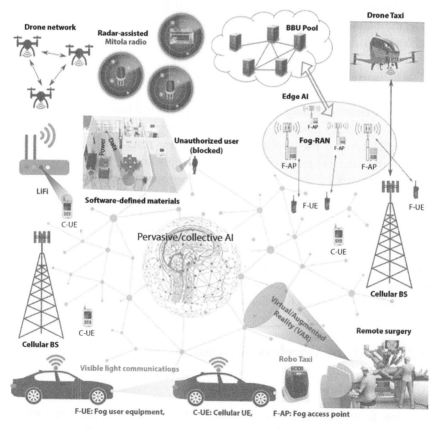

Figure 8.1 6G vision [9].

Deep learning has been commonly used in wireless networks, perceived to be the critical component of AI technologies. It will play a critical role. The role of 6G in various fields, including linguistic interactions, holistic strategic communications, computing, tracking, and resource control, etc., is driving the paradigm shift [14]. The 5G's advent introduces great challenges for mobile communication service suppliers. One of the ways the industry addresses these intricacies is to integrate artificial intelligence (AI) techniques into networks. Ericsson asked senior managers and decision makers from 132 service providers worldwide about their proposals to adopt AI in their networks, both present and potential. 6G would be aiming for another big jump from 5G, which would only be feasible if it were possible to achieve deep learning. Here we share evolving methods, implementations and complexities which might contribute significantly to wireless communication that would allow 6G in about two decades [15].

The aim of this study is to provide readers with profound learning customized for 6G wireless communication and to help researchers to facilitate the 6G wireless networks driven by profound learning. This work makes the main contribution

1. Introduced by an AI groundwork, 6G wireless communication is affected.
2. A clear road map for the need for profound learning and its challenges has been provided in 6G communication.
3. Described the applications and future research directions for wireless researchers to make deep learning powered 6G networks.

This survey varies clearly from other recent surveys in the above points. It gives as much info as before. Section 8.2 discusses the wireless technology source to IA study allowing 6G wireless communication. The paper has the following structure. Section 8.3 deals with 6G Wireless Communications enabled deep learning. Section 8.4 lists and describes briefly the future directions of the research in Section 8.5.

8.2   Study of Wireless Technology

8.2.1   Overview

Wireless technology consists of software that enables us to connect without ever using wires or cables. The term can also apply to devices which, without using cables, draw power. In other words, there is wireless technology in a mobile phone that we can charge without wires. Although the word applies to interacting without wires or cables in most situations. For a long time, wireless devices in one form or another have been around. It all began when Heinrich Hertz (1857–1894), a German physicist, invented electromagnetic waves [1]. Two major forms of wireless technology currently exist:

Local Wi-Fi Networks
Wireless Internet is a technology that provides Internet access to tablets, video game consoles, printers and smartphones. Care centres, smartphones and digital audio players also use Wi-Fi. In the 1990s the phrase 'Wi-Fi,' which after 'Hi-Fi,' was an arbitrary second function, came out with the words 'Wireless' plus 'Fi.' Wi-Fi has many applications. Modern Wi-Fi deployments range from small indoor and large, campus-based networks to fully mobile aircraft and train networks. In restaurants, hotels and now mobile devices connecting to networks of 3G or 4G, users can access the Internet from wireless hotspots. These aspects of external access points often do not require a network registration or password. Subsequent to registration or a fee is paid, others may be accessed.

Cellular Networks (Mobile Phone Networks)
This feature provides electronic devices to be connected over long distances. For example, in Alaska, somebody in Australia can talk to someone else on

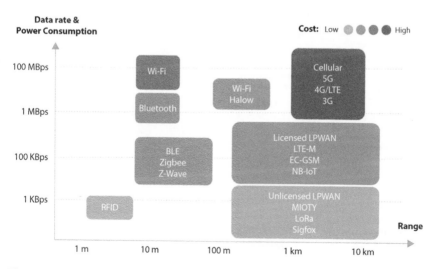

Figure 8.2 Wireless technologies—Overview.

cell phones. This can be done by mobile networks. The cells provide radios that are entered together for a wide geographical area. This means a broad range of ported transceptors can interact across the network via the base stations with each other and with fixed transceivers and telephones even if certain transceivers go via more than one cell during transmission (for example, mobile telephones, tablets or laptops with broadband modems, pagers). Figure 8.2 is showing the overview of Wireless technologies.

8.2.2   Background Study

For the last half of the nineteenth century, transmitting knowledge wirelessly was a technological curiosity. In the first place, telegraph wires became unreliable or untrusted as signals and audio contact through electromagnetic radiation was used as a wireless telegraph. Wireless networking is typically seen as wireless or RF connectivity (radio frequency). Other technologies that allow wireless links are available. As shown in Figure 8.3,

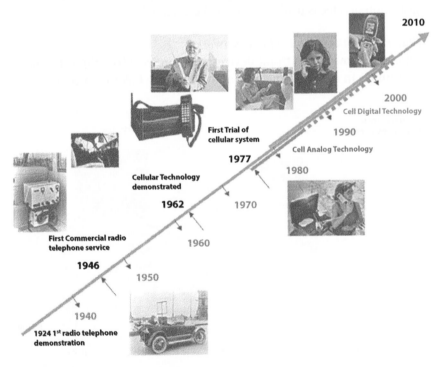

Figure 8.3 History of wireless technology [12].

there are also acoustic techniques that transfer data from point to point using frequencies outside the audio range [11].

8.2.3 6G Wireless Technology

In several parts of the world, broadband networks of 5th generation (5G) have already been deployed. Already, service providers from all over the world have derived the benefits of AI integration into their networks. Some aspects of AI will be integrated fully in their networks by more than half at the end of 2020 (53%). Some even expect that AI will be adopted in 3–5% years by the end of this year with an additional 19% schedule. By 2020, the full international rollout of 5G is expected. 5G networks could not provide a completely integrated and intelligent network, offering it as a fully immersive experience and service. While the 5G communications network, which will soon be initiated, will make substantial upgrades to existing networks, they will not be able to accommodate future smart and automation systems after ten years [9].

In comparison to 4G, the 5G network provides additional features and provides higher service efficiency (QoS). The 5G technology provides a range of new methods including the development and support of a new frequency band (e.g. one mm wave or optical spectrum), enhanced spectrum use and spectrum spectrum control, licensed and unlicensed band integration. Some devices, like VR devices, need to be above 5G (B5G) because they require a minimum data rate of 10 Gbps.

In order to adapt to the constraints of 5G, a 6th-generation wireless infrastructure with new atmospheric features will need to be installed. The 6G system will also proceed the development of previous times, including the addition of new technology to revolutionary facilities. The Six G system also converges all past features such as network densification, high performance, and high reliability. AI, smart wearables, augmentations, self-supporting vehicles, computer reality applications, 3D visualization and sensing are new services.

For cable-free 6G networks adjusting to large volumes of data and unbelievably high internet connectivity per device is most important. The 6G framework combined with a few exciting features enhance performance and enhance user QoS by 5G. The machine is safe and user data is secure. As a global communication facility, the 6G communications system is designed. It has comfortable accommodation. The 6G system can provide simultaneous wireless networking 1,000 times greater than 5G. Researchers around the world study the essence of 6G communications in 2030 and the possible drivers of successful 6G wireless communications [6, 7].

8.2.4   Influence of AI in 6G Wireless Communication

The entire world will soon be related to the exponential growth of information technology. On 6G communications, artificial intelligence has an important impact. Nowadays, all the new technologies support AI. In the years to come, we should expect the planet to be a powered AI pretty fast. The 6G can increase artificial intelligence in many respects. In the future, AI players will certainly play a key role. The driving force behind mobile technology is artificial intelligence and the framework for the development of a whole modern trend of machine learning methods.

In recent studies, the wireless community seems to be very interested in artificial intelligence and progress leads to deep learning and an increase in smartphones, extremely smart devices and big data generation. 6G communications are supposed to provide complete wireless and automatic interaction, and also enable artificial intelligence in an integral way.

Artificial intelligence is at the pivot allowing automated machine technology. The dominant force behind automation is numerous machine learning algorithms and deep learning principles. In general, artificial intelligence and machine learning power many requirements running on cell devices or smart devices. AI is crucial to 6G in different components such as conceptual connectivity, mechanical learning and deep neural network, and extensive communication, storage, and growth. The idea of ET makes a system work efficiently [2, 13]. Figure 8.4 indicates the Ai enabled 6G.

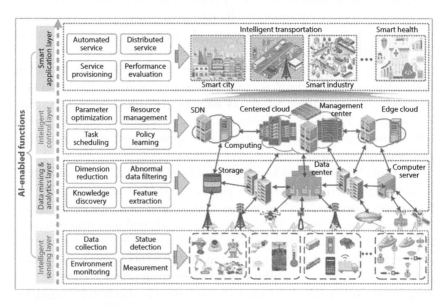

Figure 8.4 AI enabled 6G.

8.3 Deep Learning Enabled 6G Wireless Communication

In 6G wireless networks, Deep Learning (DL) would therefore play a crucial role as it is capable of modeling structures that a mathematical equation does not present. In addition, DL tools can be used to substitute heuristic or brute strength algorithms in order to optimize these localized tasks. In the meanwhile DL has been established so that 6G networks can be analyzed and controlled on a computerized zero touch basis in time. In addition, mobile devices may perform additional DL activities or forecasts, reporting them onto the network to aid with resource management decision making and render mobile devices an integrated compound. These data require rapid access by wireless devices, especially in enormous potential for growth such as real-time video surveillance and extended reality (XR). DL agents include the configuration of the radio interface, adaptive hopping methods, access control, improvisation for several functions and are used by 6G networks.

The 6G networks are now being researched by industry as well as academia during its implementation of 5G networks, in which 6G networks are expected to utilize quality services, mobile apps (for example virtual and enlarged reality, remote and holographic operation) and unlimited connectivity on a large number of intelligent devices. The first 6G networks are mainly dominated by the established 5G infrastructure such as the SDN, NFV and the network cut-off architectures in agreement with previous network evolution rules. But in comparison with 5G networks, 6G systems connect certain laws. Ultra-high data rates, ultra-low latency, high reliability and smooth connectivity, for example. Significant size, complexity, dynamic characteristics and heterogeneity establish 6G networks.

8.3.1 Deep Learning Techniques for 6G Networks

Deep learning to enable Space-Air-Ground Embedded networks to optimize their performance and use deep learning to push the routes that best suit satellite networks. Furthermore, extensive training was introduced by learning about environmental dynamism, in order to maintain reliable internet abilities for UAV networks, and simulation showed that deep strengthening learning substantially exceeds conventional methodologies. AI and 6G networks therefore promise to improve system design and system performance. Deep learning in 6G networks will be massive, inter-complex, highly vibrant and heterogeneous. 6G networks should also support wireless implementation and provide diverse Qos parameters for a range of appliances and large physical data processing. ATM technology which can be used in 6G networks to intelligently optimize performance, information retrieval, advanced learning, organizational structure and complicated decision making with powerful analysis capabilities, learning skills and smart recognition.

Recently, deep learning methodologies based on artificial neural networks have solved several learning problems (ANNs). The development of the Deep Learning Framework was primarily driven by the use of computer resources and access to large data sets. For various tasks, many deep learning strategies are used. Multi-layer vision is a commonly used fundamental for many learning tasks (MLPs). In the field of image recognition, convolutional neural networks (CNN) are widely used to decrease the input size using convolution operations. Recurrent neural networks (RNNs) are most suitable for sequential learning tasks. For dimension reduction, autoencoder-based profound learning models are used to generate samples close to the available data collection, and the generative adversarial networks (GANs). Figure 8.5 indicates the DL enabled intelligent 6G Networks.

The amount of training data available in the field of WC remains far from comparable to broad data sets for key market players, such as computer vision and speech recognition, for core profound learning applications.

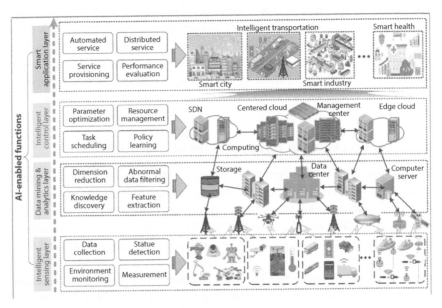

Figure 8.5 Deep learning enabled intelligent 6G networks.

Deep learning models necessitate very large training sets because of the fractal dimension of the signal cant in relation to simple models. The network complexity indicated by the coexistence of multiple mobile network operators is another limiting factor. Although standardised formats of data sets could help to create interoperability, network management feature implementations could differ significantly between different operators.

In addition, operators can choose to keep their acquired data confidential because of business-oriented principles. The fact that deep learning alone is not the best solution for all data analytical tasks in 6G networks leads to these variables. Moreover, several application and platform-dependent models will be required, even on resource-controlled platforms, for example, ultra-low-performance microcomputers [4].

8.3.2   Predicted Services in the 6G Era

8.3.2.1   Internet-of-(Every)Thing

The number of IoT devices is anticipated to rise to 18 billion by 2022, each of which will require network access. The 6G can be used in small-scale private IoT devices such as smart cities and emerging production technology for large-scale architecture situations. Small devices (Amazon Alexa, Nest Cam and Google Home) like In-house IoT can take advantage of in-depth learning to unload computer tasks into their small storage spaces. User can play videos with the desired content from their base stations or deliver videos on their cache devices based on local network conditions, which allow quality/bandwidth. Increasing ARS stores local relevant information to overlay the user interface for user latency, unlike data recovery from regional cloud data centers.

8.3.2.2   Connected Vehicles

6G would allow more large-scale new applications. Consider coordinating more and more ad hoc networks of UAVs that have to navigate in new environments, unloading computer tasks and downloading new information via near-by desktop workstation stations with close to zero vehicles traveling around their areas.

8.3.2.3   Smart Cities

6G can be used globally to improve intelligent city programmes in urban settings, by providing local activities and communities with computing and data storage points. Cloud computing and access to the internet can also be used by Smart Cities in cities for large-scale IOT, providing urban services such as electricity networks, transport networks and emergencies through more information about mobile edge computing. Using 6G to monitor the energy consumption of rising urban areas based on energy profiles and real time demand in common activities. Moreover, the edge of deep learning will help public security and police programmes in large urban environments by lightweight computer vision systems.

8.3.2.4   Robotics and Industry

6G can be used to maximize manufacturing work with robotic equipment and to analyze big data on the mobile edge of the plant in real time. Rugged 6G networks offer technological innovations which are essential to smart plants, such as system stability, low latency and attack susceptibility, in a specific area of the network. Crucial information such as Product Quality Control are automated by 6G and mobile edge computing. Computerized factory systems can then use deep learning to manage the discharge of power and energy into the local grid [8]. Figure 8.6 represents the Drone of IoT in 6G.

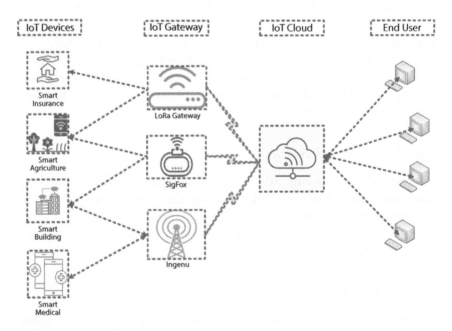

Figure 8. 6 Drone of IoT in 6G.

8.4   Applications and Future Research Directions

Conventional machine learning schemes rely on a central server and are susceptible to major security issues such as a single point of failure.

Furthermore, centralized data aggregation and processing leads to high overheads, and researchers warn against 6G being inappropriate for conventional centered ML schemes. Since AI has all facets of network systems in a 6G environment, it can link human-centered growth. 6G communications also have significantly higher privacy and protection standards.

While many features and facilities are open to uncertainty, we can confidently assume that AI has a key role to play. 6G communication revolutionizes our way of virtual communication with AR/VR. The 6G world of communication has brought a range of new infrastructures with the development of in-depth learning, integrated land and space, federated learning networks, decentralized infrastructure and trusted technology. Because 6G equipment and applications are customized, maintaining confidentiality without quality trading is a challenge. And when 6G arrived, the researchers were attempting to clear the way for a smooth transition to future research. Figure 8.7 indicates the Future of Deep learning in 6G.

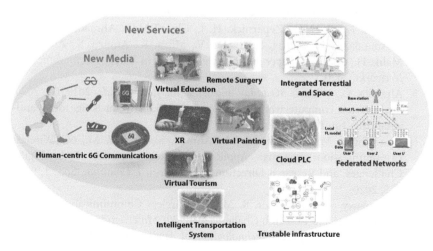

Figure 8.7 Deep learning in 6G—Future [3].

Conclusion

The unparalleled Internet of all scenarios with highly complex and demanding specifications is required to support 6G. 6G is intended to be space–aerial–terrestrial–ocean interconnected three-dimensional networks of various slice styles to meet these complex requirements effectively allowing new innovations and paradigms to make the device smarter and more versatile. As 6G networks are highly complicated, heterogeneous and diverse, achieving efficient use of resources, smooth user experience, automated management and orchestration is very challenging. By using deep learning, it is natural to solve complex 6G network problems with the advent of big data processing technologies, computational resources and the availability of rich data. Big potential attempts are made in this chapter to research the context of 6G wireless communication with the specifics of how deep learning has led to 6G wireless technology. This chapter also highlights, in the end, future research directions for wireless technology powered by deep learning.

References

1. https://marketbusinessnews.com/financial-glossary/wireless-technology
2. https://www.comsoc.org/publications/journals/ieee-tnse/cfp/ai-driven-6g-mobile-wireless-networks-key-enabling-theories
3. https://analyticsindiamag.com/6g-machine-learning-federated/
4. Ali, S., Saad, W., Rajatheva, N., Chang, K., Steinbach, D., Sliwa, B., Wietfeld, C., Mei, K., Shiri, H., Zepernick, H.-J., Chu, T.M.C., Ahmad, I., Huusko, I., Suutala, J., Bhadauria, S., Bhatia, V., Mitra, R., Amuru, S., Abbas, R., Malik, H., *6G White Paper on Machine Learning in Wireless Communication Networks*, 2020.
5. Altavilla, D., *What is 5G today and what the future holds*, 2019, 04, 2020, https://www. computerworld.Com /article/3445370/ what-is-5g- today-and-what- the- future-holds.html.
6. Chowdhury, M. Z., Shahjalal, M., Ahmed, S., Jang, Y. M., 6G Wireless Communication Systems: Applications, Requirements, Technologies, Challenges, and Research Directions. *IEEE Open J. Commun. Soc.*, 1, 957–975, 2020.
7. Elmeadawy, S. and Shubair, R. M., 6G Wireless Communications: Future Technologies and Research Challenges, in: *2019 International Conference on Electrical and Computing Technologies and Applications (ICECTA)*, pp. 1–5, UAE, 2019.

8. Letaief, K., Chen, W., Shi, Y., Zhang, J., Zhang, Y.-J., The Roadmap to 6G: AI Empowered Wireless Networks. *IEEE Commun. Mag.*, 57, 84–90, 2019.

9. Sangeetha, S.K.B., An Empirical Investigation of Securing Internet of Things Data in Wireless Sensor Network. *J. Asian Sci. Res.*, 9, 8, 95–99, 2019.

10. Tariq, T., Khandaker, M.R.A., Wong, K.-K., Imran, M.A., Bennis, M., Debbah, M., A Speculative Study on 6G. *IEEE Wirel. Commun.*, 27, 4, 118–125, 2020.

11. Viens, A., *The Future of 5G: Comparing 3 Generations of Wireless Technology*, 2019, Retrieved October 06, 2020 from https://www.visualcapitalist.com/the-future-of-5g-comparing-3-generations-of-wireless -technology/.

12. Wicks, A. and Kemerling, J., A brief early history of wireless technology. *Exp. Tech.*, 27, 11 2003, 57–58, 2003, https://doi.org/10.1111/j.1747-1567.2003.tb00140.x.

13. Winters, F., Mielenz, C., Hellestrand, G., *Design process changes enabling rapid development,* 1–13, 2004.

14. Yang, H., Alphones, A., Xiong, Z., Niyato, D., Zhao, J., Wu, K., Artificial Intelligence-Enabled Intelligent 6G Networks, 2019. *IEEE Netw.,* 34, 6, 272–280, 2020.

15. Zhao, Y., Zhao, J., Zhai, W., Sun, S., Niyato, D., Lam, K.-Y., A Survey of 6G Wireless Communications: Emerging Technologies. *Adv. Inf. Commun.,* 150–170, 2020.

Robust Cooperative Spectrum Sensing Techniques for a Practical Framework Employing Cognitive Radios in 5G Networks

J. Banumathi[1]*, S.K.B. Sangeetha[2] and R. Dhaya[3]

[1]*Dept. of Information Technology, University College of Engineering, Nagercoil, India*
[2]*School of Computing, SRM Institute of Technology, Vadapalani Campus, Chennai, India*
[3]*Dept. of Computer Science, King Khalid University-Sarat Abidha Campus, Abha, KSA*

Abstract

Cooperative communication in 5G networks is one of the most rapidly developing areas of study, and it is expected to be a crucial enabling technology for future spectrum efficiency in 5G networks. One of the most challenging tasks for cognitive radio systems is to detect the presence of primary (licensed) users over a broad spectrum at a specific time and in a specific area. The use of cooperative spectrum sensing in cognitive radio systems to improve the efficiency of detecting primary users is discussed in this book chapter. We will define spectrum sensing for cognitive radios and suggest robust cooperative spectrum sensing techniques for a realistic cognitive radios application. In a cognitive wireless relay network, we also look at mutual communications for spectrum sharing. We present a cognitive space-time-frequency coding technique that can opportunistically change its coding structure by adjusting to the complex spectrum environment in order to maximize spectrum opportunities. The concept of resource sharing among multiple nodes in a network is central to user cooperation. The exploration of user cooperation is driven by the fact that willingness to share power and computation with neighbouring nodes will result in network resource savings. Cooperative communications has recently been upgraded to one of 3GPP LTE Advanced's most

**Corresponding author*: jbanu85@gmail.com

R. Kanthavel, K. Ananthajothi, S. Balamurugan and R. Karthik Ganesh (eds.) *Artificial Intelligent Techniques for Wireless Communication and Networking*, (121–138) © 2022 Scrivener Publishing LLC

advanced features (LTEA). Cognitive radio (CR) is another groundbreaking new technology that has the ability to address the radio spectrum's stringent requirements and scarcity. Cognitive radio can use cooperative networking systems for spectrum sensing and spectrum sharing in 5G networks.

Keywords: Cooperative, spectrum, 5G networks, cognitive radio

9.1   Introduction

Cognitive Radios (CRs) are viewed as the answer for the current low use of the radio range. It is the key innovation that will empower adaptable, productive and dependable range use by adjusting the radio's working attributes to the constant states of the climate. CRs can possibly use the enormous measure of unused range in a savvy way while not meddling with other officeholder gadgets in recurrence groups previously authorized for explicit employments [2]. CRs are empowered by the quick and huge headways in radio innovations (e.g., programming characterized radios, recurrence readiness, power control, and so on), and can be described by the usage of problematic procedures, for example, wide-band spectrum detecting, constant range allotment and procurement, and ongoing estimation scattering. The multiplication of wireless administrations and gadgets for utilizations, for example, versatile correspondences, public wellbeing, WiFi, and TV broadcast fill in as the most undeniable case of how much the advanced society has gotten subject to radio range [3]. While land and energy established the most valuable abundance creation asset during the agrarian and modern periods individually, radio range has become the most significant asset of the cutting edge period .This presentation part characterizes the utilization of agreeable range detecting in cognitive radio frameworks to improve the dependability of recognizing essential clients, range detecting for cognitive radios and propose strong helpful range detecting methods for a down to earth structure utilizing cognitive radios, helpful interchanges for range partaking in a cognitive wireless transfer network [1].

9.2   Spectrum Sensing in Cognitive Radio Networks

Spectrum sensing helps a cognitive radio to measure, learn, and understand its operating environment. For instance, the accessibility of the spectrum and the presence of obstructions. When a specific recurrence band is identified as being underutilized by the primary or approved client at a specific time in a specific location, the auxiliary clients may use the spectrum, indicating that a spectrum opportunity exists. As a consequence, spectrum sensing can be applied to time, recurrence, and space. With the development of beam forming technology, multiple clients may use a similar channel/recurrence in a similar topographical region at the same time [5]. In this way, if an essential client isn't sending in all directions, spectrum openings can be created for optional clients in non-administrative ways, and spectrum sensing must also remember the point of appearances [6]. The essential clients can also use their assigned groups via spread-spectrum or recurrence jumping, and optional clients can send in a similar band at the same time without going overboard. If they receive a symmetrical code corresponding to the codes adopted by the essential clients, Spectrum Sensing in Cognitive Radio Networks has the potential to cause disturbance to the essential clients [4]. This creates code space range openings, but it also necessitates the position of the codes used by the critical clients, much like multipath boundaries. Many studies on spectrum sensing have focused on critical transmitter recognition based on the neighborhood estimations of auxiliary clients, since identifying essential clients that are accepting information is often difficult. Cognitive radio networks often provide spectrum sensing and channel checking to ensure that the cognitive MAC layer has constant spectrum/channel data. The following errands are generally carried out by spectrum sensing: (1) location of spectrum openings, (2) assurance of ghostly target for any spectrum opening, (3) assessment of the spatial bearings of an approaching meddling symbol, and (4) signal order.

The identification of spectrum openings is presumably the most difficult of these activities, and it is investigated using double theory research issues [10]. Thus, spectrum sensing refers to the detection of spectrum openings on a small recurrence band, which detects the presence or absence of critical clients in the basic band. Non-cooperative/transmitter detection and cooperative exploration are the two main classifications of spectrum sensing strategies, as shown in Figure 9.1. The discovery of signals transmitted from an important framework via the nearby experiences of cognitive radio clients is central to transmitter recognition approaches. Transmitter, or non-cooperative, recognition techniques are often based on the assumption that the critical transmitter's location is hidden from the cognitive device. As a result, cognitive clients can only rely on the discovery of frail basic transmitter signals and perform spectrum sensing using only nearby perceptions. In its inclusion territory, a cognitive system does not have full details on spectrum incidence. As a result, absolutely avoiding hurtful

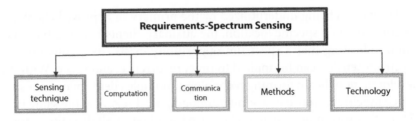

Figure 9.1 Spectrum sensing requirements.

impediment with important clients is ridiculous. Furthermore, transmitter discovery would not prevent a hidden terminal problem [9].

9.3   Collaborative Spectrum Sensing for Opportunistic Access in Fading Environments

Spectrum Sensing is authorized to clients by government offices in a fixed way where licensee has selective option to get to the allotted band. Nonetheless, with expanding interest for the spectrum and shortage of empty groups, a spectrum strategy change appears to be inescapable. Then, ongoing estimations recommend the chance of sharing spectrum among various gatherings subject to obstruction assurance limitations [7, 8]. An auxiliary client must scan approved groups and deftly submit when no critical sign is recognized to allow access to unused authorized spectrum. However, when a client is exposed to shadowing or blurring effects, identification is harmed. In such instances, the client is unable to distinguish between an unused band and a profound blur. Spectrum sensing in the community has been suggested as a way to combat such effects. Our research and simulation results suggest that a concerted effort could significantly boost sensing execution.

Spectrum accessibility for optional access could be regulated by direct spectrum sensing without coordination or motioning between critical licensee and auxiliary user(s) [13]. In this case, an optional client checks an allowed recurrence band for the existence of any important clients and shrewdly sends when none are found. At the point when the structure of essential sign is known to the optional client, the ideal identifier in fixed Gaussian commotion is a coordinated channel followed by a limit test [12]. Nonetheless, executing this sort of intelligible identifier is troublesome since an auxiliary client would require extra devoted hardware to accomplish synchrony with each kind of essential licensee. Moreover, there might be cases practically speaking where coordinated channel locator is precluded because of the absence of information about essential sign's structure. In such situations, a universally useful identifier would be significantly more attractive. A typical technique for location of obscure signs in commotion is energy identification [11].

9.4   Cooperative Sensing Among Cognitive Radios

Cognitive Radios have been progressed as an innovation for the deft utilization of under-used spectrum since they can detect the spectrum and use recurrence groups if no Primary client is distinguished. In any case, the necessary affectability is requesting since any individual radio may confront a profound blur [15]. We propose light-weight collaboration in sensing dependent on hard choices to relieve the affectability prerequisites on singular radios. We show that the "interface spending plan" that framework architects need to save for blurring is a huge capacity of the necessary likelihood of recognition. Indeed, even a couple coordinating clients (~10–20) confronting free blurs are sufficient to accomplish common sense limit levels by definitely lessening singular discovery prerequisites [14]. Hard choices perform nearly just as delicate choices in accomplishing these additions. Cooperative increases in a climate where shadowing is corresponded, is restricted by the collaboration impression (zone in which clients participate). Fundamentally, a couple of autonomous clients are heartier than many related clients [13]. Tragically, cooperative addition is exceptionally touchy to antagonistic/bombing Cognitive Radios. Radios that fall flat in a known manner (consistently report the presence/ nonappearance of a Primary client) can be made up for by controlling them. Then again, radios that flop in unmodeled ways or might be pernicious, present a bound on feasible affectability decreases [18]. As a general guideline, in the event that we accept that 1 N clients can fall flat in an obscure manner, at that point the collaboration gains are restricted to what in particular is conceivable with N confided in clients. Utilization of collaboration in remote has been concentrated widely particularly regarding accomplishing variety gains and bringing down blackout probabilities through participation of versatile clients. In the Cognitive Radio setting, we might want to misuse this cooperative impact in an alternate manner. Instead of improving certainty by expanding participation, need to keep up certainty while lessening capability! Subsequently our picked metric is the decrease in affectability prerequisites whenever collaboration is utilized [16]. Affectability of a radio is inalienably restricted by cost and defers necessities. Subsequently the gadget planner can sort out the ramifications of collaboration on the gadget detail through the surely knew metric of location affectability, consequently separating the issue from random concerns like the entrance system, and so forth Participation permits autonomously blurred radios to by and large accomplish strength to extreme blurs while keeping singular affectability levels near the ostensible way misfortune. Besides, few radios (~10–20) are sufficient to accomplish handy affectability levels [17].

- Practical "connect financial plans" for managing blurring rely unequivocally upon the objective likelihood of recognition which thusly relies upon the decent likelihood for destructive obstruction at the Primary collector and the quantity of non-participating Cognitive networks [21].
- Communicating provisional hard choices can accomplish cooperative gains almost indistinguishable from sharing delicate choices [19].
- In a related blurring climate, we can't really work heartily with the affectability levels anticipated by the investigation of free clients. For this situation, surveying a couple of autonomous clients is in a way that is better than surveying many associated clients.
- Radios that bomb in unmodeled ways or might be vindictive, present a bound on reachable affectability decreases.
- As a dependable guideline, on the off chance that we accept that a division 1 N of clients can come up short in an obscure manner, at that point the collaboration gains are restricted to what in particular is conceivable with N confided in clients [20].

Covariance Based Signal Detections for Cognitive Radio: Sensing is a major issue in cognitive radio. The measurable covariances of sign and clamor are generally different. This is utilized to differentiate signal from commotion. The example covariance grid of the got signal is figured and changed dependent on the accepting channel. At that point two identification techniques are proposed dependent on the changed example covariance network. One is the covariance outright worth (CAV) identification and the other is the covariance Fresenius standard (CFN) discovery [22]. Hypothetical examination and edge setting for the calculations are talked about. The two techniques needn't bother with any data of the sign, the channel and commotion power as from the earlier. Reproductions dependent on caught ATSC DTV signals are introduced to confirm the techniques.

Cooperative Diversity for Wireless Ad Hoc Networks: Cooperative diversity is a narrative strategy projected for passing on data in remote specially appointed networks, where tightly found single-reception apparatus network hubs cooperatively communicate or potentially get by shaping practical receiving wire clusters. For its structure obstructs, the hand-off channel and the two-transmitter, two-recipient cooperative channel, we overview the most recent go forward complete in deciding the hypothetical limit limits and depict the most excellent down to earth code plans announced up until now [23]. Both hypothesis and practice foresee that cooperative correspondence can give expanded limit and force reserve funds in impromptu networks.

A remote specially appointed network comprises of an enormous number of conceivably versatile hubs that speak with one another over remote connections. The way that there is no requirement for network frameworks—subsequently ease and straightforward reconfiguration—makes specially appointed networks alluring in both business and military applications, for example, remote LAN and MAN. Home networks, gadget networks, and sensor networks. As opposed to a conventional framework remote network (e.g., a cell network), where data is sent starting with one client then onto the next by means of a control base station, a specially appointed network permits shared correspondence from a sending hub to an objective hub [24]. Direct correspondence between two hubs can be acknowledged in a solitary bounce. Notwithstanding, since remote channels are regularly poor, single-bounce directing requires high transmission power and subsequently causes expanded obstruction. To accomplish critical force reserve funds, data ought to be passed on to an objective through different transitional hubs. While transmission over a solitary bounce channel has just been seriously contemplated and surely known [25], cooperative correspondence in multi-node networks is as yet an open examination issue, which as of late has gotten significant consideration, Since correspondence over a remote channel is restricted by obstruction, blurring, multipath, way misfortune, and tailing, the fundamental plan confront libel in concocting correspondence strategies in a decentralized network to conquer these impediments. An extra plan issue has to do with the high elements of a specially appointed network, where hubs as often as possible join and leave the network. One plan approach is to utilize different transmitter and beneficiary reception apparatuses at hubs, which builds the limit and improves vigor to blurring and obstruction by methods for spatial diversity and information rate multiplexing [26].

9.5   Cluster-Based Cooperative Spectrum Sensing for Cognitive Radio Systems

Optional clients may be aided in performing cooperative spectrum sensing in cognitive radio systems, making it easier to distinguish the critical client. In any case, the sensing execution can be severely degraded when the sensing perceptions are sent to a typical beneficiary through blurring networks. The sensing execution can be enhanced by using a group-based cooperative spectrum sensing approach. By grouping all auxiliary clients into a few groups and selecting the most ideal client from each group to respond to the primary beneficiary, the proposed strategy will take advantage of client determination diversity to improve sensing execution. Furthermore, the effects of logical execution are given for both option and energy combinations. Mathematical results indicate that, as compared to normal spectrum sensing, the sensing execution is significantly improved. Although cyclostationary highlight position can discern signs with extremely low SNR, it does require some prior knowledge of the important client. Limit ourselves to energy exploration in the spectrum sensing for ease of execution. It appears that the hidden hub problem, extreme blurring and shadowing, and other issues will cause cognitive clients' sensing execution to fail. To solve this issue, cognitive clients should collaborate on spectrum sensing. Normally, the primary beneficiary facilitates mutual spectrum sensing. After receiving permission from the usual collector, all cognitive clients begin spectrum sensing on their own and then forward their perceptions to it [27].

9.6   Spectrum Agile Radios: Utilization and Sensing Architectures

Today, the biggest and most attractive part of the radio spectrum is distributed to authorized administrations, which has brought about the notable significant shortage of this asset for arising applications. With the fast development of remote advancements, current spectrum shortage has become a difficult issue as an ever increasing number of remote applications seek almost no spectrum. Then again, the authorized spectrum designated to applications, for example, TV, cell communication and public security show almost no utilization over the long run at various topographical areas [28]. This has, consequently, genuinely impeded the advancement of fresher advances due to current administrative limitations on the activity in authorized spectrum, for example, TV groups, and is being tended to by FCC through late principle makings. In light of the objective of omnipresent correspondence, we investigate spectrum light-footed radios as another innovation empowered by such arising administrative decisions and study its points of interest over regular radios. At first, we give a straightforward numerical demonstrating to comprehend the use that is feasible by spectrum light-footed radios [30]. Next, we research a few issues identified with spectrum sensing, as it is one of the critical columns to acknowledge spectrum nimble radios. Through sensing, the spectrum dexterous radio distinguishes the so called "blank areas" in the spectrum and afterward concludes whether to consume those blank areas artfully to send information. We additionally talk about the idea of impedance temperature presented by the FCC, and propose a spectrum-mindful sensor network as an approach to address it. At last, we expand this spectrum-mindful sensor networks to acquaint another sensing engineering with distinguish and find void areas in the spectrum.

The sensing capacity in a spry radio is altogether different than those pre-owned these days in customary radios, and structures a basic piece of it. Lithe radios need to detect the remote mechanism for various reasons, and one of them is recognizing spectrum not utilized by essential clients ("spectrum void areas"). It would then be able to send in these blank areas with power levels, for example, not to make any impedance these essential clients Another explanation behind spry radios to detect the remote medium is to identify the transmission of other optional gadgets. For this situation, the dexterous radio necessities to share a few or the entirety of the channels involved by different secondary's hence diminishing its own obstructing likelihood [29]. Figure 9.2 shows the spectrum agile radio architecture. The sensing capacity in spry radios is not the same as customary radios in another regard also, specifically, regular radios are intended to impart the medium to like gadgets as it were. For instance, think about the IEEE 802.11 remote LAN innovation. Here, all gadgets utilize similar sensing limits to decide whether the channel is inert before a transmission. Then again, coordinated radios need to recognize the presence of the essential sign at edges that are under sign levels of essential gadgets. As a rule, the discovery affectability of the light-footed radio ought to beat essential radio framework by a huge edge to forestall what is basically called as concealed terminal issue. This is one of the central points of contention that

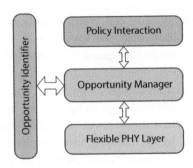

Figure 9.2 Spectrum agile radio.

makes spectrum sensing an extremely testing research issue. Meeting the affectability necessity in each band, which has diverse essential clients with various qualities, would be troublesome [31]. This is done with the goal that the lithe radio can decide the send power, and the transmission and obstruction sweep craftily.

9. 7   Some Fundamental Limits on Cognitive Radio

Cognitive radio alludes to remote designs in which a correspondence framework doesn't work in a fixed doled out band, yet rather searches and finds a fitting band wherein to work to the key prerequisites for such framework that attempts to evade obstruction to likely essential clients of a band to convey genuine increases, cognitive radios must have the option to distinguish un-decodable signs by telling the best way to assess the trade-off between auxiliary client power, accessible space for optional activity, and obstruction assurance for the essential recipients. As a rule, the exhibition of the ideal locator for identifying a powerless obscure sign from a realized zero-mean heavenly body resembles that of the energy indicator show that the presence of a realized pilot sign can help incredibly which is shown in Figure 9.3.

Impedance Controlled: The essential permit holder could specify for instance maximal allowable optional client obstruction levels, in actuality ensuring the essential clients certain transmission rates. This could permit essential and auxiliary clients to send in the very groups, that is, in a similar time frequency-space-code blocks. The idea of obstruction temperature has been presented with objective of staying away from the trade-off of the essential clients.

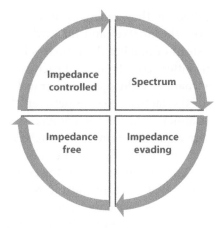

Figure 9.3 Fundamental limits on cognitive radio.

Spectrum: Auxiliary gadgets should control their emanations with the end goal that the total impedance at the essential clients is under a specific level (or obstruction temperature).

Impedance Evading: A subset of the obstruction controlled system is that in which the essential licensee just permits optional clients to utilize its spectrum relying on the prerequisite that its client endures of no obstruction at all. Such frameworks are substantially more prohibitive than impedance controlled frameworks, yet are normal in cognitive radio writing [22, 25]. The optional client could stick to this severe necessity by filling in ghastly openings. That is, an auxiliary client would communicate just without essential clients.

Impedance Free: When cognitive gadgets exist in a network however have no data of their own to send, they might go about as transfers, and work together with the essential clients. As opposed to make obstruction the essential connection, they help it. Dismissing some other conceivably dynamic cognitive bunches this framework is without obstruction.

9.8 Cooperative Strategies and Capacity Theorems for Relay Networks

For hand-off organizations, coding systems that make use of hub collaboration are developed. Transfers can either read or forward the source message to the objective, or they can pack and forward their channel yields to the objective. The unravel and-forward strategy is similar to multihopping, but instead of making the transfers interpret the message sequentially, the transmitters coordinate and each beneficiary uses a few or all of its previous channel yield squares to translate [32]. The transfers take advantage of the factual reliance between their channel yields and the objective's channel yield for the compress and -forward strategy. The techniques are applied to remote channels, and it is shown that if stage data is only accessible locally and the transfers are close to the source centre, translate and forward achieves the ergodic limit with stage blurring. Despite the fact that the transmitting radio wires are not collocated, the ergodic limit agrees with the speed of a circulated receiving wire show with complete participation. The limit results cover a wide range of topics, including multi antenna transmission with Rayleigh blurring, single-skip blurring, semi-static blurring problems, situations where halfway channel information is available at the transmitters, and situations where neighbourhood client cooperation is permitted. Multisource and multi-destination organisations, such as multi-access and broadcast transfer networks, will benefit from the results.

IEEE 802.11: The first worldwide wireless standard based on cognitive radios: Wi-FAR (IEEE Std 802.22-2011), the IEEE 802.22 standard for wireless regional area networks (WRANs), aims to use the unused TV band channels in the VHF and UHF classes to provide fixed and roaming, high-throughput, long-range correspondences. This norm is used for remote and regional broadband Internet access, Frugal 5G for e-Education, e-Health, e-Banking, e-Payments, boat to shore interchanges, country security, outskirt insurance and reconnaissance, environment checking, smart framework applications, for example, administrative control and information procurement (SCADA), and low inactivity applications, for example, for e-Learning, e-Health, e-Banking, e-Payments, country security, outskirt ISO has approved IEEE Std. 802.22-2011, and the White Space Alliance is conducting interoperability testing under the business brand name Wi-FAR., the 802.22 architecture establishes a fixed point-multipoint (P-MP) remote air interface in which a base station (BS) deals with its own cell4 and all associated Consumer Premise Equipment (CPEs). The BS manages medium access in its cell and communicates with the various CPEs via the downstream path, which then respond to the BS via the upstream path. The 802.22 system uses an exacting expert/ slave arrangement to ensure the security of officeholder benefits, with the BS serving as the expert and the CPEs as the slaves. No CPE is allowed to communicate without first receiving valid approval from a BS, which also controls all of the CPEs' RF attributes. Aside from the standard function of a BS, which is to monitor data transmission within a cell, an 802.22 BS deals with a one-of-a-kind feature of appropriated detecting [33]? The BS inclusion range, which can go up to 100 km if power isn't an issue, is a distinguishing feature of 802.22 WRAN, when compared to current IEEE 802 guidelines. WRANs, as shown in figure, have a much wider inclusion spectrum than current organisations, owing to their higher power and the good propagation characteristics of TV recurrence classes. This expanded inclusion spectrum presents one-of-a-kind specialized challenges and circumstances.

9.9   Research Challenges in Cooperative Communication

Spectrum sensing is a critical capability of cognitive radio for avoiding harmful interference with approved clients and identifying the available spectrum for better spectrum use. In either case, multipath blurring, shadowing, and collector vulnerability issues often jeopardize recognition execution. Cooperative spectrum sensing has been shown to be a viable technique for improving recognition execution by exploiting spatial variation to alleviate the effects of these issues. Although cooperative addition can lead to improvements in recognition execution and a loosening of affectability criteria, cooperative sensing can result in participation overhead. Any additional sensing time, deferral, resources, and activities devoted to cooperative sensing, as well as any presentation corruption caused by cooperative sensing, are all referred to by the overhead. To address the issues of cooperation technique, cooperative increase, and participation overhead, the best in class overview of cooperative sensing is given. The components of cooperative sensing, which include participation models, sensing procedures, theory testing, information mixture, control channel and detailing, client choice, and information base, are breaking down the collaboration strategy in particular. In addition, the influencing factors of possible cooperative addition and acquired participation overhead are discussed. Sensing time and deferral, channel limitations, energy effectiveness, teamwork proficiency, versatility, security, and wideband sensing issues are all viable variables. The accessible exploration challenges associated with each cooperative sensing problem are also discussed [34]. Figure 9.4 shows the research challenges in cooperative communication.

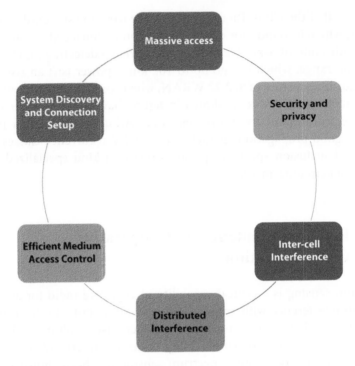

Figure 9.4 Research challenges in cooperative communication.

- *Massive access*: When compared to normal human-to-human traffic in cell networks, a large number of M2M devices in a cell can pose real system challenges in terms of RAN blockage and over-burdening. To resolve the RAN over-burden problem, various proposals have been proposed in 3GPP, such as ease of transition, access class excepting, and M2M prioritization. Nonetheless, each of these strategies has advantages and drawbacks, and no one strategy is widely accepted as the strongest.
- *Security and privacy*: Various normalization bodies have discussed security extensively. For example, M2M protection in ETSI M2M revolves around a few attributes of a client and their interactions, such as authenticity, authority, integrity, and privacy. M2M protection is critical for enabling widespread M2M administrations and, in particular, improving buyer recognition. Different M2M applications and areas (such as e-health and smart metering) may have different

security requirements that must be considered right from the start of the framework design [35].

- *Inter-cell Interference*: Inter-cell interference is one of the most serious issues with HetNets. This is particularly problematic in the case of unplanned small cell deployment, where the operators have little to no control over the small cell's location. Furthermore, the activity of small cells and standard macro cells at the same time can result in irregularly formed cell sizes and hence interior interference, necessitating advanced power management and resource allocation to prevent inter-cell interference.

- *Distributed Interference*: Distributed interference avoidance will be needed in the deployment of access points where there is little to no coordination, such as between WLANs. If more devices use unlicensed spectrum to supplement their throughput, this will become increasingly important.

- *Efficient Medium Access Control*: This is especially important in dense deployments of access points and user terminals, such as WLANs, where medium access is distributed. In such cases, user throughput will be low, latency will be high, and hotspots will be unable to supplement cellular infrastructure to provide high throughput. To maximize channel use, existing medium access control would need to be revamped for such an environment.

- *System Discovery and Connection Setup*: When a large number of devices are present, there can be problems with non-network assisted device discovery in D2D communications. Furthermore, establishing and maintaining relations with multiple parties, particularly when operating on the same frequency, can be difficult.

9.10 Conclusion

This chapter covers Spectrum Sensing, Collaborative Spectrum Sensing, cooperative sensing among cognitive radios, Covariance dependent signal detections for cognitive radios, Cooperative diversity for wireless ad hoc networks, and Cluster-based cooperative spectrum sensing techniques for a functional framework employing cognitive radios in 5G networks. Relay network communication methods and power theorems Collaboration research issues. Spectrum sensing utilizes dynamic spectrum model without upsetting the essential clients. This may improves the radio recurrence utilization of spectrum and it is done when both unlicensed and authorized lessening impedance and furthermore by use of authorized clients for distinguishing the void areas. Utilization of agreeable range detecting in cognitive radio frameworks is done to improve the dependability of the 5G Networks. With the expanding interest for the spectrum and the shortage of empty groups, a spectrum strategy change appears to be unavoidable. Cooperative diversity is a novel strategy to pass on data in remote impromptu organizations where firmly found single-radio wire network hubs cooperatively communicate or potentially get by framing virtual reception apparatus exhibits. Cooperative diversity offers high added substance rate picks up when contrasted with the noncooperation case and the key in accomplishing these increases lies in coding with side data. We look forward that our learning would stimulate spectrum sensing techniques to encourage and investigate this exhilarating research subject and expand more inventive and computationally realistic Cognitive Radio Frameworks frame works specially intended for 5G Networks.

References

1. Nakamura, T., Nagata, S., Benjebbour, A., Kishiyama, Y., Tang, H., Shen, X., Yang, N., Li, N., Trends in Small Cell Enhancements in LTE Advanced. *IEEE Commun. Mag.*, 51, 2, 98–105, Feb 2013.
2. Marzetta, T.L., Noncooperative Cellular Wireless with Unlimited Number of Base Station Antennas. *IEEE Trans. Wireless Commun.*, 9, 11, 3590–3600, Nov 2010.
3. Larsson, E.G., Tufvesson, F., Edfors, O., Marzetta, T.L., Massive MIMO for Next Generation Wireless Systems. *IEEE Commun. Mag.*, 2013.
4. McKeown, N. *et al.*, OpenFlow: Enabling innovation in campus networks. *ACM SIGCOMM Com. Commun. Rev.*, 38, 2, 69–74, 2008.
5. Yap, K. *et al.*, Blueprint for Introducing Innovation into Wireless Mobile Networks. *ACM VISA*, 2010.
6. Li, L.E., Mao, Z.M., Rexford, J., Toward Software-Defined Cellular Networks, in: *European Workshop on EWSDN*, 2012.
7. Rappaport, T.S. *et al.*, Millimeter Wave Mobile Communications for 5G Cellular: It Will Work! *IEEE Access*, 1, 1, 335–349, May 2013.
8. Nakamura, T., Nagata, S., Benjebbour, A., Kishiyama, Y., Tang, H., Shen, X., Yang, N., Li, N., Trends in Small Cell Enhancements in LTE Advanced. *IEEE Commun. Mag.*, 51, 2, 98–105, Feb 2013.
9. Hoymann, C., Larsson, D., Koorapaty, H., Cheng, J.-F., A Lean Carrier for LTE. *Commun. Mag., IEEE*, 51, 2, 74–80, 2013.

10. Marzetta, T.L., Noncooperative Cellular Wireless with Unlimited Number of Base Station Antennas. *IEEE Trans. Wireless Commun.*, 9, 11, 3590–3600, Nov 2010.
11. Ahlswede, R., Multi-way communication channels, in: *ProcISIT*, September 1973, Google Scholar.
12. Aref, M.R., *Information flow in relay networks*. Technical report, Stanford University, 1980, Google Scholar.
13. Biglieri, E., Proakis, J., Shamai, S., (Shitz), Fading channels: Information-theoretic and communication aspects. *IEEE Trans. Inf. Theory*, 44, 6, 2619–2692, October 1998, zbMATHCrossRefMathSciNetGoogle Scholar.
14. Caire, G. and Shamai, S., On the achievable throughput of a multi-antenna gaussian broadcast channel. *IEEE Trans. Inf. Theory*, 49, 7, 1691–1705, July 2003, CrossRefMathSciNetGoogle Scholar.
15. Carleial, A.B., Interference channels. *IEEE Trans. Inf. Theory*, IT-24, 1, 60–70, January 1978, zbMATHCrossRefMathSciNetGoogle Scholar.
16. Costa, M., On the gaussian interference channel. *IEEE Trans. Inf. Theory*, 31, 5, 607–615, September 1985, zbMATHCrossRefGoogle Scholar.
17. Costa, M.H.M., Writing on dirty paper. *IEEE Trans. Inf. Theory*, IT-29, 439–441, May 1983, zbMATHCrossRefGoogle Scholar.
18. Cover, T., Comments on broadcast channels. *IEEE Trans. Inf. Theory*, 44, 6, 2524–2530, September 1998, zbMATHCrossRefMathSciNetGoogle Scholar.
19. Cover, T. and Thomas, J.A., *Elements of Information Theory*, John Wiley & Sons, New York, 1991.
20. Cover, T.M. and Gamal, A.E., Capacity theorems for the relay channel. *IEEE Trans. Inf. Theory*, 25, 5, 572–584, September 1979.
21. Csiszár, I. and Körner, J., *Information Theory: Coding Theorems for Discrete Memory less Systems*, Academic Press, New York, 1981.
22. Devroye, N., Mitran, P., Tarokh, V., Achievable rates in cognitive networks, in: *2005 IEEE International Symposium on Information Theory*, September 2005.
23. Devroye, N., Mitran, P., Tarokh, V., Achievable rates in cognitive radio channels, in: *39th Annual Conf. on Information Sciences and Systems (CISS)*, March 2005.
24. Devroye, N., Mitran, P., Tarokh, V., Achievable rates in cognitive radio channels. *IEEE Trans. Inf. Theory*, 52, 5, 1813–1827, May 2006.
25. Zhang, W., Mallik, R.K., Letaief, K.B., Optimization of Cooperative Spectrum Sensing with Energy Detection in Cognitive Radio Networks. *IEEE Trans. Wireless Commun.*, 8, 12, 5761–5766, December 2009.
26. Devroye, N., Mitran, P., Tarokh, V., Cognitive decomposition of wireless networks, in: *Proceedings of CROWNCOM*, March 2006.
27. Sim, M.S., Chung, M., Kim, D., Chung, J., Kim, D.K., Chae, C.B., Nonlinear self-interference cancellation for full-duplex radios: From link-level and system-level performance perspectives. *IEEE Commun. Mag.*, 55, 9, 158–167, 2017.

28. Politis, C., Maleki, S., Tsinos, C., Liolis, K., Chatzinotas, S., Ottersten, B., Simultaneous sensing and transmission for cognitive radios with imperfect signal cancellation. *IEEE Trans. Wireless Commun.*, 99, 1–1, 2017.

29. Adams, M. and Bhargava, V.K., Use of the recursive least squares filter for self interference channel estimation, in: *2016 IEEE 84th Vehicular Technology Conference (VTC-Fall)*, Sept 2016, pp. 1–4.

30. Gao, H., Ejaz, W., Jo, M., Cooperative wireless energy harvesting and spectrum sharing in 5G networks. *IEEE Access*, 4, 3647–3658, 2016.

31. Kang, X., Ho, C.K., Sun, S., Full-duplex wireless-powered communication network with energy causality. *IEEE Trans. Wireless Commun.*, 14, 10, 5539–5551, Oct 2015.

32. Sahai, A., Patel, G., Dick, C., Sabharwal, A., On the impact of phase noise on active cancelation in wireless full-duplex. *IEEE Trans. Veh. Technol.*, 62, 9, 4494–4510, Nov 2013.

33. Korpi, D., Anttila, L., Valkama, M., Feasibility of in-band full-duplex radio transceivers with imperfect RF components: Analysis and enhanced cancellation algorithms, in: *Proc. 9th Int. Conf. on Cognitive Radio Oriented Wireless Networks and Communications (CROWNCOM)*, June 2014, pp. 532–538.

34. Tsakmalis, A., Chatzinotas, S., Ottersten, B., Interference constraint active learning with uncertain feedback for cognitive radio networks. *IEEE Trans. Wireless Commun.*, 16, 7, 4654–4668, July 2017.

35. Tong, Z. and Haenggi, M., Throughput analysis for full-duplex wireless networks with imperfect self-interference cancellation. *IEEE Trans. Commun.*, 63, 11, 4490–4500, Nov 2015.

10

Natural Language Processing

S. Meera* and S. Geerthik

Agni College of Technology, Chennai, India

Abstract

The AI approach applies to natural language processing. The AI communication approach uses intelligent systems. These intelligent systems, such as English, use natural languages. The process of Natural Language required a smart machine such as a robot to act as per human orders when you want to hear decisions from a clinical expert system based on dialogue. The field of Natural Language Processing (NLP) includes designing a program to perform some useful natural language tasks. NLP is usually used for human use. The input and output of the structures of an NLP are: 1. Speech and 2. Written Text. Two components are used in Natural Language Processing. One is Natural Language Understanding (NLU). The second one is Natural Language Generation (NLG). This Input involves Mapping and Analyzing different aspects of language. It refers to the internal representation of Text planning, Sentence Planning, and Text Realization.

Keywords: NLP Terminology, context-free grammar, Top-Down Parser, expert system capabilities, knowledge base

10.1 Introduction

Natural language processing (NLP) is a branch of computer science and artificial intelligence that studies how computers and humans communicate in natural language. NLP's ultimate aim is to allow computers to understand language as well as humans do.

Corresponding author: meeraselvakumar@gmail.com

R. Kanthavel, K. Ananthajothi, S. Balamurugan and R. Karthik Ganesh (eds.) Artificial Intelligent Techniques for Wireless Communication and Networking, (139–154) © 2022 Scrivener Publishing LLC

Literature Review:

1. Cross-Lingual Ability of Multilingual BERT: An Empirical Study
Karthikeyan K, Zihan Wang, Stephen Mayhew, Dan Roth 26 Sept 2019
(modified: 11 Mar 2020) ICLR 2020 Conference
Recent research has shown that multilingual BERT (M-BERT) has surprising cross-lingual skills, despite the fact that it was equipped with no cross-lingual goal and no aligned results [1]. We present a detailed analysis of the contribution of different components in M-BERT to its cross-lingual potential in this paper. The effect of linguistic properties of the languages, model architecture, and learning objectives is investigated [3]. The experiment is conducted using two conceptually distinct NLP tasks, textual entailment and named entity identification, in three typologically different languages: Spanish, Hindi, and Russian. One of our main findings is that lexical overlap between languages has a minor impact on cross-lingual performance, while network depth is critical. On our project page, you can find all of our templates and implementations.

2. Structural Similarity and Architecture
ICLR 2020 Conference Paper2020 Authors 16 Nov 2019ICLR 2020
Structural similarity: We discovered that the structural similarity causes some concern among reviewers and others, owing to its abstract nature [2]. We also added an overview of two sub-components of structural similarity to explain and clarify the importance of structural similarity: (1) Effect of Word-ordering (a) Words are organized differently between languages [6]. In English, for example, the subject–verb–object order is used, while in Hindi, the subject–object–verb order is used. This aspect of structural similarity is investigated.

(b) During pretraining, we shuffled a percentage of the words in sentences, destroying word-ordering, which is one aspect of structural similarity [5]. Both the source (Fake-English) and target languages are shuffled (shuffling any one of them would also be sufficient). The structure's word ordering portion is thus concealed from B-BERT. We shuffle 25, 50, and 100% of the words in the sentence at random while holding the rest in their original places. Each sentence can be treated as a Bag of Words when it is fully shuffled.

3. Word Ordering Similarity
ICLR 2020 Conference Paper2020 Authors 16 Nov 2019ICLR 2020
(c) It's worth noting that we don't permute during fine-tuning because cross-lingual ability comes from pretraining, not fine-tuning [4]. (d) We conclude

that while word order is essential, cross-linguality can still be preserved even when the entire sentence is shuffled. For more details, WORD-ORDERING SIMILARITY.

4. More Insights on Architecture and Multilingual Settings
ICLR 2020 Conference
The architecture experiments yielded no clear recommendations for a minimum number of parameters or width. ** — — We acknowledge that we did not display a specific minimum number of parameters, but we have now added a few more findings for number of parameters, and we believe the pattern is now apparent (There is a drastic drop in performance when the number of parameters is changed from 11.83M to 7.23M, this is kind of threshold, at least for 12 layers and 12 attention settings [7]). Please see the appendix section "FURTHER ARCHITECTURE DISCUSSIONS" for more information. —The trend with scope, we believe, is mostly evident. For the English language.

After a depth of 6, the output is almost saturated. For Russian (for multilingual purposes): It's nearly saturated at 12 o'clock (still the performance increases slightly) Also, as we go from 18 to 24 layers, the output of English drops slightly [9]. As a result, this selection is ideal for cross-linguistic transition. If these findings were replicated with the 100+-language edition, how might they differ?—We did not do the 100+-language version, but we have now added the 4-language version to the appendix (we assume the findings are comparable also for the 100+-version).—Our findings also show that with as few as 15% of the parameters and single focus, we can achieve comparable results.

NLP's Components
As given, two components are NLP.
Understanding Natural Language (NLU)
Knowledge of natural language comprises the following tasks:

1. In the form of useful representation based on the input, natural languages are given. These inputs are mapped.
2. Study of various aspects of languages.

Generation Natural Language (NLG)
Natural Language Generation is the process of generating meaningful phrases and sentences. It is from natural representation, in the form of natural language.

This includes different aspects of

1. Planning Text
2. Planning Sentence
3. Realization of Text.

Planning Text
It requires operations being recovered. Based on the related content, retrieving operations. This Knowledge Base Material.

Planning Sentence
From sentence preparation, it is possible to choose the appropriate term. These words form the definition of full sentences and the sound of the sentence is also set.

Realization of Text
This is used especially in sentence plan mapping. The Sentence Plan is translated into the form of sentences.
Note: Knowing Natural Language is harder than producing natural language.

NLU's Problems
NL has an amazingly rich architecture and structure. It's highly vague. Different levels of uncertainty may occur:

Lexical ambiguity, such as word-level, is at a very primitive point. Treating, for instance, the word 'Rain' as a noun or verb?
Syntax Uncertainty for stage: It is possible to parse a sentence in various ways.
"He lifted the beetle with a red cap, for example."—Did he raise the beetle with a cap or did he lift the beetle with a red cap?
Referential ambiguity—Using pronouns to refer to someone. For example, Rima went to Gauri. "She said, Tired, I am."—Who exactly is tired?
Diverse meanings can be represented in one entry.
One thing can be interpreted with the same meaning.

Terminology of NLP:
Systematical sound studies are structured by phonology.

Morphology—Significant primitive units of word research construction.

In a language, morpheme—primitive meaning.

Syntax—To create a sentence, it's just arranging phrases. In phrases and sentences, it involves the structural function of words.

The semantics—The meaning of the words is largely concentrated and the mechanisms of integrating the words are clarified. Words are described as complete sentences and phrases.

Pragmatics—it deals with a phrase's use. These sentences are readily understood in different situations and how the meaning of the word is influenced.

Discourse—This based on how immediate proceedings are influenced by the sentence [10].

Global Knowledge—Includes general world knowledge.

Steps in processing natural language:

Five measures can be referred to as

Study of Lexicon:
Identify and evaluate the structure of terms. One of these languages is the Lexicon. In a language, this means the set of terms and phrases. The entire chunk of text was sprayed into paragraphs, terms and phrases by this review.

(Parsing) Syntactic Analysis:
Words are analyzed using the technique of parsing. For grammar and arranging phrases, words are fully analyzed in the sentence. Words are structured in a way that indicates the connection between the terms. The English Syntactic Analyzer refuses the expression "the church goes to the priest."

Study of Semantics:
It provides from the text the exact meaning or the dictionary meaning. It checks every email. This offers important context. It is achieved by mapping. The mapping is based on the syntactic structure and the artifacts of the task domain. The semantic analyzer's negligence term, such as "hot-ice-cream."

Discourse Integrating:
The importance of the expression depends on the context of the word before it. It provides the feeling in the presence of the immediate good sentence.

Study of Pragmatics:

What was already mentioned in this pragmatic study is seen at various points in what was originally meant. It interested and includes the derivation of those language elements that needed knowledge of the real world.

In the flowchart below, the following five definitions are viewed:

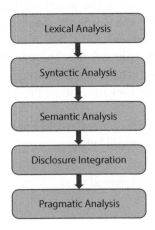

Syntactic Analysis Implementation Aspects

All algorithms for syntactic analysis have been developed by researchers. Yet we concentrated on basic processes.

Context free grammar is the first technique. The Top-Down Parser is the second solution.

Detailed contextual vision Free grammar is

Context-Grammar for Free

It is composed of rules. It concentrated on the left side of the rewriting rules with a single symbol. Let's see the instance of creating grammar and parsing a sentence with that grammar.

"The Bird pecks the grains."

DET (Articles)—a | a | Nouns—birds | birds | crops | grains | grains | grains | grains | grains

Noun Phrase (NP)—Item + Noun | Item + Adjective + Noun | Item + Adjective + Noun = DET N | DET ADJ N = DET N N N N = DET N

Verbs—pecks | pecking | pecking | pecking | Verb Phrase (VP)—NP V | V NP NP Phrase (VP) Adjectives (ADJ) | small | lovely | chirping | beautiful

Using the parse tree, sentences are broken. In order to break down the word into ordered bits, the parse tree is mainly used. And the computer can easily comprehend it. And it is processed by the machine. In order for the algorithm to parse tree parsing, it is possible to construct and rewrite the rules. This determines which one is legal and which one needs to be mounted.

These rules explain the fact that a certain symbol can be ordered by other symbols in the tree. Consider two strings on the basis of the logic of the first order. Noun pharse, another verb pharse, is one of them. Strings are combined by a sentence that is NP followed by VP. For the sentences, The laws are rewritten like this:

S × NP VP VP
NP • DET N | DET ADJ N N | DET ADJ N
VP × V NP VP N | DET ADJ N VP × V NP

Lexocon –

DET a | the |
Lovely ADJ | Perching
N?? insect | birds | seed | grains | grains
V • peck | pecks | pecking | pecking | pecking | pecking

As shown, the parse tree can be generated

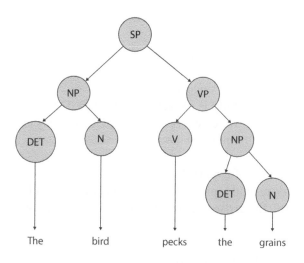

Now accept the rewritten instructions. Since V can be replaced by either both "peck" or "pecks," phrases such as "the bird peck the grains" can be wrongly allowed. An inconsistency in the subject–verb agreement is accepted as true. Merit: Merit:
The grammatical style is quite basic. Therefore, one commonly used.

The demerits:
It is not known as highly reliable. Consider the syntactically accurate example of "The grains peck the bird". Parser makes the corrective way of sentencing, even though it makes no sense.

Grammar with several sets needs to be planned in order to achieve high precision. Different rule sets are followed. This high accuracy involves completely different sets of parsing rules. The emphasis of this parsing was singular and plural combinations, passive words, etc. This can lead to unmanageable laws that are enormous.

Parser Top-Down
Consider that parsers begin with the symbol S and several attempts to rewrite it. It can be formed into a terminal symbol sequence. These terminal symbols fit the word classes in the input sentence, otherwise they can be considered as terminal symbols.

It is possible to verify these with the input sentence. Testing to see if the If Not method is matched is began again with a new set of rules. This is repeated until the basic rules defining the sentence structure are reached.

Merit: Merit:
It is very easy to execute.

The demerits
If a mistake happens, the repetitive search process renders it inefficient.

The speed of work is very sluggish.
One of the fields of study is expert systems (ES). One of the influential research fields is AI. Researchers at Stanford University are introducing this field. Dept. of Computer Science.

What are Structures of Experts?
It is a computer-related topic that focuses on complex problem solving in a specific domain. Expertise is generally referred to as extra ordinary human experience.

Expert Applications characteristics
The majority of human activities are conducted by language, whether directly articulated or recorded using natural language. There is an even greater need to learn the languages we use to communicate as technology is gradually making the tools and channels on which we communicate more and more accessible. Natural Language Processing (NLP) [8, 10] allows computers to read text by simulating the human ability to interpret

language by incorporating the power of artificial intelligence, computer linguistics and computer science.

- Reliable
- Extremely reactive
- High quality.

Expert Technologies' capabilities
The professional systems are capable of

- Advising
- Illustrating
- Diagnosis.

Instruction and human support in decision-making

- Deriving a solution
- Explaining
- Input interpretation
- Forecasting outcomes

Justifying the assumption
Suggesting potential solutions to a dilemma
Expert Systems components
It encompasses

- Foundation of Expertise
- Engine of Inference
- User experience

Let us briefly see them one by one—
Let us briefly see them one by one—

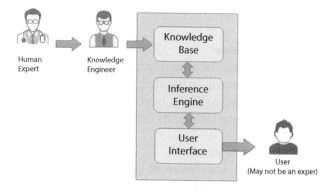

Method of Knowledge-Based Management:
This is analogous to the management structure of a database in an information system. Building a knowledge base of knowledge and rules is its key purpose.

Working place
A memory area used to define the current problem and to store intermediate outcomes is a work area or blackboard.

Facility for Clarification
There is a clarification facility for most expert systems. It shows you how the Excluded User recommendations will understand how the expert system has reached the answer, why some choices have been disclaimed, why some data has been requested, etc. By relation to system priorities, data feedback and decision rules, the clarity function addresses these questions. For example, in the case of reviewing the loan request, the explanation of the expert system would be explained on the facility inquiry why an application was accepted and why the other was denied. In the case of a medical specialist system such as Mycin, this function builds trust in the expert system and the user provides this issue with the solution.

Ability Rationale
The specialist framework has the ability to assess whether its solution has failed or has succeeded in improving its solution methods.

Engine for Inference
In the disassembly support system, the intensive motor model works. Manipulate a set of guidelines using the strategies of forward chewing and backward chaining. The following is a sequence of ahead-checking engines. Then search the scenario. Responses are based on a special solution. Ingestion The engine begins with the target and tests whether the conditions that go to that objective are present in the techniques of backward chains.

Interface with the Consumer
In order to produce ideas, the system provides an interface for users to communicate with the system. In the support system, this decision is similar to the contact function. Artificial Intelligence Technology aims to provide a natural language interface for its users.

Explain the Expert System Structure:
Knowledge Base—It is a warehouse of particular heuristics or regulations that are specifically used by knowledge, facts (productions). It has

information that is needed for understanding, formulating, and solving problems.

Working Memory—This helps to describe and record intermediate performance of the current running problem.

Intermediate Hypothesis & Decisions Records: 1. Blueprint, 2. Tagesordnung, 3. The Solution

Inference Engine—It is the heart of the expert system and helps control the entire framework of the expert system and offers numerous reasoning methodologies.

Explanation Method—Through asking questions and responses, [8] such as why, how, when, where, where, who, it helps to track transparency and explain the actions of the expert system.

User Interface—It allows users to use their own Natural Language Processing menus and graphics to insert their questions.

Knowledge Engineer—The primary objective of this engineer is to build a system with the use of an expert system shell for particular problem areas. It is possible to rely on many techniques [11, 14] of information representation. Two of these approaches include:

1. Frame-based schemes

   – Are used for the construction of very strong ESs. A frame defines the attributes of a complex object, and frames have defined relationships for different object types.

2. Laws of Production

   – Are the most common methods of representation of information used in industry. Expert systems based on rules are systems of expertise in which information is defined by the rules of production.

Device Engineer—Designing the user interface and declarative knowledge base format and building the inference engine

Users are non-expert people who wish to obtain direct guidance.

Shell's Expert System

The special software development environment is included in the expert system shell and has fundamental components of the expert system such as the knowledge-based management system, workplace, explanation facility, reasoning capability, inference engine [12, 15], user interface. This shell is connected by configuring these components together with a pre-defined method for designing different applications.

Shell example: Example:

CLIPS-CLIPS (C Language Integrated Production System)

OPS5, ART, Eclipse, and JESS

Expert Systems Production and Maintenance

Steps in the methodology for the iterative development and maintenance process of ES include:

1. Identification of a problem and Feasibility Analysis:

   - The problem must be sufficient for the expert system to solve it.
   - would look for an expert for the project
   - The cost-effectiveness of the system must be identified (feasibility).

2. Identifying Device Architecture and ES Technology:

   - Development of the device. It establishes the required degree of integration with other subsystems and databases.
   - concepts which best reflect the knowledge of the domain are worked out
   - with sample, the best way to represent the information and to conduct inferencing should be developed.

3. Prototype Development:

   - The knowledge engineer works with the expert to put the initial knowledge kernel in the knowledge base.
   - Information must be conveyed in the language of the particular instrument selected for the project.

4. Prototype Research and Refinement:

   - The prototype is checked using sample cases, and defects in performance are noted. End users are testing the ES prototypes.

5. Complete and Field the ES: it guarantees and checks the ES's relationship with all elements of its environment, including users and other information systems [13, 16]. ES is recorded and user training is performed.

6. Maintain the Scheme:

- by updating the knowledge base, the framework is mostly kept up to date.
- It is also important to establish interfaces with other information systems, as such systems develop.

Expert Applications Advantages

An ES is no replacement for the overall success of the problem-solving project of an information worker. But these systems will significantly decrease the amount of work that a person needs to do to solve a problem [17, 19], leaving people with the imaginative and inventive aspects of problem solving.

Some of the potential organizational advantages of specialist systems are:

1. An ES can complete its part of the duties much more quickly than a human expert.
2. The error rate of effective systems for the same assignment is low, often much lower than the human error rate.
3. Consistent recommendations are made by ESs
4. ESs are a simple way of taking difficult-to-use sources of information to the point of application.
5. The scarce knowledge of a uniquely trained specialist can be captured by ESs.
6. In comparison to the experience of people in the organization, ESs may become a tool for building up organizational knowledge.
7. For novices, ESs result in a quicker learning curve when used as training vehicles.
8. In environments hazardous to humans, the company can operate an ES.

Expert Systems' Drawbacks

A simple and complete solution is not provided by any technology. Large systems are expensive and need considerable time and computer resources for development [18]. The ESs have their weaknesses as well, including:

1. Technology's weaknesses
2. Knowledge acquisition challenges
3. Operational domains as the key field of application of ES
4. Holding human intelligence in organizations.

10.2   Conclusions

Being able to communicate in conversational human languages to computers and making them understand us in an AI researcher target. Systems for natural language processing are becoming widespread. At this time, the key use for natural language systems is as an expert and database systems user interface.

A general overview of NLP, which is a young discipline, was provided by this book, but one that, especially during this decade, has reached a significant applicational maturity. NLP's recent success, particularly in the application domains, is due to both technological development and the historical conditions of today.

With regards to technology, the Internet has become an integral aspect of society. On a daily basis, billions of individuals around the world use search engines available on the Internet for personal and professional purposes. Opinion mining and emotion analysis have become significant for target marketing experts, as well as contact directors for political or creative figures. For instance, similar instruments have found a place within management software in the context of decision support systems. By analyzing the content of electronic messages circulating on the Internet in public spaces and by analyzing the content of social messages circulating on the Internet in public spaces, these methods make it possible to survey the views of employees in an organization on a given topic. Some go so far as to examine the morale of workers using similar instruments, although this activity is not without ethical issues and it is not the instrument itself that should be challenged, as with any technology, but the purpose of the individual wielding it.

As far as historical circumstances are concerned, in addition to the development of Multilingual governing bodies such as the need for multilingual services that can respond to the growing demand for communication between people who do not share a common language is therefore increasingly connected to the European Union in general and the world. This makes NLP technologies, including machine translation and multilingual databases, far more important for the future.

References

1. Arora, S., Khandeparkar, H., Khodak, M., Plevrakis, O., Saunshi, N., A theoretical analysis of contrastive unsupervised representation learning, in: *Proc. of ICML*, 2019.

2. Bachman, P., Hjelm, R.D., Buchwalter, W., Learning representations by maximizing mutual information across views. *arXiv preprint 1906.00910*, 2, 2019.

3. Belghazi, M.I., Baratin, A., Rajeswar, S., Ozair, S., Bengio, Y., Courville, A., Hjelm, R.D., Mine: Mutual information neural estimation, in: *Proc. of ICML*, 2018.

4. Dai, A.M. and Le, Q.V., Semi-supervised sequence learning, in: *Proc. of NIPS*, 2015.

5. Dai, Z., Yang, Z., Yang, Y., Carbonell, J., Le, Q.V., Salakhutdinov, R., Transformer-XL: Attentive language models beyond a fixed-length context, in: *Proc. of ACL*, 2019.

6. Devlin, J., Chang, M.-W., Lee, K., Toutanova, K., BERT: Pre-training of deep bidirectional transformers for language understanding, in: *Proc. of NAACL*, 2018.

7. Donsker, M.D. and Varadhan, S.R.S., Asymptotic evaluation of certain markov process expectations for large time. IV. *Commun. Pure Appl. Math.*, 36, 2, 183–212, 1983.

8. Gutmann, M.U. and Hyvarinen, A., Noise-contrastive estimation of unnormalized statistical models, with applications to natural image statistics. *J. Mach. Learn. Res.*, 13, 307–361, 2012.

9. Hjelm, R.D., Fedorov, A., Lavoie-Marchildon, S., Grewal, K., Bachman, P., Trischler, A., Bengio, Y., Learning deep representations by mutual information estimation and maximization, in: *Proc. of ICLR*, 2020.

10. Howard, J. and Ruder, S., Universal language model fine-tuning for text classification, in: *Proc. of ACL*, 2018.

11. Peters, M.E., Neumann, M., Iyyer, M., Gardner, M., Clark, C., Lee, K., Zettlemoyer, L., Deep contextualized word representations, in: *Proc. of NAACL*, 2020.

12. Poole, B., Ozair, S., van den Oord, A., Alemi, A.A., Tucker, G., On variational lower bounds of mutual information, in: *Proc. of ICML*, 2019.

13. Radford, A., Narasimhan, K., Salimans, T., Sutskever, I., *Improving language under- standing by generative pre-training*. Technical report, OpenAI, San Francisco, 2018.

14. Radford, A., Wu, J., Child, R., Luan, D., Amodei, D., Sutskever, I., *Language models are unsupervised multitask learners*. Technical report, OpenAI, San Francisco, 2020.

15. Rajpurkar, P., Zhang, J., Lopyrev, K., Liang, P., SQuAD: 100,000+ questions for machine comprehension of text, in: *Proc. of EMNLP*, 2016.

16. Rajpurkar, P., Jia, R., Liang, P., Know what you don't know: Unanswerable questions for squad, in: *Proc. of ACL*, 2018.

17. Song, K., Tan, X., Qin, T., Lu, J., Liu, T.-Y., MASS: Masked sequence to sequence pre-training for language generation, in: *Proc. of ICML*, 2020.

18. Tschannen, M., Djolonga, J., Rubenstein, P.K., Gelly, S., On mutual information maximization for representation learning. arXiv preprint 1907.13625, 2, 2020.

19. van den Oord, A., Li, Y., Vinyals, O., Representation learning with contrastive predictive coding. arXiv preprint 1807.03748, 2, 2020.

11

Class Level Multi-Feature Semantic Similarity-Based Efficient Multimedia Big Data Retrieval

D. Sujatha[1], M. Subramaniam[2]* and A. Kathirvel[3]

[1]*DCSE, St. Peters College of Engineering and Technology, Chennai, India*
[2]*Dept. of Information Technology, Sree Vidyanikethan Engineering College, Sree Sainath Nagar, Tirupati, Andhra Pradesh, India*
[3]*Dept. of CSE, Karunya Institute of Technology and Sciences, Karunya Nagar, Coimbatore, Tamil Nadu, India*

Abstract

The development of information technology has given different dimensions for the form of data and has opened the gate to manage data in different ways. Earlier days involved data management in a basic way as they were classified simply. The technology development in information management opened the gate for the users to combine various relational data to form a single entity. This increased the phenomenon of combining various personal details to form a big data. Storage and retrieval of multimedia big data has been handled with several techniques based on different features. The number of approaches has been discussed earlier but suffers to achieve higher performance in big data retrieval. To solve this issue, an efficient class level multi-feature semantic similarity measure based approach has been presented in this paper. The method receives the input query and estimates class level information similarity, class level texture similarity, class level semantic similarity measure for different classes. Using these measures, the method computes the multi-feature semantic similarity towards each class available. At last, a class which is having maximum similarity is identified and the result set is produced accordingly.

*Corresponding author: subbu.21074@gmail.com

R. Kanthavel, K. Ananthajothi, S. Balamurugan and R. Karthik Ganesh (eds.) Artificial Intelligent Techniques for Wireless Communication and Networking, (155–174) © 2022 Scrivener Publishing LLC

Keywords: Multimedia data sets, big data, information retrievals semantic similarity, MFSS

11.1   Introduction

The modern representation of data has changed the type of storage medium. Also, representing the data in different ways has given different dimensions for the data being maintained. The earlier data management systems have considered the data of either textual or alphanumeric. The growing information technology and the entry of image based data representation have supported the emerging of multimedia data. Later in the previous decade, representing the information through pictures, images, and videos has come. However, the growth of information technology has supported different ways of representing the information; the management of the diverse data has become a more challenging one. The textual information are just considered as text where the data types like imaging and voice, video cannot be considered just as they have various features included. For an image, there are many properties available, like objects, color, texture and shapes. These features increase the dimension of the data when it is being represented. When the features are presented in the form of images and videos, the way of presenting the information has changed. However, such presentation of information should be considered at the information retrieval. In earlier days, the documents are clustered and grouped according to the text features. When the text features are considered for document clustering the method estimates the similarity according to the text features only. But, as the way of presenting the feature has changed, considering only the text features is not enough. It is necessary to consider different other features like image, video and so on.

Multimedia data set is the collection of data points which has the combination of above mentioned features. Like relational database, the information related to the particular entity has been combined to produce or form a multimedia data and big data. Consider, there exists a person or patient, whose details can be stored in the form of big data. By combining the professional, personal, medical and diagnosis information, the big data related to a person can be generated. The multimedia content would have various properties like, the MRI (multi resolution image) captured through the device, X-ray, blood reports, disease information, treatment details, treatment history can be presented in form of big data as it is produced from multimedia. Such data points are used to perform various activities like disease prediction, web search, and so on.

The application of multimedia data has no extend and has been used in several problems. As the size of data and dimensions of the data gets increased, identifying the related data points has become more challenging. There exist numerous techniques toward indexing multimedia data. The methods either consider the text feature or keywords in clustering the data points. When it becomes multimedia data points, the methods consider color features in grouping the images. But they suffer to achieve higher performance because of missing features. Most approaches do not consider many features in grouping them.

On the other side, the search engines and information management systems have the headache of presenting results according to the user's interest. To perform this, the query has to be handled in an intelligent way. For example, the user would simply produce a query like "Hospital" which has been produced with the list of hospital names by the existing algorithms. But, the user intension would be the list of hospitals near to the user location. So it is necessary to handle the query in a more efficient way. This increases the requirement of considering the meaning of the query. It is necessary to identify the relations between the query and the terms. By considering this, the multimedia retrieval can be performed efficiently.

Semantic ontology has been used in various domains of information systems. The ontology maintains a set of classes and their properties with the relation between them. By grouping the multimedia big data based on semantic relationship, the clustering efficiency can be improved. Towards this scope, there are a number of methods that have been presented earlier, but struggles in achieving the performance. The reason behind this is, the way the data points are grouped. The similarity between the data samples are measured according to the terms of ontology. However, it is more essential to consider, the relations being covered by the data. For example, when the dataset indexes the climate information, it is necessary to index them in more efficient manner. This would help to analyze the climate conditions and could be able to predict the upcoming natural disasters and would be helpful in predicting the weather condition. The climate data would contain regional properties, rainfall data, satellite images, weather report, air properties and so on. Such data would have no restriction in their dimension. All these increase the requirement of efficient indexing scheme for multimedia big data.

Towards increasing retrieval efficiency, a class level semantic similarity orient scheme is discussed. The method performs information retrieval according to the similarity values on various features like Information, Texture and Semantics. Section 11.1 presents the detailed introduction and Section 11.2 discusses the detailed review. Section 11.3 details the proposed approach and Section 11.4 discusses the result and analysis. Section 11.5 details the conclusion.

11.2   Literature Review

The problem of multimedia data retrieval has been approached by several techniques. Such methods are discussed in detail in this part. In [1], a data hiding technique has been presented towards ubiquitous data. The method uses data hiding technique with the combination of semantics to perform retrieval. The DHSR uses the semantic information in data retrieval. Similarly, in [2], the author presented an optimized BoW (Bag of Words) model named SPBoW towards mapping exact document through semantic features. The method measures the semantic distance between the words of the corpus. The same has been used to generate code book. This reduces the gap between the documents.

The map reduce has been considered as more important in semantic retrieval [3]. The author presented a programming model. The model aims at reducing the computation time in semantic retrieval. In [4], a cross model approach is presented towards multimedia retrieval. The method uses SIFT features to perform image retrieval where the topical features are used to extract text information. Canonical analysis is performed to measure the correlation between the data. The model improves the retrieval accuracy. In [5], the relation between the same class and relation between another class has been considered for the data retrieval. The method estimates the cross media similarity based on inter and intra media correlation measures. The data retrieval is performed using HSNN (Heterogeneous Similarity Nearest Neighbor) measure.

In [6], the problem of large scale multimedia retrieval is approached using semantic graphs. The method measures the similarity between different multimedia data using multi-modality semantic relationship graph (MSRG) which has been used to measure the correlation between the data.

The problem of multimedia retrieval has been approached with the feedback obtained from the uses in [7]. The method ranks the data based on the feedback obtained and use them for data retrieval. The author presented a global alignment algorithm with regression which uses the laplacian matrix to perform ranking. In [8], the author presented a combined approach for multimedia retrieval. The method measures correlation, semantic and cross model matching measures for each document. The method estimates semantic correlation matching score to perform data retrieval. Transitive Hashing Network for Heterogeneous Multimedia Retrieval [9], extracts relationship from dataset and query. Using such relations, a cross model correlation is measured to perform retrieval.

In [10], a semantic feature orient multimedia retrieval technique is presented, which clubs heterogeneous feature to include semantic, topical measures in estimating their closeness. In [11], a semantic ontology based document retrieval algorithm is presented. The method considers the big data tools to perform data retrieval. The method initially extracts the semantic information and performs document retrieval. The problem of multimedia retrieval is approached with a cross model technique in [12], which uses text features and image features. The text features are mapped to image classes. The semantic operators are used to map the text features to images. Based on the mapping, the document retrieval is performed.

In [13], the author presented a healthcare document merging scheme in hadoop. The method considers the small sized files and merges them to big files to handle the storage problem. The method reduces the storage cost towards data retrieval. A range free localization technique has been presented in [14], which identifies the nearest nodes in extracting data in wireless sensor nodes. The distance between the nodes has been used as the key in data retrieval. Similarly, in [15] an efficient search algorithm is presented which uses the document tags. The algorithm performs searching using RFID and reduces the energy consumption.

An adaptable sentiment analysis approach is presented in [16], which has been applied on social posts which extracts opinions of users by constructing dynamic dictionary of words according to hash tags.

A feature selection scheme towards sentiment analysis is presented in [17], which extracts n grams to perform sentiment analysis. A combined approach of sentiment analysis is presented in [18], which combines rule-based reasoning and case-based reasoning. Similarly, a novel approach has been presented in [19], that utilizes aspect level sentiment detection, which focuses on the features of the item. In [20], sentiment analysis methods and techniques are presented that are used in the medical domain.

The methods analyzed above suffer to achieve higher efficiency in multimedia big data retrieval and suffer with higher time complexity.

11.3   Class Level Semantic Similarity-Based Retrieval

The proposed class level multi-feature semantic similarity based multimedia retrieval algorithm reads the input multimedia data set and removes the data points with missing values. The preprocessed data points have been used to extract the features. The features extracted have been used to measure class level multi-feature semantic similarity measure. The similarity measure has been measured in each dimension, with the semantic features. For the query, the method computes both semantic similarity and feature similarity. A set

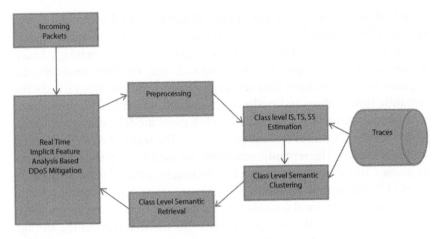

Figure 11.1   Architecture of proposed multimedia big retrieval system.

of tuples are identified according to the two measures. The same has been used to extract the relevant results from multimedia big data set.

The functional architecture of proposed multimedia big data retrieval system has been pictured in Figure 11.1. The detailed stages and functional components has been explained briefly in this section.

Preprocessing
Input: Multimedia Data Set Mds
Output: preprocessed Data set Pds.

Start

    Read input data set Mds.
    Identify the possible dimensions of data points.

$$\text{Dimension list Dls} = \int_{i=1}^{size(Mds)} \sum Dimension(Mds(i) \not\exists Dls$$

    For each data point di

        If $\int_{i=1}^{size(Mds)}$ if $(Mds(i) \not\exists \forall Data\ points$ then

            Remove data point

        Else

$$Pds = \sum (Di \in Pds) \cup Di$$

        End

    End

Stop

The pre-processing scheme finds incomplete data points and removes them from the data set. The data set which is noise removed is used to perform clustering and retrieval.

Class Level Multi-Feature Semantic Clustering:
The clustering algorithm performs grouping of high dimensional multimedia data based on the similarity of data points which has been measured in number of levels. As the data points have much dimension, it is necessary to measure the similarity between the data points in each dimension. According to this, the method measures class level information similarity, class level texture similarity and class level semantic similarity measures. Using all these measures, the method estimates multi-feature semantic weight. Estimated weight has been used to identify the class.

The class level Informative similarity is measured as follows:

Consider, the dataset has N number of documents which are classified into k number of classes and each class has p number of documents, then the value of information similarity of the document towards the class c has been measured as follows:

$$\text{CIS} = \int_{i=1}^{size(C)} \frac{\sum_{j=1}^{size(C(i))} C(i) \in Di}{size(C(i))}$$, where C is the class which has number

of terms related to the concept of the class. According to that, the value of CIS is computed according to the number of terms contained in the document from the concept of the class considered and the total number of terms contain in the class. So, for any document Dk to become a member of the class considered, it should contain minimum terms of the concept in the document so that you can justify or conclude that the document speak about the topic or concept.

Similarly, the texture similarity on multimedia data has been measured by computing the texture similarity among the images present in the document and the images present in the class. For example, the images and the objects on the images can be classified under different classes. The document class of cricket would contain number of images related to the cricket. By considering the images of the class cricket and its features, the similarity of any given document towards the class cricket can be measured. To measure the texture similarity, the texture features are extracted from the images of any document and the texture features belongs to the class. As the method maintains a set of texture features for any class, with the list of texture features of the class and the texture feature obtained from the document image, the method estimates the distance among the texture features. By computing the distance between the texture features and counting the list of features which has distance less than threshold value, the value of Class Texture Similarity (CTS) is measured. The value of CTS is measured as follows:

$$CTS = \int_{i=1}^{size(C)} \frac{\sum_{j=1}^{size(C(i))} Dist(C(i)(j), Di(j)) < Th}{size(C(i))}$$, which defines a func-

tion which measure the distance between the texture features and by computing the ratio of texture matches with the total number of textures present in the class, the value of CTS is measured. The CTS value defines the similarity of texture features among the images and multimedia data present in the document. By measuring the CTS value, the relevancy and similarity between the documents at their multimedia features can be measured which supports the improvement of information retrieval.

Finally, the class semantic similarity (CSS) is measured towards various classes to support information retrieval. The value of CSS is measured according to the semantic ontology present in the document feature and the number of semantic terms presents the ontology of the class. According to both values, the value of CSS is measured for the document towards single class and in the same way, the value of CSS can be measured towards various classes.

The value of CSS is measured for the given document Di towards the class C as follows:

$$CSS = \frac{\int_{i=1}^{size(Di)} \sum Di(i) \in C(O)}{size(C(O))}$$, where Di is the document given, O is

the ontology where C is the class and the size (C(O)) represents the total number of semantic terms present in the ontology of the class C.

Now using the value of CIS, CTS, and CSS the value of multi-feature semantic weight can be measured. It has been measured as follows:

$$\text{Multi-feature semantic weight MFSW} = \frac{CIS}{CSS} \times \frac{CTS}{CSS}$$

Now according to the value of MFSW, the class of the document can be identified. The class with maximum value of MFSW has been selected as the resultant class and the document has been indexed to the identified class.

Algorithm:
Input: Multimedia Data Mds, Semantic Ontology O.
Output: Cluster Set Cs.

Begin

Read input Multimedia data Mds, O.

For each data point Di

For each class C

Compute information similarity $CIS = \int_{i=1}^{size(C)} \dfrac{\sum_{j=1}^{size(C(i))} C(i) \in Di}{size(C(i))}$

Compute Texture similarity $CTS = \int_{i=1}^{size(C)} \dfrac{\sum_{j=1}^{size(C(i))} (C(i)(j), Di(j)) < Th}{size(C(i))}$

Compute semantic similarity $CSS = \dfrac{\int_{i=1}^{size(Di)} \sum Di(i) \in C(O)}{size(C(O))}$

Compute multi-feature semantic weight $MFSW = \dfrac{CIS}{CSS} \times \dfrac{CTS}{CSS}$

End

Class C = Choose the class with maximum multi-feature semantic weight.

Index the data point to selected class.

End

Stop.

The class level multi-feature semantic clustering algorithm estimates similarity towards information, texture and semantic features. Based on the measures, the value of multi-feature semantic weight is measured to identify the class of data point.

Class Level Semantic Retrieval

The retrieval phase starts with reading the input query submitted, and for the input query, the method estimates the class level information similarity, class level texture similarity, and class level semantic similarity measures. The above mentioned measures are estimated on each class of data points in each level. According to the value of measures estimated, the value of semantic weight is computed. According to the semantic weight, a single class which is having higher value is selected. The data points of selected class are produced as result.

Algorithm:

Input: Query IQ, Cluster Set ClS, Ontology CO

Output: results Set Rs.
Start

    Read IQ, Cls, CO.

    Extract textual features from IQ as $\text{Tf} = \sum Key\ words \in IQ$

    Extract texture features from IQ as $\text{Tef} = \sum Texture\ Features \in IQ$

    Extract semantic terms from IQ as $\text{SF} = \sum Key\ words(Q) \in IO$

    For each class C

        For each level l

    Compute information Similarity $Is = \dfrac{\sum Attributes(C(l)) \in TF}{size(C(l))}$

Compute Texture similarity $TS = \dfrac{\sum_{j=1}^{size(Tef)}(Dist(Tef(j), C(l(i))) < Th) \forall Datapoints(C(l))}{size(C(l))}$

Compute Semantic Similarity $Ss = \dfrac{\sum relations(CO(C(l))) \forall SF}{size(CO(C(l)))}$

    Estimate multi-feature semantic weight $MFSW = \dfrac{IS}{SS} \times \dfrac{TS}{SS}$

    End

    End

    Choose the class with maximum MFSW.

    Retrieve data points of identified class to produce result.

Stop

The above discussed algorithm performs multimedia retrieval based on the multi-feature semantic weight being measured. The MFSW has been measured based on the information similarity, texture similarity and semantic similarity. The class with higher weight has been selected to retrieve the results.

11.4   Results and Discussion

The proposed multi-feature semantic weight based multimedia retrieval algorithm has been implemented using Advanced Java. The method has been validated for its performance under varying number of classes and features. The results obtained are presented in this part.

Table 11.1 Experimental details.

Parameter	Value
Tool Used	Advanced Java
Number of Classes	20
Number of sub class	5
Total documents	1 million

The experimental setup being used for the evaluation of proposed algorithm is shown in Table 11.1. The evaluation on performance has been measured and presented below:

11.4.1   Performance Analysis vs Number of Classes

The performances of the methods are measured on different parameters according to different number of classes of documents. Obtained results are presented in this section shown in Table 11.2.

Analysis on clustering accuracy has been performed on different methods towards varying number of class of multimedia data. However, the proposed multi-feature semantic weight based approach has produced higher clustering accuracy. The inclusion of semantic features in the measurement of MFSW improves the performance of clustering.

The clustering accuracy produced by the proposed method is measured at different number of classes of documents in the environment. In each case, the performance is measured for different approaches and the MFSW scheme identified as capable of producing higher clustering accuracy and the respective graph is plotted for the same and shown in Figure 11.2.

Table 11.2 Analysis on clustering accuracy vs no. of classes.

Performance on clustering accuracy vs no. of classes			
Method	30 classes	50 classes	100 classes
DHSR	71	76	82
SPBoW	74	82	86
MSRC	79	85	89
MFSW	86	92	98

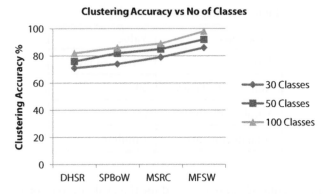

Figure 11.2 Comparison on clustering performance vs no. of classes.

Performance of methods in retrieving the relevant document is measured among different methods at various numbers of classes of documents in each class shown in the Table 11.3. Among them, the proposed MFSW algorithm has shown great retrieval accuracy than others which is shown through Figure 11.3. The inclusion of semantic features to estimate the weight has influenced the retrieval accuracy highly.

Table 11.3 Performance analysis in retrieval accuracy vs no. of classes.

Performance on retrieval accuracy vs no. of classes			
Method	**30 classes**	**50 classes**	**100 classes**
DHSR	82	86	89
SPBoW	84	88	91
MSRC	86	89	92
MFSW	91	94	98

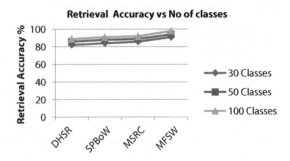

Figure 11.3 Comparison on retrieval accuracy vs. no. of classes.

The comparative result on retrieval accuracy has been measured between different methods. The MFSW approach shows higher retrieval accuracy among various approaches.

The performance on false classification ratio has been measured for different methods. The results obtained have been analyzed towards other methods outcome where the MFSW approach shows least false classification, which is shown in Table 11.4.

The false ratio in classification generated by various approaches are measured and plotted in Figure 11.4, and MFSW approach keeps least false ratio from other approaches.

The time complexity on multimedia retrieval has been measured for different methods. At each class of data in the Table 11.5, the proposed MFSW algorithm has produced less time complexity compared to other methods.

The time complexity generated by various schemes are measured and plotted in Figure 11.5, where MFSW approaches have shown least time complexity.

Table 11.4 Performance on false classification ratio vs no. of classes.

Performance on false classification ratio vs no. of classes			
Method	30 classes	50 classes	100 classes
DHSR	28	26	18
SPBoW	25	18	14
MSRC	21	15	11
MFSW	13	8	3

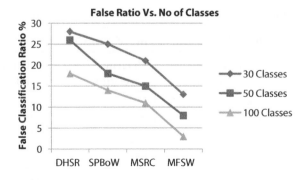

Figure 11.4 Comparison on false classification ratio vs no. of classes.

Table 11.5 Performance analysis on time complexity vs no. of classes.

Performance on time complexity vs no. of classes			
Method	30 classes	50 classes	100 classes
DHSR	46	68	87
SPBoW	39	63	83
MSRC	33	55	71
MFSW	8	21	29

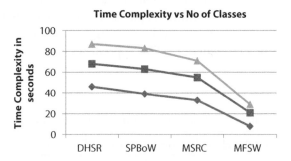

Figure 11.5 Comparison on time complexity vs no. of classes.

11.4.2   Performance Analysis vs. Number of Terms/Relations

The performance of the methods is measured by varying the number of terms and relations in the semantic ontology. According to the method estimates the similarity measures to perform information retrieval.

Table 11.6 Performance on clustering accuracy vs no. of terms/relations.

Performance on clustering accuracy vs no. of terms/relations			
Method	30 terms/ relations	50 terms/ relations	100 terms/ relations
DHSR	69	73	79
SPBoW	71	78	83
MSRC	77	83	87
MFSW	86	92	98

Table 11.6 shows the analysis on clustering accuracy has been performed on different methods towards varying number of Terms/Relations under each class of multimedia data. However, the proposed multi-feature semantic weight based approach has produced higher clustering accuracy. The inclusion of semantic features in the measurement of MFSW improves the performance of clustering.

The clustering accuracy produced by the proposed method is computed and plotted in Figure 11.6, where proposed MFSW approach shows great achievement in clustering accuracy among the methods compared.

Performance of methods in retrieving the relevant document are measured and plotted in Table 11.7, where the MFSW approach is identified as capable of producing higher retrieval accuracy. The inclusion of semantic features to estimate the weight has influenced the retrieval accuracy highly.

The comparative result on retrieval accuracy has been measured between various schemes and plotted in Figure 11.7. The MFSW approach generated higher accuracy on document retrieval among the methods considered.

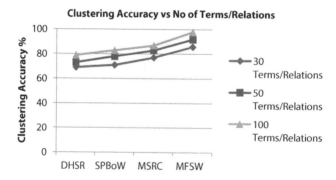

Figure 11.6 Comparison on clustering performance vs no. of terms/relations.

Table 11.7 Performance analysis in retrieval accuracy vs no. of terms/relations.

Performance on retrieval accuracy vs no. of terms/relations			
Method	30 terms/relations	50 terms/relations	100 terms/relations
DHSR	78	82	85
SPBoW	82	85	88
MSRC	85	87	91
MFSW	91	94	98

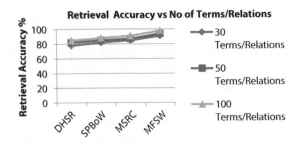

Figure 11.7 Comparison on retrieval accuracy vs. no. of terms/relations.

The analysis on false classification ratio has been measured for different methods. The results obtained have been analyzed with the performance of other approaches. The MFSW approach generated least false ratio among the methods compared as shown in Table 11.8.

The false ratio in classification produced by different approaches are measured and plotted in Figure 11.8. The MFSW approach has produced least false ratio among the methods considered.

Table 11.8 Analysis on false classification ratio vs no. of terms/relations.

Performance on false classification ratio vs no. of classes			
Method	30 terms/ relations	50 terms/ relations	100 terms/ relations
DHSR	22	18	15
SPBoW	18	15	12
MSRC	15	13	9
MFSW	9	6	2

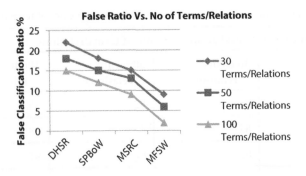

Figure 11.8 Comparison on false classification ratio vs no. of terms/relations.

Table 11.9 Performance analysis on time complexity vs no. of terms/relations.

Performance on time complexity vs no. of terms/relations			
Method	30 terms/ relations	50 terms/ relations	100 terms/ relations
DHSR	56	72	95
SPBoW	49	65	86
MSRC	38	57	67
MFSW	8	21	29

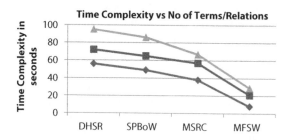

Figure 11.9 Comparison on time complexity vs no. of terms/relations.

The time complexity on multimedia retrieval has been measured for different methods. At each class of data, the proposed MFSW algorithm has produced less time complexity compare to other methods, the comparative values are shown in Table 11.9.

The value of time complexity generated by various approaches on document retrieval are computed and plotted in Figure 11.9. The MFSW approach is identified as least time complex approach among the methods considered.

Conclusion

In this chapter, an efficient multi-feature semantic similarity based multimedia retrieval in big data has been proposed. The input data has been preprocessed which eliminates the noisy data points first. Second, the method computes information, texture and semantic similarity measures in each class of data points. Based on these measures, the method computes MFSW value to identify the exact class of the document. In retrieval, the same set of measures has been estimated to identify the class and the method returns the result to the user based on that. The proposed method improves the performance of multimedia indexing and retrieval with higher accuracy. The time complexity and false ratio has been hugely reduced.

References

1. Guo, K., Ma, J., Duan, G., DHSR: A novel semantic retrieval approach for ubiquitous multimedia. *Wireless Pers. Commun.*, 76, 779–793, 2014.

2. Wu, L., Hoi, S.C., Yu, N., Semantics-preserving bag-of-words models and applications. *IEEE Trans. Image Process.*, 19, 1908–1920, 2010.

3. Dean, J. and Ghemawat, S., MapReduce: simplified data processing on large clusters. *Commun. ACM*, 51, 107–113, 2008.

4. Rasiwasia, N., Costa Pereira, J., Coviello, E., Doyle, G., Lanckriet, G.R., Levy, R., Vasconcelos, N., A new approach to cross-modal multimedia retrieval, in: *Proceedings of the ACM international conference on Multimedia*, Firenze, Italy, pp. 251–260, 2010.

5. Zhai, X., Peng, Y., Xiao, J., Cross-media retrieval by intra-media and inter-media correlation mining. *Multimed. Syst.*, 19, 395–406, 2013.

6. Lu, B., Wang, G.R., Yuan, Y., A novel approach towards large scale cross-media retrieval. *J. Comput. Sci. Technol.*, 27, 1140–1149, 2012.

7. Yang, Y., Nie, F., Xu, D., Luo, J., Zhuang, Y., Pan, Y., A multimedia retrieval architecture based on semi-supervised ranking and relevance feedback. *IEEE Trans. Pattern Anal. Mach. Intell.*, 34, 723–742, 2012.

8. Costa Pereira, J., Coviello, E., Doyle, G., Rasiwasia, N., Lanckriet, G., Levy, R., Vasconcelos, N., On the role of correlation and abstraction in cross-modal multimedia retrieval. *IEEE Trans. Pattern Anal. Mach. Intell.*, 36, 521–535, 2014.

9. Cao, Z., Long, M., Wang, J., Yang, Q., Transitive Hashing Network for Heterogeneous Multimedia Retrieval, in: *AAAI*, pp. 81–87, 2017.

10. Guo, K., Pan, W., Lu, M., Zhou, X., Ma, J., An effective and economical architecture for semantic-based heterogeneous multimedia big data retrieval. *J. Syst. Software*, 102, 207–216, 2015.

11. Guo, K., Liang, Z., Tang, Y., Chi, T., SOR: An optimized semantic ontology retrieval algorithm for heterogeneous multimedia big data. *J. Comput. Sci.*, 2017. http://dx.doi.org/10.1016/j.jocs.2017.02.005

12. Pereira, J.C. and Vasconcelos, N., Cross-modal domain adaptation for text-based regularization of image semantics in image retrieval systems. *Comput. Vision Image Understanding*, 124, 7, 123–135, 2014.

13. He, H., Du, Z., Zhang, W., Chen, A., Optimization strategy of Hadoop small file storage for big data in healthcare. *J. Supercomput.*, 72, 10, 3696–3707, 10, 2015.

14. Zhang, S., Liu, X., Wang, J., Cao, J., Min, G., Accurate range-free localization for anisotropic wireless sensor networks. *ACM Trans. Sens. Netw.*, 11, 3, 1–28, 2015.

15. Zhang, S., Liu, X., Wang, J., Cao, J., Min, G., Energy-efficient active tag searching in large scale RFID systems. *Inf. Sci.*, 317, 10, 143–156, 2015.
16. El Alaoui, I., Gahi, Y., Messoussi, R., Chaabi, Y., Todoskoff, A., Kobi, A., A novel adaptable approach for sentiment analysis on big social data, Springer. *J. Big Data*, 5, 1, 12, 2018.
17. Le, B. and Nguyen, H., Twitter Sentiment Analysis Using Machine Learning Techniques, in: *Advanced Computational Methods for Knowledge Engineering*, pp. 279–289, Springer, 2015.
18. Berka, P., Sentiment analysis using rule-based and case-based reasoning, Springer. *J. Intell. Inf. Syst.*, 55, 51–66, 2020.
19. Nandal, N., Tanwar, R., Pruthi, J., Machine learning based aspect level sentiment analysis for Amazon products, in: *Spatial Information Research*, Springer, 2020.
20. Abualigah, L., Alfar, H.E., Shehab, M., Hussein, A.M.A., Sentiment Analysis in Healthcare: A Brief Review, in: *Recent Advances in NLP: The Case of Arabic Language. Studies in Computational Intelligence,*,Abd Elaziz M., Al-qaness M., Ewees A., Dahou A (eds.) vol. 874, Springer, Cham, 2020, https://doi.org/10.1007/978-3-030-34614-0_7.

Supervised Learning Approaches for Underwater Scalar Sensory Data Modeling With Diurnal Changes

J.V. Anand[1], T.R. Ganesh Babu[2], R. Praveena[2*] and K. Vidhya[3]

[1]Department of Electronics and Communication Engineering, Siddartha Institute of Science and Technology, Chittoor, Andhra Pradesh, India
[2]Department of Electronics and Communication Engineering, Muthayammal Engineering College, Namakkal, India
[3]Department of Electronics and Communication Engineering, Saveetha School of Engineering, Saveetha University, Chennai, India

Abstract

Spatial patterns of underwater temperature data, its impact of depth and associated temperature are taken from SEAONE obtained from Temperature Data Logger UA-002. The different geographical locations of data logger and different depths namely 5 and 12 m have been modeled for classification using a supervised learning approach. The first approach deals with inter depth variation profile in line with latitude and longitude in a particular area. Classification is obtained incorporating multilayer perceptron with dependant variables and its covariates to intercept the impact of temperature variations in day and night cycles. The second approach deals with calculating attenuations the temperature coefficient of real data sets and attribute of attenuation in a frequency dependant loss. Thus the idiosyncratic nature of underwater and coefficients of temperature and attenuations is systematically analyzed using realistic temperature data in simulation models with statistical tools.

Keywords: Multilayer perceptron, absorption and transmission loss analysis

Corresponding author: praveenajuhi@gmail.com

R. Kanthavel, K. Ananthajothi, S. Balamurugan and R. Karthik Ganesh (eds.) *Artificial Intelligent Techniques for Wireless Communication and Networking*, (175–192) © 2022 Scrivener Publishing LLC

12.1   Introduction

Ocean stratification varies from surface to bottom across different depths. Thus measuring temperature and salinity across varying depth is vital. The parameter of temperature and salinity determines the optimal frequency of communication and the buoyancy frequency for density stratification [1]. The impact on *in situ* temperature in acoustic communication has been discussed using "High frequency acoustic thermometry". It uses Global Positioning System (GPS) for calculating the propagation times between two stations [2]. Incorporating GPS signals is not feasible in all depth due to high frequency attenuation characteristics of underwater. In [3], discussion on underwater sensor signals are subjected to mismatch in synchronization which affects the sound speed profile in networking wireless sensors. The work focuses upon link breakage and restoration rather than considering the impact of attenuation profile using synthetic data. Supervised machine learning approach with linear regression [4] states that consolidated impact of sensors "offered load" and performance metrics such as energy consumption and throughput. The work is confined to communication void in sensors without explicit calculation of attenuations. In [5], the relationship in localized sensor nodes for timely transmission is dealt with autoregressive moving model. However, the chance of single mismatch observation tends to burden the waiting time of next transmission. The proposed work is designed in two folds. In the first half of the work real time sensor data obtained from "Temperature Data Logger UA-002" as in [6], is used for classification using statistical tools. Subsequently, independent values of frequency and propagation range are assigned to estimate transmission loss and absorption loss [14].

This chapter is organized into the following sections. Section 12.2 deals with discussion on temperature calculations and underwater channel models. Section 12.3 deals with methodological descriptions on statistical analysis of real time temperature data and attenuation calculations of conventional model with changes in temperature. Section 12.4 deals with the overall results accomplished via statistical and underwater wireless attenuations. Section 12.5 concludes the overall work and scope of future work.

12.2   Literature Survey

The process of calibrating hydrophones in underwater spanning from 30 Hz to 2 kHz has been worked with vibrating water columns. Standard reference hydrophones have been used for calculating the uncertainties within the lab conditions [1]. The limitation of overcoming the uncertainties across different depth with associated temperature and pressure data is lagging. Supervised learning has been worked with realistic data for classification. Spectrometer approaches with two types of detectors namely "3 × 3 detector" and "2 × 2 detector". It states that peak shift occurs as a result of variance in temperature and electronic factors [7]. Underwater gliders where used to measure the hydrodynamic data the errors which occurs in sea trail. Compared to laboratory data the associated errors are predominantly due to salinity and conductivity [8].

12.2.1 Underwater Channel Models

Temperature and air bubble fluctuations which alters the channel conditions in salty and fresh water has been discussed with "Exponential Generalized Gamma distribution model" [9]. The entire work in [9] has been carried out in underwater optical communication with attenuation coefficient suitable for a particular wavelength with prior attenuation calculations. In [10], joint estimation of temperature and depth has been studied using "optic fiber based sensors". The results sensor measurements states that the values are in close proximity to reference sensors. However, salinity measures are excluded from the calculation. The discussion of temperature associated linearly with salinity does not work in all geographical locations [11]. Hence, measuring the buoyancy periods for up-cast and downcast profiles is needed to estimate Conductivity Temperature and Depth (CTD).

In-situ measurement with a radiation sensor has been discussed with nonlinear impact of temperature on high voltage. It states that a correction step is needed followed by prediction to analyze the temperature rate changes [12]. Time frequency relationship of source changes with location and to discriminate noise the work in [13] uses four data loggers. Three where arranged in an equilateral triangle manner with the fourth logger positioned at the center. However, the process involves setting the data logger multiple times which increase the overhead.

12.3 Proposed Work

This work contributes to the modeling of underwater channel with conventional models for attenuation calculations. The impact of temperature used has been inputted from real time data set from SEAONE [6].

12.3.1   Statistical Analysis Using Software Tools

The "time of sampling" relates the acquire time during day or night. The "depth" has been taken as factor and the measured temperature is taken as dependant variable from the dataset [6]. Subsequently, samples are taken in day and night to observe the variations in temperature across the exogenous impact.

Sample 1:

Table 12.1 SeaOne temperature data considered during day time.

Time of sampling	Depth(m)	Temperature (degree centigrade)
12:00:03	12	24.448
12:20:04	12	24.545
12:40:05	12	24.448
13:00:06	12	24.351
13:20:07	12	24.351

Table 12.2 SeaOne temperature considered during night time.

Time of sampling	Depth(m)	Temperature (degree centigrade)
20:20:28	12	25.125
20:40:29	12	25.028
21:00:30	12	25.416
21:20:31	12	24.931
21:40:32	12	25.125

Table 12.3 SeaOne temperature data considered during day time.

Time of sampling	Depth (m)	Temperature (degree centigrade)
13:35:26	5	23.677
13:55:26	5	23.966
14:15:26	5	23.292
14:35:26	5	23.581
14:55:26	5	23.581

Table 12.4 SeaOne temperature considered during night time.

Time of sampling	Depth (m)	Temperature (degree centigrade)
21:55:26	5	22.812
22:15:26	5	22.717
22:35:26	5	22.621
22:55:26	5	22.429
23:15:26	5	22.525

Tables 12.1 to 12.4 are taken across the same latitude and longitude coordinates. The timing interval taken is around 20 min. Table 12.1 shows temperature measures at day and Table 12.2 shows the temperature measured at night measure across a depth of 12 m.

Table 12.3 shows temperature measures at day and Table 12.4 shows the temperature measured at night measure across a depth of 5 m.

Sample 2:
Tables 12.5 to 12.8 are taken across the same latitude and longitude coordinates. The timing interval taken is around 20 min. Table 12.5 shows temperature measures at day and Table 12.6 shows the temperature measured at night measure across a depth of 12 m.

Table 12.7 shows temperature measures at day and Table 12.8 shows the temperature measured at night measure across a depth of 5 m.

Table 12.5 SeaOne temperature data considered during day time.

Time of sampling	Depth (m)	Temperature (degree centigrade)
12:16:00	12	20.424
12:36:00	12	20.519
12:56:00	12	20.424
13:16:00	12	20.615
13:36:00	12	20.71

Table 12.6 SeaOne temperature considered during night time.

Time of sampling	Depth (m)	Temperature (degree centigrade)
20:36:00	12	19.662
20:56:00	12	19.853
21:16:00	12	19.853
21:36:00	12	19.948
21:56:00	12	19.853

Table 12.7 SeaOne temperature data considered during day time.

Time of sampling	Depth (m)	Temperature (degree centigrade)
12:31:15	5	16.332
12:51:15	5	16.523
13:11:15	5	16.618
13:31:15	5	16.618
13:51:15	5	16.713

Table 12.8 SeaOne temperature considered during night time.

Time of sampling	Depth (m)	Temperature (degree centigrade)
21:31:15	5	17.379
21:51:15	5	17.284
22:11:15	5	17.284
22:31:15	5	17.189
22:51:15	5	17.094

12.4   Results

12.4.1   Statistical Works

The section deals with statistical analysis between the different depths of 5 and 12 m as factors. The temperature across the depth has been taken as dependant variable. In the total 10 samples of case processing summary is done using seven training and three testing variables from sample-1.

The network level information along the statistical level is shown excluding bias has been shown in Table 12.9. The superscript denoted as "a" indicates the excluding bias function. The activation function used for hidden layer is "hyperbolic tangent" and output layer is identity.

Figure 12.1 shows the multilayer perceptron model across different depth at daytime.

Table 12.9 Network information in statistical analysis for sample-1.

	Factors	**1**	**Depth**
Input layer	**Number of units**[a]		**2**
Hidden Layer(s)	Number of Hidden Layers		1
	Number of Units in Hidden Layer 1[a]		3
Output Layer	Dependent Variables	1	Temperature
	Number of Units		1
	Rescaling Method for Scale Dependents		Standardized
	Error Function		Sum of Squares

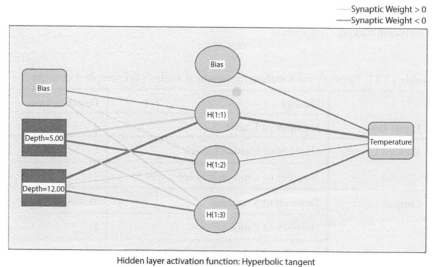

Synaptic Weight > 0
Synaptic Weight < 0

Hidden layer activation function: Hyperbolic tangent

Output layer activation function: Identity

Figure 12.1 Multi-layer perceptron model using different depth coordinates.

The model summary for relative error calculations is shown in Table 12.10. The superscript "a" in table denotes error computations for testing data.

The calculations using night time across different depth is analysed in Tables 12.11 and 12.12. The different depth and temperature coefficients are taken with six training and four testing variables has been for case processing at night time from sample 1.

The network level information along the statistical level is shown excluding bias has been shown in Table 12.11. The superscript denoted as "a" indicates the excluding bias function. The activation function used for hidden layer is "hyperbolic tangent" and output layer is identity.

Figure 12.2 shows the multilayer perceptron model across different depth at night.

Model Summary

Table 12.10 Model summary for calculating relative errors in testing data.

Training	Sum of Squares Error	.317
	Relative Error	.106
	Stopping Rule Used	1 consecutive step(s) with no decrease in error[a]
Testing	Sum of Squares Error	.664
	Relative Error	.353

Dependent Variable: Temperature.

Table 12.11 Network information in statistical analysis for sample-1 at night.

	Factors	1	Depth
Input layer	**Number of Units[a]**		2
Hidden Layer(s)	Number of Hidden Layers		1
	Number of Units in Hidden Layer 1[a]		1
Output Layer	Dependent Variables	1	Temperature
	Number of Units		1
	Rescaling Method for Scale Dependents		Standardized
	Error Function		Sum of Squares

[a] Excluding the bias unit.

Model Summary

Table 12.12 Model summary for calculating relative errors in testing data at night.

Training	Sum of Squares Error	.035
	Relative Error	.014
	Stopping Rule Used	1 consecutive step(s) with no decrease in error[a]
Testing	Sum of Squares Error	.023
	Relative Error	.015

Dependent Variable: Temperature.
[a] Error computations are based on the testing sample.

The model summary for relative error calculations is shown in Table 12.12.

Data from along different spatial coordinates from sample 2 used for calculations from Tables 12.6 and 12.8. Case processing summary value is taken for analysis from sample-2. The different depth and temperature coefficients are taken with seven training and three testing variables.

The network level information along the statistical level is shown excluding bias has been shown in Table 12.13.

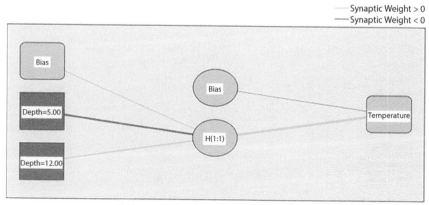

Hidden layer activation function: Hyperbolic tangent

Output layer activation function: Identity

Figure 12.2 Multi-layer perceptron model using different depth coordinates at night.

Network Information

Table 12.13 Network information in statistical analysis for sample-2.

	Factors	1	Depth
Input layer	Number of Units[a]		2
Hidden Layer(s)	Number of Hidden Layers		1
	Number of Units in Hidden Layer 1[a]		1
	Activation Function		Hyperbolic tangent
Output Layer	Dependent Variables	1	Temperature
	Number of Units		1
	Rescaling Method for Scale Dependents		Standardized
	Activation Function		Identity
	Error Function		Sum of Squares

[a] Excluding the bias unit.

Figure 12.3 shows the multilayer perceptron model across different depth at daytime.

The model summary for relative error calculations is shown in Table 12.14 for night time.

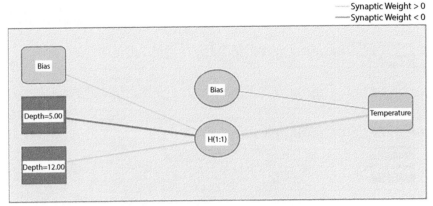

Hidden layer activation function: Hyperbolic tangent

Output layer activation function: Identity

Figure 12.3 Multi-layer perceptron model using different depth coordinates at night.

Table 12.14 Model summary for calculating relative errors in testing data at night time.

Training	Sum of Squares Error	.012
	Relative Error	.004
	Stopping Rule Used	1 consecutive step(s) with no decrease in error[a]
Testing	Sum of Squares Error	.015
	Relative Error	.011

Dependent Variable: Temperature.
[a] Error computations are based on the testing sample.

The value in Tables 12.5 and 12.7 has not been used for statistical analysis since the relative error is high across the samples.

12.4.1.1   Auto Correlation and Partial Auto Correlation Analysis of Depth and Temperature

Table 12.15 shows the case processing summary for sample Table 12.1. Since the temperature data shows similar values an autocorrelation function is done as shown in Table 12.16.

Figures 12.4 and 12.5 show an ACF and PACF lag diagram with the temperature data from sample 1.

The case processing summary for Table 12.2 data is shown in Table 12.17.

Table 12.15 Case processing summary for sample 1 data obtained from Table 12.1.

		Temperature
Series Length		5
Number of Missing Values	User-Missing	0
	System-Missing	0
Number of Valid Values		5
Number of Computable First Lags		4

Autocorrelations

Series: Temperature

Table 12.16 ACF function for Table 12.1 data.

Lag	Autocorrelation	Std. Error[a]	Box–Ljung Statistic		
			Value	Df	Sig.[b]
1	.343	.338	1.029	1	.310
2	−.386	.293	2.764	2	.251
3	−.400	.239	5.564	3	.135

[a] The underlying process assumed is independence (white noise).
[b] Based on the asymptotic chi-square approximation.

Auto correlation and Partial Auto correlation functions for Tables 12.18 and 12.19 are based on Table 12.2 data from sample 1.

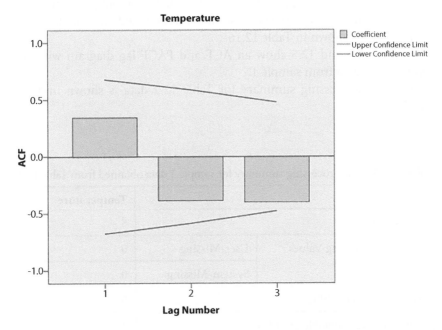

Figure12. 4 Autocorrelation function and lag for temperature data in Table 12.1.

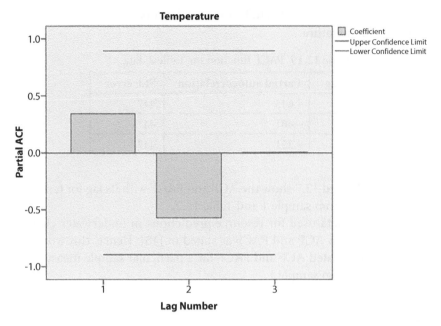

Figure 12.5 Partial Autocorrelation function and lag for temperature data in Table 12.1.

Table 12.17 Case processing summary for sample 1 and Table 12.2 data.

		Temperature
Series Length		5
Number of Missing Values	User-Missing	0
	System-Missing	0
Number of Valid Values		5
Number of Computable First Lags		4

Autocorrelations

Series: Temperature

Table 12.18 ACF function for Table 12.2 data.

Lag	Autocorrelation	Std. Error[a]	Box–Ljung Statistic		
			Value	Df	Sig.[b]
1	-.643	.338	3.616	1	.057
2	.143	.293	3.854	2	.146
3	.000	.239	3.854	3	.278

[a] The underlying process assumed is independence (white noise).
[b] Based on the asymptotic chi-square approximation.

Partial Autocorrelations

Series: Temperature

Table 12.19 PACF function for Table 2 data.

Lag	Partial autocorrelation	Std. error
1	−.643	.447
2	−.461	.447
3	−.351	.447

Figures 12.6 and 12.7 show the ACF and PACF with its lag for temperature data taken from sample 1 and Table 12.2.

Time series data used for resource predictions in underwater channel must be free from ACF and PACF as stated in [15]. Hence, this work calculates the associated ACF and PACF for a particular sample measured at day and night from sample 1.

12.4.2 Attenuation Results

The frequency dependant calculation of absorption loss and frequency independent transmission loss is calculated using [14]. The attenuation

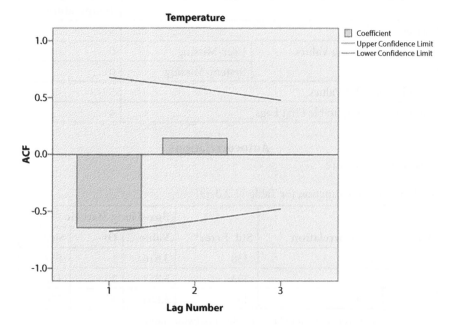

Figure 12.6 Autocorrelation Function and lag for temperature data in Table 12.2.

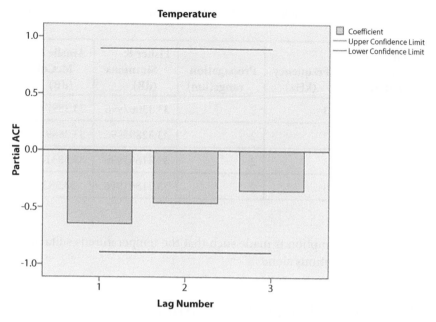

Figure 12.7 Partial Autocorrelation function and lag for temperature data in Table 12.2.

calculations one sample value from real time temperature data inputted from Tables 12.3, 12.4, 12.7 and 12.8. Highest temperature within each set of sample value is taken and inputted to analyze the inevitable impact of attenuations.

In Tables 12.20 and 12.21 two attenuation models are being considered for analysis namely: Fisher and Simmons [16] and Ainslie & McColm [17]. Lyman and Fleming standard of salinity 35 parts per trillion and pH 8 is considered. The range of validity in all cases is considered to be less than 7 km.

Table 12.20 Absorption loss in underwater environment for input of real time temperature data.

Temperature (degree centigrade)	Frequency (kHz)	Fisher & Simmons (dB/km)	Ainslie & McColm (dB/km)
23.966	3	0.16019	0.18972
22.812	3	0.15932	0.1893
16.618	3	0.15334	0.18642
17.379	3	0.15416	0.18676

Table 12.21 Transmission loss in underwater environment for input of real time temperature data.

Temperature (degree centigrade)	Frequency (kHz)	Propagation range(km)	Fisher & Simmons (dB)	Ainslie & McColm (dB)
23.966	3	2	33.33067996	33.38974
22.812	3	2	33.32893996	33.3889
16.618	3	2	33.31697996	33.38314
17.379	3	2	33.31861996	33.38382

In this work assumption is made such that the temperature is suitable for theoretical calculations alone.

12.5   Conclusion and Future Work

Temperature data measured with varying depth under the same latitude and longitudinal coordinates are initially considered for training using Multilayer perceptron. Subsequently, the values of testing data and relative errors are being obtained using statistical tools of SPSS. In the second half, the information rate with transmission loss and attenuation loss incorporated with diurnal changes of temperature from ocean observation data has been estimated. The limitation of this study is issues like Doppler tracking and sensor mobility and other networking related studies is not discussed throughout this work. Further research would include estimating the performance of sensory data along with the deployed sensors for theoretical attenuations obtained and the impact of networking used for diverse applications.

References

1. Cui, S. and Khoo, D.W.Y., Underwater Calibration of Hydrophones at Very Low Frequencies from 30 Hz to 2 kHz. *IOP Conf. Ser.: J. Phys.: Conf. Ser.*, 1065, 072015, 2018.
2. Yu, X., Zhuang, X., Li, Y., Zhang, Y., Real-time observation of range-averaged temperature by high-frequency underwater acoustic thermometry. *IEEE Access*, 7, 17975–17980, 23-Jan-2019.

3. Anand, J.V. and Sivanesan, P., Certain investigations of underwater wireless sensors synchronization and funneling effect. *Int. J. Comput. Appl.*, 43, 5, 423–430, 2021.

4. Anand, J.V. and Titus, S., Regression based analysis of effective hydrocast in underwater environment. *TENCON 2014-2014 IEEE Region 10 Conference*, Oct-2014, pp. 1–6.

5. Anand, J.V., Sundeep, K., Rao, N.D.P., Underwater Sensor Protocol for Time Synchronization and Data Transmissions using the Prediction Model. *2020 International Conference on Inventive Computation Technologies (ICICT)*, Feb-2020, pp. 762–76.

6. Edson, F.-J. and Lindner, A., *An underwater temperature dataset from coastal islands in Santa Catarina, southern Brazil: High accuracy data from different depths*, Francais, SEANOE, https://doi.org/10.17882/62120, 2019.

7. Zeng, Z., Pan, X., Ma, H., He, J., Cang, J., Zeng, M., Cheng, J., Optimization of an underwater *in-situ* LaBr3: Ce spectrometer with energy self-calibration and efficiency calibration. *Appl. Radiat. Isot.*, 121, 101–108, 2017.

8. Lv, B., Liu, H.-L., Hu, Y.-F., Wu, C.-X., Liu, J., He, H.-J., Chen, J., Yuan, J., Zhang, Z.-W., Cao, L., Li, H., Experimental study on integrated and autonomous conductivity-temperature-depth (CTD) sensor applied for underwater glider. *Mar. Georesour. Geotechnol.*, 1–11, 39, 9, 1044–1054, 2020.

9. Zedini, E., Oubei, H.M., Kammoun, A., Hamdi, M., Ooi, B.S., Alouini, M.S., Unified statistical channel model for turbulence-induced fading in underwater wireless optical communication systems. *IEEE Trans. Commun.*, 67, 4, 2893–2907, Apr-2019.

10. Duraibabu, D.B., Leen, G., Toal, D., Newe, T., Lewis, E., Dooly, G., Underwater depth and temperature sensing based on fiber optic technology for marine and fresh water applications. *Sensors*, 17, 6, 1228, 2017.

11. Van Haren, H. and Gostiaux, L., Characterizing turbulent overturns in CTD-data. *Dyn. Atmos. Oceans*, 66, 58–76, 2014.

12. Naumenko, A., Andrukhovich, S., Kabanov, V., Kabanau, D., Kurochkin, Y.A., Martsynkevich, B., Shoukavy, D., Shpak, P.V., Autonomous NaI (Tl) gamma-ray spectrometer for *in situ* underwater measurements. *Nucl. Instrum. Methods Phys. Res. Section A: Accel. Spectrom. Detect. Assoc. Equip.*, 908, 97–109, 2018.

13. McCauley, R.D., Thomas, F., Parsons, M.J., Erbe, C., Cato, D.H., Duncan, A.J., Salgado-Kent, C.P., Developing an Underwater Sound Recorder: The Long and Short (Time) of It. *Acoust. Aust.*, 45, 2, 301–311, 2017.

14. http://www.tsuchiya2.org/absorption/absorp_e.html, 31-Aug-2020.

15. Anand, J.V. and Titus, S., Energy efficiency analysis of effective hydrocast for underwater communication. *Int. J. Acoust. Vibr.*, 22, 1, 44–50, 2017.

16. Fisher, F.H. and Simmons, V.P., Sound absorption in sea water. *J. Acoust. Soc. Am.*, 62, 3, 558–564, 1977.

17. Ainslie, M.A. and McColm, J.G., A simplified formula for viscous and chemical absorption in sea water. *J. Acoust. Soc. Am.*, 103, 3, 1671–1672, 1998.

Multi-Layer UAV Ad Hoc Network Architecture, Protocol and Simulation

Kamlesh Lakhwani[1]*, Tejpreet Singh[2] and Orchu Aruna[2]

[1]Department of Computer Science and Engineering, JECRC University, Jaipur, Rajasthan, India
[2]Department of Computer Science and Engineering, Lovely Professional University, Phagwara, India

Abstract

Wireless Networks allow communication between nodes without any support from existing infrastructure. In this manner, nowadays industries are showing interest in ad-ad hoc networks. Relatively a new research area introduced in ad hoc networks called Flying Ad hoc Networks (FANETs). It consists of a collection of nodes called Unmanned Aerial Vehicles (UAVs) that fly in the air autonomously based on pre-programmed flight plans. There is no need to link all UAVs to a ground station in FANET, only one backbone UAV connects with the ground station, and remaining all UAVs communicate with each other in an ad hoc manner. FANETs are more effective to provide data connectivity as opposed to ground-based networks such as MANETs and VANETs. Communication between mobile nodes is a big challenging-issue in FANETs due-to the high-mobility of nodes in the network area. Many routing protocols were developed for MANETs and VANETs can't be applied directly on FANET applications. It is necessary to design an efficient and reliable routing protocol for FANETs to provide efficient communication among the UAVs. Within the performance of routing protocol, mobility-model acts a major role in-FANETs. In FANET, the selection of a suitable mobility model is a critical task for researchers. In this chapter, communication architecture is suitable for FANETs, what is the needs of routing protocol and mobility model for data delivery in the network and, which protocol and mobility model provides strong communications between UAV-to-UAV networks is discussed.

Keywords: FANETs, communication architecture, routing protocols, mobility, UAVs, HAPs, MAC protocol

*Corresponding author: kamlesh.lakhwani@gmail.com

R. Kanthavel, K. Ananthajothi, S. Balamurugan and R. Karthik Ganesh (eds.) *Artificial Intelligent Techniques for Wireless Communication and Networking*, (193–210) © 2022 Scrivener Publishing LLC

13.1   Introduction

In today's time, UAV (Unmanned-Air-Vehicles) are used in various operations. There are different areas where the UAVs are very much important such as military operations. Moreover, it can also be used for personal and commercial applications. The recent development in the electronics field makes it possible to design and produce a portable UAV. The small size UAV is very much helpful in performing various operations, but on the other side, it has a disadvantage also. The performance of small size UAVs is not so good. To overcome this issue, a new type of network has been developed. Such a network is called FANET.

13.1.1   Flying Ad Hoc Networks (FANETs)

Flying Ad Hoc-Networks (FANETs) are the collection of several small-size UAVs that are connected with the help of ad hoc-network, as shown in Figure 13.1. These UAV systems work like an expert team to attain highly complicated goals [1]. UAV stands for Unmanned Aerial Vehicle. These vehicles contain a jet engine and are controlled remotely with the help of programming based PDA. They don't require any human to be sat in it as a pilot and controlling its movement [2]. In recent times, the Ad hoc network-based UAVs are becoming very much useful for scientific operations also. UAVs contain many features in it such as self-organization and identifying the location of neighboring nodes. In the case of infrastructure-less area, a FANET can extend the range of communication and connectivity. A FANET is a kind of network that can be deployed at a very fast rate. It is a much more flexible and very much cost-effective network [3]. The high-level goals can be achieved by using such kind of FANET which contains very small size based UAVs. These UAVs are always connected in an ad hoc manner. Coordination is required among various UAVs to achieve the objective. It is very much important to establish better quality based communication architecture and routing protocols to attain the high level goals which can be achieved by using such kind of FANET which contains very small size based UAVs. These UAVs always connected in an ad hoc manner. Coordination is required among various UAVs to achieve the objective. It is very much important to establish a better quality based communication architecture and routing protocols to attain a robust and a reliable communication [10].

The process of information exchange or the method of information exchange related to the UAV and station at base or intra-UAVs can be identified with the help of communication architecture. In FANET, an ad hoc

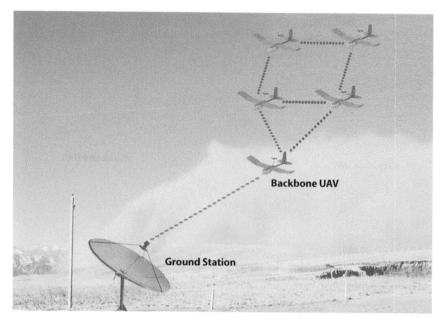

Figure 13.1 Flying-ad hoc-networks.

based approach is used to condense real-time communication between UAVs. Due to this ad hoc based approach, the requirement of infrastructure can be reduced and it resolves the issue of limited communication range [4]. Three aspects give a reason for the implementation of FANETs. The first is architecture, the second is real-time communication and the third is communication range. The prime issue that is encountered in UAVs is their connection and disconnection from the network. UAVs connect and disconnect from the network more frequently and that's why we need an ad hoc network. Decentralized communication-based architecture could also be used for establishing a robust communication [10, 13, 14, 17].

13.1.2   Multi-Layer-Based UAVs Ad Hoc Network

Figure 13.2 shows a multiple layer ad hoc network based on UAV. This communication design represents various heterogeneous UAVs of a single ad hoc network. All the UAVs of a single group are connected with the help of multiple links. There are two layers in this network: one is the upper layer and the other is the lower layer. The communication between various UAVs is carried out by using the upper layer whereas the lower layer is used for providing the message passing among the backbone-UAV of all

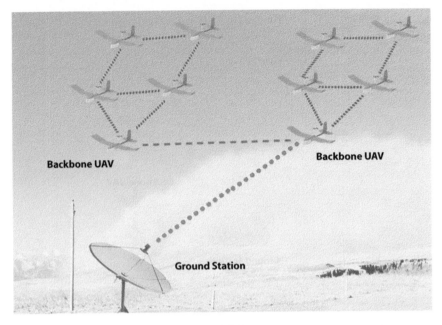

Figure 13.2 Multi-layer UAV ad hoc network [6].

the connected-groups and the station at the ground. When two different groups want to communicate then they need not communicate through the station at the ground [4]. This type of design for communication will be implemented for those cases when we need to establish one-to-many UAVs based communication.

13.2   Background

Nadeem *et al.* [4] classified existing ad hoc network routing protocols which one is suitable for FANETs and list out open research issues and challenges of FANETs. Tareque *et al.* [9] clearly illustrated the distinction between the MANETs, VANETs, and FANETs. The multi-hop communication between multi-UAV systems and a survey of communication protocols in FANETs are depicted. Khan *et al.* [10] clearly outline the importance of FANETs and how it is useful to our society and also discussed problems with existing research. Maxa *et al.* [11] proposed a secured routing-protocol for FANET using Model-Driven Development (MDD) approach. Shahbazi *et al.* [12] examined ad hoc network transportation networks and the complexity of existing routing protocols. Due to the complexity of communication protocol, Quality of Service in data transformation is a hard task for the researchers. Bazzi *et al.* [15] discussed delay-constrained routing based on a stochastic model and outlines open issues, link connectivity and void region problems need to be solved in FANETs. In FANETs nodes having mobility and in this literature models related to the mobility of the nodes have been discussed. One of the mobility models that is discussed, is the Paparazzi Mobility model. Paparazzi Mobility model is a stochastic model. Based on the state machine this model mimics the paparazzi UAV response. The routing process is a huge challenge in FANETs. Earlier, DCF (distributed coordinate function) MAC and omnidirectional antennas were used. Nowadays in FANETs, DMAC protocols and directional are used as an alternative application [22]. In [23], an efficient location-oriented-directional-medium-access-control Protocol (LODMAC) is defined. It is much better than DMAC-protocol in terms of fairness, utilization, throughput, and average-network-latency. It was adapted for 3D scenarios. Muzaffar *et al.* [10] discussed four-routing protocols, and a Route Switching algorithm has been proposed. This algorithm holds the track of all possible routes from source to destination. Moreover when a link in FANETs fails automatically another route will be selected with the help of this algorithm. Rosati *et al.* [13] proposed a specifically FANET based routing protocol. It is having Linux based implementation of an algorithm i.e. Predictive Optimum Link State Routing (P-OLSR) algorithm It takes the GPS information of the UAVs to predict the quality of the link. Gu *et al.* [18] proposed Hierarchical State Routing Protocol for wireless ad hoc networks. It is the extension of the existing HSR protocol, improves the scalability of the network.

13.3   Issues and Gap Identified

After reading various literatures and reviewing them extensively following issues and gaps have been identified:

- Communication is the major challenging issue for the design of UAVs systems for multiple nodes.
- The performance of FANET can vary expressively with diverse mobility models, and to choose a suitable mobility model is very difficult in FANETs applications because of the high mobility of nodes.
- Many protocols for routing that is based on projected for traditional ad hoc networks like MANETs, VANETs cannot

be applied directly on FANETs because of the high mobility nature of UAVs. It is necessary to design a reliable and energy-efficient routing protocol for robust communication among the UAVs.

- The use of UAVs are surprisingly increasing in civilian and military based applications. Therefore ad hoc-routing among UAVs are highly required. Such ad hoc-routing among the UAVs are done by FANETs airborne-networks. The FANET-applications require a scalable communication network, a high range of coverage, low latency and, efficient data transfer among intermediate nodes. Because of the following issues like the complexity of routing-protocol, dynamic nature of computing resources, radio bandwidth, preserving QoS in data-transfer is a very complex task.

- Propagation of audio/video data in flying ad hoc networks requires high bandwidth. Bandwidth requirement is a key constraint in such a scenario. If high bandwidth is used during data transmission, the noise will be introduced in actual data.

- Security is the biggest challenge in FANETs. There are several numbers of attacks (Hardware attack, wireless attack, denial of service attack) that occur in FANET. These attacks occur due to malicious nodes enter the network.

- To solve routing-related issues in FANET, topology-based-routing is the most considerable approach. In the FANET, topology-based routing protocols improve the efficiency and throughput FANETs in terms of network load, and end-to-end delay.

13.4   Main Focus of the Chapter

This chapter mainly focuses on the mobility of a node, routing, and efficient communication architecture for Flying Ad hoc Networks (FANETs). The prime objectives of this chapter are to enlighten about which architecture is best suited for communication for FANETs, and how to provide an efficient routing with the help of FANET routing protocols, and finally how to simulate results on simulation. For the simulation of a result, the mobility model plays an important role in FANETs. Flying Ad hoc Networks (FANETs) with Multi-Layer UAVs ad hoc Network-Communication-Architecture are also discussed in this chapter.

13.5   Mobility

First, we concentrate on mobility. For high mobility of UAVs in ad hoc networks a realistic spatial dependency mobility model is used which is the Reference Point Group Mobility Model. In ad hoc networks, the mobility model represents every movement of a node and how the location was changed dynamically. Mobility plays an important role in the result of the simulation. The FANET is best suited for the following scenarios such as: where real time communication is required, where communication rang is constrained, and applications where providing infrastructure is a very difficult task. For the above-said scenarios, the Multi-Layer UAV Ad hoc Network is a good choice. This architecture is also suited for one of many UAVs' communication operations. In Flying Ad hoc Networks (FANETs), the identification of neighbor location is the major problem for data transfer because the topology was changed dynamically. For solving that problem we are using high altitude platforms (HAPs) with the conjunction of directional antennas. This conjunction provides several advantages compared with a traditional network like satellites, ground-based stations, etc. With the use of directional antennas, we phase several problems like a hidden terminal problem, the problem in hearing, etc. For solving these problems we are using an efficient medium access control protocol. In Ad hoc networks, the topology was changed continuously with high mobility of nodes. So, we can concentrate on topology-based algorithms. Finally, the results will be simulated on a network simulator, Aerial Vehicle Network Simulator (AVENS).

13.5.1   Mobility Model

Due to the mobility of the nodes, change in their velocity, location, and acceleration over time is reported and, mobility models are implemented to represent these variations. Mobility models are used for simulation purposes. Whenever new navigation or communication techniques are experimented such mobility models are often used for simulation and testing purposes [5, 7]. It is essential to select an appropriate mobility model while evaluating FANET protocol.

13.5.2   Reference-Point-Group Mobility Model (RPGM)

This mobility-model can also be used to simulate a cluster of UAVs to perform self-governing military operations without the use of any centralized system to control the nodes as shown in Figure 13.3. Reference-Point-Group Mobility-Model is a type of Spatial Dependency approach [7]. The

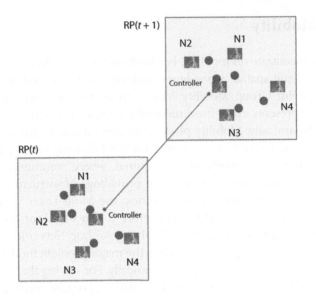

Figure 13.3 A group of five mobile node movements using the RPGM model [7].

total number of nodes is divided into groups and every group has a group controller node (Reference Point) to control the movement of every node in a cluster that moves on a predefined path. The direction vector and speed vector of each node in the cluster be governed by Reference-Point made by self and, randomly group controller node deviation [8].

13.5.3 Spatial Dependency-Based Mobility Model

Spatial-dependency of the mobility-nodes occurs while UAVs move collectively in a cluster. The mobility of one node may be influenced by the mobility of the other node [8]. The Reference-Group-Mobility model is one type of spatial dependency approach.

13.5.3.1 Degree of Spatial-Dependency

The degree of special dependency between two closest mobile nodes is the amount of correlation between their velocities.

Formula to calculate spatial degree is represented through following equation:

$$\text{Spatial Degree } (p, q, t) = \text{RD}(\overline{vp}(t).\overline{vq}(t) * \text{SR}(\overline{vp}(t).\overline{vq}(t))$$

- Where, Spatial Degree (p, q, t): describes the spatial-degree of node-q and node-p at a particular time instance 't'.
- RD($vp(t).vq(t)$): represents the relative direction between the node q and node p at a particular time instance t.
- S($vp(t).vq(t)$): represents speed-ratio among the node-y and node-x at a particular time-instance 't'.
- The value of spatial-degree will be high at what time both the nodes will move almost in identical speed in identical direction.
- The value of spatial degree will decrease gradually decreases while relative speed ratio reduces or change relative direction.

13.6   Routing Protocol

For data transmission it is very important to find an appropriate path, Routing protocols are used to serve this purpose [9, 19]. In FANET, to manage routing among UAVs is a very critical task because of the highly dynamic nature of UAVs. Developing a routing protocol that can be suitable for all scenarios and conditions of UAVs in FANET is a challenging task and still is under research.

13.6.1   Data-Centric-Routing-Protocol (DCRP)

DCRP is an auspicious paradigm of routing-mechanism. DCRP can also be amended for Flying Ad hoc Networks (FANETs). It is possible to implement Data-centric-routing algorithms for FANETs. In this algorithm instead of receivers or senders ID, data requested and collected with the reference of data characteristics. Figure 13.4 shows a data-centric-routing based model. There is wireless communication between the UAVs in FANET, therefore multicasting is preferred instead of unicasting [3, 15, 16, 18].

DCRP-protocols are decoupled in the following three dimensions:

1. Space decoupling: in this type of coupling, communicating-UAVs can be anywhere, and it is not mandatory for UAVs to know each other's location and ID.
2. Time decoupling: in this type of coupling, communicating UAVs can forward data to-the, subscribers, promptly-or-later, so it is not required for UAVs to be online simultaneously.
3. Flow decoupling: in this type of coupling, the asynchronous structure of communication is used to accomplish reliable delivery of data.

Figure 13.4 Data-centric routing.

This type of routing-model can be adopted while the nodes in FANETs having a predetermined flight-plan and number-of nodes are fewer in the network and also involves in minimum-assistance among the clusters.

13.7   High Altitude Platforms (HAPs)

The mobility of nodes in FANETs is higher than the mobility of the nodes in MANETs [20, 21]. In FANET UAVs can have velocity in the range of 20 to 40 m/s. Currently, many models of FANETs are using a traditional omnidirectional antenna and DCF (Distributed coordinate function) MAC. Due to the high speed of nodes in FANET, the network topology between nodes changes rapidly [24].

Therefore an alternative is required for DCF based and traditional omnidirectional antenna-based systems. So as an alternative, nowadays directional MAC protocols and directional antennas are projected to be deployed in FANET. There are many advantages of using a directional antenna on UAVs in FANETs, but still, the discovery of a neighbor node in FANET is a challenging task, therefore High Altitude Platforms (HAPs) are used for this purpose. HAPs are used to provide continuous location information in FANETs. In Figure 13.5 a HAP-based scenario is illustrated. It can be observed from Figure 13.5 that HAP resides above the FANET. In FANET, during the flight, it is not necessary that all UAVs communicates with the ground station. Often only one UAV or node chosen as a cluster

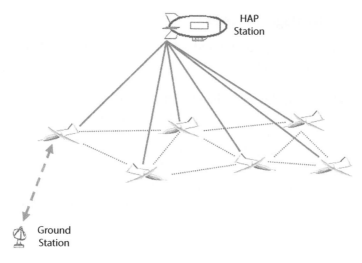

Figure 13.5 FANET augmented with a HAP station.

head is adequate to communicate with the ground station. Moreover, all UAVs have to be connected to the HAP station during a complete flight.

13.7.1 Characteristics of HAP

In the air and above the FANETs, the HAP station works as a wireless repeater. HAP station having the following characteristics:

- High Altitude Platforms (HAPs) can play a governing role in communication between UAVs, remote sensing, and observations.
- HAPs improve spectrum efficiency, communication capacity, and reduces system complexity and cost.
- HAPs having a small decline path than terrestrial communication, therefore it having a smaller communication delay than satellite communication.
- The area covered by HAPs is depended on the altitude of the UAVs at which it operates.
- The higher altitude of HAPs covers large coverage areas, such as if altitudes of HAPs is higher than 50,000 ft. the coverage area would be 150 km.
- The projected altitudes of HAPs is above civil-air-routes, and power for the HAPs station can be used through solar panels.

13.7.2   Advantages of HAPs

As compared to the ground-based-satellite system, HAP systems having the following advantages:

- Flexible deployment than the ground-based satellite.
- The ability of wide-area coverage (depending on the projected altitudes).
- Line-of-sight (LOS) propagation.
- Low cost and easy to maintain the payload.
- Higher rate of packet propagation.
- Reduced latency in packet delivery and less propagation loss.

13.8   Connectivity Graph Metrics

In ad hoc network performance of the routing protocols depends on the connectivity-graph of mobile nodes. Therefore analyzing the connectivity graph between mobile nodes is an important activity because the connectivity metrics provides the link between the performance of the mobility model and routing protocols.

$$G = (V, E)$$

The Graph G is a connectivity graph
i.e. $|V| = N$ vertices at time t,
Whereas $(x, y) \in E$ if Distance $(x, y) < T R$
Whereas Distance (x, y) is the distance between mobile nodes x and y.
TR is the mobile node transmission range.
Where $A(x, y, t) = 1$; is a random indicator, for a particular time 't' it indicates the link between nodes x and y.

13.8.1   Link Changes Counts

It represents, so many times the link associated with two nodes x and y changes from up-to-down and down-to-up. The number of link changes can be calculated with the help of the following equitation:

$$LC(x, y) = \sum X(x, y, t) T$$

In this equation LC(x,y) is the link change;
T represents the simulation-time;
X(x,y, t) is a random-variable such as:

$$X(x, y, t) = \begin{cases} 1, & A(x,y,t-1)=0 \\ 0, & A(x,y,t)=1 \end{cases}$$

13.8.2   Link Duration

Link duration represents the link durability between two mobile nodes. It
is used to define the average-number of link-durations among two nodes
such as between node-x and node-y.

$$Link\ Duration(x, y) = \begin{cases} \dfrac{\displaystyle\sum_{t-1}^{T} A(x,y,t)}{LC(x,y)} & if\ Link\ \ Changes \neq 0 \\[4mm] \displaystyle\sum_{t-1}^{T} A(x,y,t) & Otherwise \end{cases}$$

In this equation T represents the total simulation time; (x,) is a random
variable having value-1 if there is a link between the mobile nodes-x and
node-y.

13.8.3   Path-Availability

It shows the availability of path between two mobile node-x and node-y at
a time-instance-t. It can be calculated with the help of following equation:

$$Path\ Available(x, y) = \begin{cases} \dfrac{\displaystyle\sum_{t=start(x,y)}^{T} A(x,y,t)}{T-start(x,y)}, & if\ T-start(x,y)>0 \\[4mm] 0, & Otherwise \end{cases}$$

Where A(x, y, t) = 1; is a random value indicator, for a particular time 't' it indicates the link between nodes x and y.

Otherwise, it will have value = 0;

13.9   Aerial Vehicle Network Simulator (AVENs)

AVENS is a hybrid aerial network simulation framework. The main purpose of this simulator is to provide a platform to researches and scientist for mobile and ad hoc network analysis; whereas mobile nodes such as UAVs shares a wireless network and shares information and messages among them. AVENS provides the virtual environment and test-bed for experimenting (virtually) FANETs model. AVENS is used in various major research projects to provide a simulation environment and that requires the provision of a testbed to simulate AV flight and control, using different, controlled, and changeable configurations.

The main goal of using AVENS is to use a flight simulator that can also be used as a network simulator to obtain network measurement parameters and its values such as transmission-rate, Received-Signal-Strength Indication (RSSI), number of retransmission, packet loss, and throughput.

In AVENS two base simulation platforms are integrated with LARISSA. These two simulation platforms are the X-Plane Flight Simulator and the OMNeT++ Network Simulator. For an abstract UAVs modeling, an automatic OMNeT++ code is generated by LARISSA. AVENS receives mobility model information from X-Plane's navigation pattern also updates UAVs positions on OMNeT++. By doing these tasks AVENS provides an accurate and reliable simulation environment. In the mobility model, while nodes are moving, their positions are generated by the X-Plane, and OMNeT++ uses this information to simulate the network conditions of moving nodes. In this current mobility model node's position is determined while the node's connectivity is not considered.

In the future, a new version will be available, which will have a mobility model including network connectivity between UAVs nodes for simulation. It will provide realistic mobility models and protocols for FANETs. Multiple simulators are integrated with each other such as a module on the OMNeT++ side and a plug-in on the X-Plane side, both exchange the information with each other through an XML file. The INET Framework is an open-source OMNeT++ model suite for networks. The structure of Aerial Vehicle Network Simulator (AVENs) is shown below in Figure 13.6.

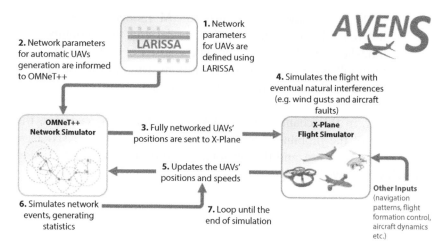

Figure 13.6 Aerial vehicle network simulator integration.

13.10   Conclusion

In Flying Ad hoc Networks (FANETs), communication is the main challenging issue among small UAVs. In this chapter, the communication network between UAVs and mobility model for efficient data transfer with the help of routing protocol are discussed. The conclusion of this chapter have been described in the following points:

- One-to-many UAVs communication, this architecture is a good choice. The use of this architecture reduces the communication overhead and processing load on the ground station because the ground station has to process only the information that intends to the final result. This communication architecture doesn't have a single point of failure therefore it can be considered as a robust architecture.
- A Data-Centric Routing Protocol (DCRP) is a good choice for this architecture for transferring data packets between sources to destination through intermediate UAV nodes in FANETs. DCRP is a promising model of routing-mechanism and can be used for Flying Ad hoc Networks (FANETs). The core advantage of this routing-algorithm is, it can only report the content to the registered subscribers.
- To select an appropriate mobility model to evaluate FANETs protocols is an important task. For that, an RPGM model

could be an adequate choice. RPGM model stands for Reference-Point-Group Mobility model and that mobility model can also be used to simulate a cluster of UAVs to perform self-governing military operations, without the use of any centralized system to control the nodes.

Moreover, in this chapter, several FANETs application scenarios, the importance of the mobility model and routing protocol for FANETs, a review of the literature, and the advantages and disadvantages of existing research work have been discussed.

References

1. Bekmezci, I., Sahingoz, O.K., Temel, S., Flying Ad Hoc Networks (FANETs): A survey. SciVerse ScienceDirect, www.elsevier.com/locate/adhoc. *Ad Hoc Networks*, 11,3, 1254–1270, 2013.
2. Mukherjee, A., Dey, N., Satapathy, S., Flying Ad hoc Networks: A Comprehensive Survey, Springer, 569–580, 2016, https://www.research-gate.net/publication/308362895.
3. Maakar, S., Singh, Y., Singh, R., Considerations and Open Issues in Flying Ad Hoc Network. *Int. J. Sci. Eng. Res. (IJSER)*, 5, 7, 397–402, 2017
4. Nadeem, A., Alghamdi, T., Yawar, A., Mehmood, A., Siddiqui, M.S., A Review and Classification of Flying Ad Hoc Network (FANET) Routing Strategies. *J. Basic Appl. Sci. Res.*, 2018.
5. Singh, K. and Verma, A.K., Adaptability of Various Mobility Models for Flying Ad hoc Networks—A Review, Springer, 51–63, 2017, https://www.researchgate.net/publication/317445668.
6. Bujari, A., Calafate, C.T., Cano, J.-C., Manzoni, P., Palazzi, C.E., Ronzani, D., Flying ad hoc network application scenarios and mobility models. *Int. J. Distrib. Sens. Netw.*, London, England, 13, 10, 2017.
7. Bouachir, O., Abrassart, A., Garcia, F., Larrieu, N., Mobility, A., Model For UAV Ad hoc Network. *International Conference on Unmanned Aircraft Systems (ICUAS)*, 2014.
8. Bilal, R. and Khan, B.M., Analysis of Mobility Models and Routing Schemes for Flying Ad Hoc Networks (FANETS). *Int. J. Appl. Eng. Res.*, 12, 3263–3269, 2017.
9. Tareque, M.H., Hossain, M.S., Atiquzzaman, M., On the Routing in Flying Ad hoc Networks. *Proceedings of the Federated Conference on Computer Science and Information Systems*, vol. 5, 2015.
10. Khan, M.A., Safi, A., Qureshi, I.M., Khan, I.U., Flying Ad Hoc Networks (FANETs): A Review of Communication architectures, and Routing

protocols, Flying ad hoc networks, 1–9, 2017, https://www.researchgate.net/publication/319310847.

11. Maxa, J.-A., Mahmoud, M.S.B., Larrieu, N., Secure Routing Protocol Design for UAV Ad Hoc Networks. *IEEE/AIAA 34th Digital Avionics Systems Conference*, 2015.

12. Bekmezci, I., Senturk, E., Turker, T., Security Issues in Flying Ad Hoc Networks (FANETs). *J. Aeronaut. Space Eng.*, 9, 2, 13–21, 2016.

13. Rosati, S., Krużelecki, K., Heitz, G., Floreano, D., Rimoldi, B., Dynamic Routing for Flying Ad Hoc Networks. *IEEE*, 1690–1700, 2015.

14. Wen, S. and Huang, C., Delay-Constrained Routing Based on Stochastic Model for Flying Ad Hoc Networks. *Hindawi Mob. Inf. Syst.*, 2018, https://doi.org/10.1155/2018/6056419.

15. Zheng, X., Qi, Q., Wang, Q., Li, Y., An adaptive density-based routing protocol for flying Ad Hoc networks, 1890, 1, 040113, 2017, https://doi.org/10.1063/1.5005315.

16. Khan, M.A., Safi, A., Qureshi, I.M., Khan, I.U., Dynamic Routing in Flying Ad Hoc Networks Using Topology-Based Routing Protocols, 2, 3, 27, 2018, www.mdpi.com/journal/drones.

17. Resmi, S. and Sivan, R., Flying Ad Hoc Network—Survey on The Mobility Models and Routing Protocols. *IJCRT*, 5, 4, 2740–2745 2017.

18. Gu, D.L., Pei, G., Ly, H., Gerla, M., Hong, X., *Hierarchical Routing for Multi-Layer Ad Hoc Wireless Networks with UAVs, NSF under contract ANI-9814675, in part by DARPA under contract DAAB07-97-C-D321 and in part by Intel.* 1, 310–314, 2000.

19. Walia, E., Bhatia, V., Kaur, G., Detection Of Malicious Nodes in Flying Ad Hoc Networks (FANET). *SSRG Int. J. Electron. Commun. Eng. (SSRG-IJECE)*, 5, 9, 6–12, 2018.

20. Khan, M.A., Khan, I.U., Javed, U., Khan, M.W., On the Performance of Flying Ad hoc Networks (FANETs) with Directional Antennas, 1–8, 2018, https://www.researchgate.net/publication/324594020.

21. Temel, S. and Bekmezci, I., On the performance of Flying Ad Hoc Networks (FANETs) Utilizing Near Space High Altitude Platforms (HAPs). *IEEE*, 461–465, 2013.

22. Gururaj, H.L. and Ramesh, B., Time As A Distance (TAAD)—A new routing protocol for FANETS. *Int. J. Pure Appl. Math.*, 119, 16, 1217–1223, 2018.

23. Liu, X., Liu, C., Liu, W., Zeng, X., High Altitude Platform Station Network and Channel Modeling Performance Analysis. *Math. Comput. Sci.*, 1, 1, 10–16, 2016.

24. Liu, X., Zeng, X., Liu, C., Liu, W., Zhang, Y., The Channel Estimation and Modeling in High Altitude Platform Station Wireless Communication Dynamic Network. *Discrete Dyn. Nat. Soc.*, Hindawi, 2017.

14

Artificial Intelligence in Logistics and Supply Chain

Jeyaraju Jayaprakash*

Department of Mechanical Engineering, Advanced Research Institute (ARI), Dr. MGR Educational and Research Institute, Chennai, India

Abstract

Supply chain is an integrating process of material flow, from suppliers to end users. It consists of selection of suppliers, scheduling & quantities of goods from suppliers, selection of routes, vehicle capacity, mode of transports, loading goods based on delivery schedule, scheduling goods in multi-depot loading & unloading goods, planning & forecasting of fluctuating demand, multi-Echelon logistics, distributed network manufacturing, fluctuation of raw materials and parts Inventories in store. This chapter focused on various research avenues in supply chain network, particularly vendor selection, transportation, inventory routing, agent-based modeling, reverse logistics. Recent days researchers have triggered very high interest with Artificial Intelligence (AI) tools in the supply chain network problems.

Real-world problems like controlling 5G IIoT data distribution network, regulating logistics and supply chain network distribution are complex in nature (like NP hard) and input data are uncertain, high volume & more ambiguity. For such condition, AI is the only choice to resolve all these issues in a reasonable time with higher optimal values. Some of the AI tools like, Neural Network, Fuzzy Logic, Genetic Algorithm, Scatter Search Algorithm, ANT Colony Algorithm, Simulated Annealing Algorithm have been used many researchers in supply chain network performance improvement. Each AI tool have their own mechanism of convergence either by population based or single point.

Keywords: Logistics, supply chain network, artificial intelligence, simulation

Email: profjaya@gmail.com

R. Kanthavel, K. Ananthajothi, S. Balamurugan and R. Karthik Ganesh (eds.) Artificial Intelligent Techniques for Wireless Communication and Networking, (211–234) © 2022 Scrivener Publishing LLC

14.1   Introduction to Logistics and Supply Chain

Agriculture

Logistics and Supply Chain Network (SCN) is an integrating process of material flow and information flow from suppliers to end customers in various stages of any industrial business process models. Transfer of raw materials from various suppliers to company owned material warehouse is an example of logistics distribution [1]. Let's take an example of agriculture harvesting paddy. Company or Government collects the required quality of paddy from various farmers during the harvesting season and would be stored the paddy bags near the field. After accumulated required quantities, they assign vehicles to carry the paddy bags from all temporary storage yard to company or Government material warehouse. Company or Government triggers the entire procurement processes in continuous or whenever they required quantities. Another example, consider tomato sauce or fruit juice manufacturers. They follow the same procurement processes from various groves, based on their plant production capacity. The critical parameters are distance from field to company, shelf life of the product, availability of required quantities and its unit price. Company will change their procurement quantities based on the critical parameters, like availability (surplus/shortage) of tomato, unit cost (high/low) and seasonal demand of the end product. In summer high demand exist of fruits and juice. So, manufacturers started to increase purchasing of raw material quantities. Logistics and supply chain network concept on market would regulate their dynamic procurement strategies with profit without material loss.

Some of the important challenges in logistic and SCN are decision making strategies. They are selection of right suppliers [2], sequence and quantities of goods purchase from suppliers, selection of routes, vehicle capacity, mode of transports, loading goods based on delivery schedule, schedule goods in multi-depot loading and unloading goods, planning and forecasting fluctuating demand of goods, multi-echelon logistics, distributed network manufacturing, fluctuation of raw materials and parts inventories in store [3]. Particularly, in the agriculture sector, farmers were affected with less than minimum support price due to uncertain surplus production of food items in the same period.

Manufacturing

In a manufacturing plant, the important issues are buffer inventories between machines, fluctuation in factory work-in-process (WIP) inventories. Nearly one third of total procured raw material inventories are held up as WIP within company as semi-finished product. Any machine failure or overproduction situation, management should be balanced the shortfall of required raw materials by buffer inventories. Management failed to balance these situations; it will lead to blocking and starving of material flow within production line. Most of the manufacturers producing 'n' number of models and each model have 'm' number of version. Let's consider, Maruti Suzuki India Ltd., having 15 different car models (swift, Alto, Dzire, Breeza…) and each model having a minimum of five versions (SWIFT LXI, VXI, VXI AMT, ZXI, ZXI+, ZXI+AMT) in India. Each model has a minimum of 30,000 number of parts and nearly 5,000 number of suppliers both India and abroad. It is very difficult for the company to communicate the required order quantity to all suppliers, regulate number of parts required based on fluctuation market and simultaneously balance mixed model assembly line production set-up, multi-machine, multi-product production schedule.

After finished product gets ready, time being shifted to company finished goods warehouse. Based on the national wide company sales shown room customers' requirement, they prepare dispatch schedule of multi-product and transport to multi-warehouse, warehouse network distribution channel. In the competitive environment, product demands are not static. It keeps on fluctuating with various constraints. Uncertainty in supply and demand of goods is produced bullwhip effect in both outbound and inbound logistics [4].

Due to global warming, most of the manufactures focused on circular economy [5]. After the end-of-life of white goods, retrieve the used products from customers and workout the conditions of reuse, recycle. DELL and other leading computer manufacture started refurbishing business. In reverse logistics, refurbishing business focused on used goods recovery mechanism after end-of-life, disassemble the end-of-life products with various sequence based on their need, reexamine the product quality, reuse with some percentage of product, recycle the defective items are called green supply chain [6, 7].

Artificial Intelligence (AI) Tools

Recently most of the researchers have focused on Artificial Intelligence (AI) tools. Prof. Hawking and Mr. Elon Musk had given serious caution to mishandling of AI tools "our biggest existential threat". But on the other side our existing real-world problems like 5G high speed data distribution, logistics and supply chain integrated network distribution of material flows are complex in nature (like NP hard problem) and uncertain input data, high volume & more ambiguity. For such condition, AI is the only choice and resolves all these issues in a reasonable time and high level of optimal point. Some of the AI tools are Genetic Algorithm (GA), Scatter Search Algorithm (SS), ANT Colony Algorithm, Simulated Annealing Algorithm (SA), Neural Network (NN), Fuzzy Logic, etc. Recent research listed number of meta-heuristic algorithms that have focused more than 185 tools. Each AI tool has their own mechanism of convergence either by population based or by single point [8].

Digital technology in recent decades has influenced supply chain network into becoming more transparent and traceable. For example, block chain technology leads supply chain network operations into being financially transparent in each level. Industrial IoT accurately integrates all companies' international operations without any time delay. Big data analytics retrieved required a large volume of logistics and SCN information from cloud for quick decision making based on market conditions at any situation, like COVID19 [9]. For any product development or modification of existing model, big data analytics helps to evaluate the tradeoff level of customer satisfaction, expectation and optimal product cost.

Transportation

Logistics means transfer of goods from sender to receiver by road transport or rail or ship or flight. In traditional logistics, sender must pack the goods, handover to logistics office and send the hard copy of the invoice receipt to the receiver by separate post. In logistic office, they segregate the goods based on delivery zone, size of the parcel and condition of material handling etc., and loading goods to transport. Logistic transports have a predefined route, delivery schedule. In the delivery site, the receiver must show invoice receipt and collect the goods from the delivery office. Logistics activities focused on moving and storing goods.

These sets of traditional logistics procedures are having more hurdles to the customer and company requirements. Corporate companies mainly focused on process integrations, process automation and cost-cut measures are the most key parameters. So, they integrate process from reliable raw material supplier, multi-layer collection centers, maintain optimal level in company raw material warehouses, production control and regulating material flow with the factory, make to order (MTO) level finished goods warehouse inventory, channelized distribution centers and final sales showroom. Minimize the non-productive activities and cost associated with the entire integration process is called supply chain. Supply chain focused on managing transfer of goods, regulating material flow and information flow, coordinating and controlling demand items. Logistics is subset of in the supply chain network.

14.1.1   Elements of Supply Chain Network

Supply chain network can be considered as shown in Figure 14.1 which consists of three main parts. They are

- Inbound logistics (transfer of goods from suppliers to factory)
- Production flow (transfer of goods within factory)
- Outbound logistics (transfer of goods from factory to End customers).

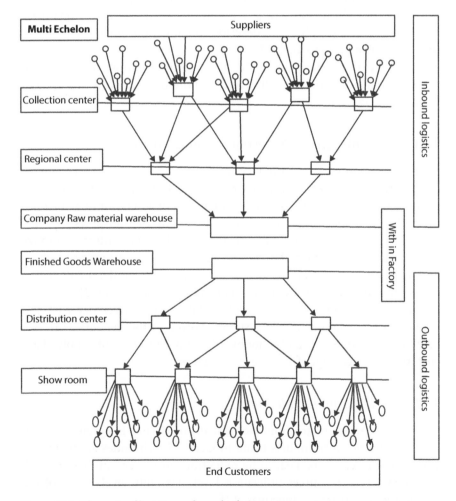

Figure 14.1 Elements of logistics and supply chain.

Inbound or inward logistics are the function of transfer of materials either raw materials or semi-finished parts, from suppliers to factories [10]. In the inbound logistics, two or more layers of multiple centers are used to accumulating the right quantity of goods, cleaning, grading and packing.

Production flow is the function of managing transfer of material handling within factory and between machines or stores: minimize the material handling in production flow, introduce robotic automation, factory layout modification and schedule the production sequence of goods & machines.

The function of outbound logistics is transferring semi-finished products or finished products from factory to end customers. In the outbound Logistics, two or more layers of multiple warehouses are used to accumulating the right quantity of goods and separating goods regional wise requirement. The supply chain describes the total journey of materials as they move 'from dirt to dirt' [11].

Automate this integrated materials and information transfer from inbound logistics, production flow and outbound logistics are proposed in Industry 4.0 concept.

14.1.2   Supply Chain Performances and Costing

Supply chain network performances and costing are interrelated elements (both direct and inversionally proportional). Optimal Inventory routing, supplier rating on delivery schedule and quality of goods, optimal loading/ unloading of goods, selection of size and mode of transports, optimal inventory level in each purchase centers and delivery centers, minimize total material flow and buffer size between machine, minimize blocking and starving of material flow inside the factory, minimize total carbon emission in the network are the few performance measures [12].

Minimize procurement cost, transportation cost, inventory cost and quality cost are the few cost measures involved in the network [13]. Net profit on sales in SCN can be doubled by only reduction of supply chain cost into 50 percentages from the existing level.

14.1.2.1   Performance Measure

Continuous performance improvement in micro and integrated level of supply chain network models using modern AI techniques are inevitable with recent researchers. Lead time reduction, customer satisfaction level, inventory levels, resources utilization level, flexibility levels some of the important performance objectives [14].

14.1.2.2   Procurement Cost

Right supplier, right price, right time and right quantity are the most important principles for purchasing raw material to make quality product with economic. In recent days E-commerce portals like Amazon, Flipkart, Tata CLiQ, IndiaMART, Alibaba, Walmart have simplified the procurement process between B2B (Business to Business), B2C (Business to Customers). This procurement cost is involved in purchasing raw materials or semi-finished products for company requirements. Nearly 20 to 60% of final product unit cost depends on raw material cost. Recent business models trigged towards in bulk purchase of raw materials to cut short competitive selling price.

14.1.2.3   Transportation Cost

This cost is associated with carrying goods depends on size (1–25 ton), mode of transport (road, air, ship using single or mixed mode) and route of the vehicles from suppliers to end customers. This cost influences significant contribution to overall cost. Recently researchers focused on optimizing multimode dynamic transportation routing and costing in different supply chain network models by considering length of traffic flow and alternative routes future traffic conditions using artificial intelligence [15].

14.1.2.4   Inventory Cost

Balancing a single or multiproduct stock level between availability on-hand to customer requirements is more complex in nature because consumption rate of the customers and procurement rate from suppliers are uncertain behaviors due various parameters like fluctuation of purchasing capacity of the customers, environment conditions, availability (shortage, surplus), technology changes [16]. These parameters lead to an increase in inventory cost by overstock or shortage of non availability of goods in any collection centers, warehouses, company stores. Inventory cost consists of ordering cost, carrying cost, unit cost. Nowadays research has focused on optimizing stock levels by using big data analytics, IoT, AI and cloud computing.

14.2   Recent Research Avenues in Supply Chain

In this section, some of the important research avenues are categorized as vendor selection, transportation model, inventory routing, agent modeling and reverse logistics.

14.2.1   Vendor Selection

Reliable long-term suppliers are incredible assets to supply chain network. For single part-family product making companies like bolt and nut manufacture (TVS Fasteners) needed nearly more than 200 numbers of reliable suppliers to meet out their international business orders. Complex Decision Support System (DSS) is most important for selection of suppliers. Analytic Hierarchy Process (AHP), Decision Making Trial and Evaluation Laboratory (DEMATEL), Fuzzy, fuzzy TOPSIS, Neural network, machine learning algorithm, etc. are contributed by recent researcher [17].

14.2.2   Transportation

Transportation is the backbone of any industrial business supply chain network. Recently, China invested $900 billion for developing the New Skill Road scheme, which connects Europe and other Asian countries. In the competitive market, reaching the product on-time delivery to the customer is the most important key parameter of sustaining customers. The maximum number of world busiest goods carrying capacity ship ports are operated from China. Travel salesman problem is the solution of transportation problem. This problem has to minimize the total distance travelled by the salesman.

Vehicle routing and Inventory routing problems have taken number of vehicles, quantity of goods, and alternative routes from depot to customer or reverse order. In Figure 14.2, the transportation model focused on inbound logistic model for collecting vegetables from various fields to local collection center. Time being warehouse in one day to one week period depends on life of the product. The purpose of the local center is separating types of vegetables, cleaning, grading different quality and packing based on customer orders. After accumulated right quality, right quantity of

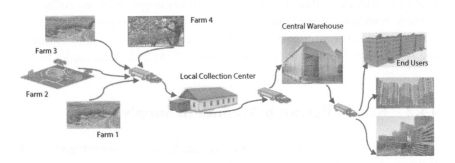

Figure 14.2 Transportation network model.

goods then transfers to various wholesalers based on their ordered quantity of different types of vegetables before the due date [18].

14.2.3   Inventory Routing

Travel salesman, vehicle routing and inventory routing problems are benchmark applications for testing effectiveness of different optimization algorithms. In supply chain network, Inventory routing problem (IRP) is a combination of grouping destinations, selecting short route in each group and distribution of multiproduct, varying stock level in each group for each destination. Figure 14.3 shows having one central stock depot and 16 collection destinations. First, group destinations are based on inventory requirements based on vehicle capacity and four different routes are calculated. Second, the shortest route in each group is generated.

The real-world problems are having multi-central manufacturing plant in different countries, having multi-central stock warehouse, having multi-destinations (more than 20,000 nos.), having multi-model transport, multi-vehicle capacity, multi-trip/shift for 'N' number of vehicles with dynamic demand in each destination [19]. AI based multi-agent, genetic algorithm, scatter search algorithm has proved inventory routing problems by many researchers.

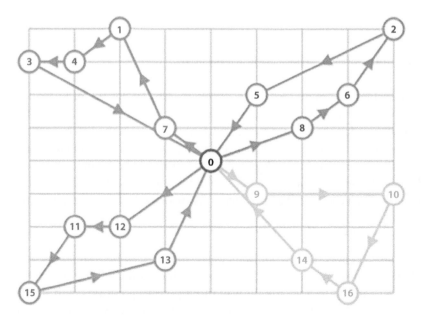

Figure 14.3 Inventory routing problem.

14.2.4   Agent-Based Modeling

Agent-based modeling is one of the simulation modeling techniques and each agent has a specific task like collection center, warehouse in SCN [20]. This modeling technique can be easily simulated before implementing any transportation/inventory problem in offline and online modeling. A group of customer agents and distributor agents are connected together and share their information in the form of messages in a case study of product distribution system as shown in Figure 14.4 using JADE Multi-Agent based open-source simulation software.

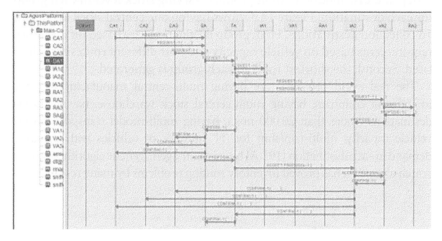

Figure 14.4 Inventory routing problem using JADE.

Consider outbound logistics distribution, have 'n' for no. of warehouses, 'm' for no. of distribution centers, and 'k' for no. of retail showroom. In any one of the retail showrooms facing shortage of goods, immediately agents will start sending messages to other neighboring showroom, distribution centers simultaneously. Customer Agent 1 (CA1) in retail showroom as shown in Figure 14.5, sending message request to supplier agent (SA) based on customer request. Then check with a time agent (TA) with a schedule to supply request.

14.2.5   Reverse Logistics

Partially recover some reusable parts for reassembly/remanufacturing from the consumer is discarded as end-of-life product. The reverse logistics (RL) function goes a long way in empowering entities with the skill of better utilization of eco-energy and resources. News paper, used cars, laptop (Dell Recycling program), mobile phone (Samsung), machine parts, are practicing reverse logistics [21, 22].

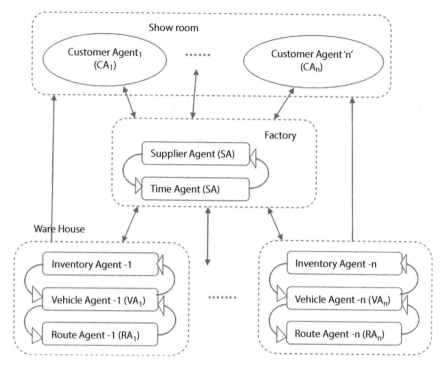

Figure 14.5 Inventory routing problem using multi-agent model.

Green manufacturers have to collect End-of-Life (EOL) products from the customers' location or propose exchange schemes and transfer to disassembly plant, for example battery manufacturers, chemical suppliers, pharmaceutical drugs (after date of expired). Then they segregate working parts, inspect working condition and then send to the remanufacturing plant as shown in Figure 14.6. Defective parts are sent to recycling process.

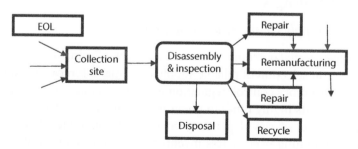

Figure 14.6 Overview of reverse logistics.

Recently many international players have started with the RL business model in their regular routine model due to global warming and carbon footprint [23].

14.3 Importance and Impact of AI

Abnormal condition of raw material supply in surplus and shortage period, high fluctuation of sales, process delay, transpiration delay of perishable goods, blocking and starving in inventory warehouses and manufacturing plants, improper coordination, communication and information sharing are leads to supply chain problems into complex. Different meta-heuristic methods were carried out by many researchers for all these problems individually. There is need of AI based tools to recover all the shortfalls of all these problems in integrated approach. Industrial IoT, Industry 4.0, Big data analytics, Integrated information with AI are research gap in dynamics behavior of logistics and supply chain network in industrial sector [24]. AI classified as neural network, machine learning, fuzzy logics and agent-based system. Will discuss benefits and challenges of AI based SCN.

14.3.1 Benefits

Some of the benefits of supply chain networks which integrate with AI based tools are:

- Demand forecasting using neural network
- Optimal transport routing using simulated annealing
- Optimize warehouse inventory management using multi-agent
- Automate vehicles in distribution centers using AI.

14.3.2 Challenges

14.3.2.1 Supply Chain Risk Estimation

Risk is the expected outcome of an uncertain event. Evaluation of uncertain occurrence in selection of reliable suppliers, demand forecasting, demand planning, inventory control, regulation uniform production flow is not an easy task and its highly random phenomena (stochastic). Company must decide the level of risk depending on level of confidence, like 10–20% risk of maintaining over or less inventory level of raw material [25, 26]. This decision may lead to balance fluctuation of raw material market and eliminate under stock and overstock. Company can take risk of 5% over or less sales forecasting. This decision may lead to eliminating final product shortage. Recently AI based tools like neural network, fuzzy, genetic algorithm with Markova chain models is used to minimize risk errors. Markova chain models have contributed mathematics-based approaches to more unpredictable events.

14.3.2.2   Green Supply Chain (GSC)

Green supply chain is an integration of environmental parameters into the organization. It consist of green suppliers, green purchase, green manufacturers, green packing, green warehouse, green transport and green customers as shown in Figure 14.7. Green supplier should have environmental sense to follow-up supply of raw material or spare parts. Green manufacture should follow less carbon footprint process in the product conversion process. In each sector, the coordinator must focus alternative methods or materials to minimize carbon emission.

Environmental benefits of GSC are reducing waste, increasing energy efficiency, reducing air pollution, water and land pollution and social

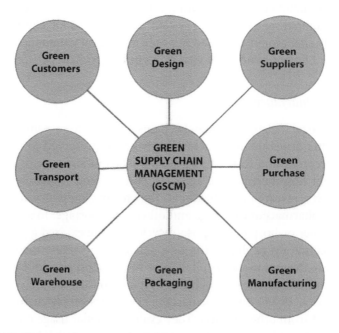

Figure 14.7 Elements of green supply chain.

benefits like healthcare, safety and security. AI based tools have given the best alternative solutions to minimize environmental pollution.

14.4   Research Gap of AI-Based Supply Chain

Recently logistics and supply chain triggered many new research avenues like, healthcare, networked manufacturing, supply chain resilience and humanitarian supply chain network.

14.4.1   Healthcare

In growing population, healthcare and food industries are playing vital roles in balancing availability and scarcity of goods. Recently corona virus (COVID-19) spread into all countries causing a pandemic situation. This virus has affected nearly 2% of the world's population and keeps on spreading with muted form. The World Health Organization (WHO) recommended that lockdown is the only solution. This sudden pandemic situation has created scarcity of base vaccines and medical equipments (ventilator, oximeter) and even all developed countries suffered extremely high. Recently a healthcare supply chain network focused to eliminate or zero shortage quantity by maintaining minimum level of surplus level based on cloud-based AI computing distribution system as in Figure 14.8. Clinical operation supply chain mainly focused not only for critical pandemic situations, but also for lifesaving and other vital drugs in supply chain network [27, 28].

14.4.1.1   *Pharmaceutical*

Pharmaceutical logistics and supply chains have one to one small inbound system. After drugs are manufactured, it has to be preserved with temperature tag recorder and RFID. Its outbound distribution systems consist of government hospitals, private agencies, clinics, drug wholesale distributors, retailers, research organizations. The challenging issues are one side surplus of pharmaceutical drugs and other side shortage. In surplus condition, retailer or hospitals dispose/recycle the date expired goods. But in shortage condition of drugs, the hospitals can't postpone their surgery/ services. So, the end users/hospitals have to maintain an additional buffer for life saving drugs. The level of buffers depends on arrival rate, occurrence rate and cost of drugs. This pharmaceutical logistics supply chain networks are different from other models. They evaluate regular usage rate of drugs and uncertain epidemic conditions using stochastic model/AI models.

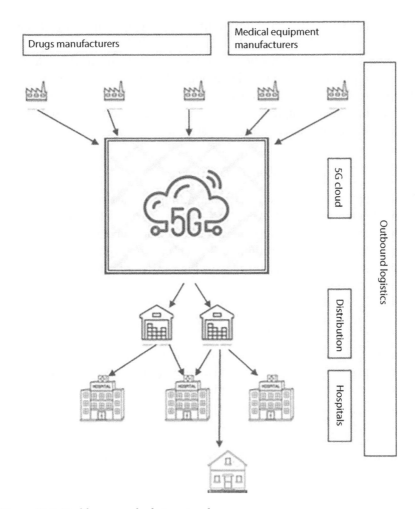

Figure 14.8 Healthcare supple chain network.

14.4.1.2   Medical Devices

X-ray, ECG, EMG, EEG and CMR, and ventilator are some of critical medical scanning devices and digital blood pressure, sugar tester, oximeter are used for diagnosing and conformation of disease. Recently AI based wearable digital medical devices like Apple watch, sweat sensor bandage, portable dialysis device have increased for convenient means of monitoring many physiological real time features. Any abnormal conditions, these devices send signal to doctors, send the existing location to emergency ambulance services, send signals to hospitals for any emergency surgery, send signals to check availability of life saving drugs. These are also part of service supply chain network bound in hospital system. They pick up the critical patient from his house or working place, meanwhile alert the service supporting system is called inbound logistics. In hospital, immediately process different scanning and surgical process is called production/service flow. After completion of service, shifted to normal ward and discharge the patient is called outbound system.

14.4.1.3 Fast Moving Consumer Goods

Retail shop and E-commerce is a playground of fast-moving consumer goods. Walmart, TESCO, Amazon Reliance mart are leading retail and E-commerce players. First, they evaluate the list of 'n' fast moving goods and their certain consumption rate. Then they procure directly from manufacturers in very large quantity with high discount rate and time being placed in central warehouses [29].

Discrete event system simulation, agent based simulation and system dynamics are simulation methods. They have been used in many consumer goods applications and evaluate customer service time, waiting time, length of queue, total time spent in the system using various mathematical probability theories. Figure 14.9 described Discrete-Event-System (DES) simulation of hospital outpatient treatment process using ARENA simulation software. Entry and registration, Preliminary check, Lab testing, review lab test report and Pharmacy, outpatients are various sets of events. Number of patients, waiting time for registration, lab testing, report checking, time taken in each lab test/patient, report review/doctor/patient are recorded

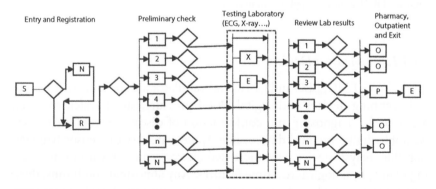

Figure 14.9 Hospital outpatient simulation model.

as elements. The objective of the case study is to improve the quality of services in case hospital and there by trade-off the increased outpatient population with increased resources in reasonable service level. Simulation results were compared with increased outpatient flow by 5, 10 and 15% and compared with increased recourses in Gamby Teaching General Hospital (GTGH) in Bahir Dar City, Ethiopia.

System dynamics (SD) has recently been used in stochastic nature models. It can predict higher order complex time varying systems of nonlinear and time-delay application qualitative and quantitative to solve the social, economic and other complex large system problems. Figure 14.10 shows a SD simulation model using Vensim simulation software of case study of multi-product and multi-period of expired and shortage of perishable products replenishment quantity problem in Bahir Dar City consumer product trade business unit warehouse in Ethiopia. They place multi order based on sales rate, stock-on-hand, remaining life of unsold items, arrival rate, lead time and so on. This model focused to eliminate stock out items and unsold items after expired date.

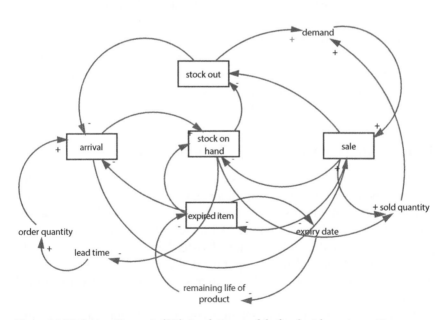

Figure 14.10 System Dynamic (SD) simulation model of replenishment quantity.

Based on consumption rate of each item, they replenish it to their 'n' retail shops by 'm' vehicles. They can assign different strategies of replenishment. It is highly impossible to follow-up 'k' number of fast-moving goods consumption rate, because there are different parameters influencing, like, weather, fashion, and festivals. Nowadays researchers focus on AI based tools to predict consumption rate with all constraints.

14.4.2   Networked Manufacturing

Traditional manufacturing system has their product catalogue to be manufactured. Customer has to select any one of the product and they have limited options to select on the base model in the product catalogue. Globalized economy and recent development in information & communication technologies introduced significant changes in traditional manufacturing are called networked manufacturing as shown in Figure 14.11. Networked manufacturing means based on customer requirements, design enterprises, manufacturers and warehouses are interconnecting and give best price, fixed delivery time and more flexible product design.

The March 2011 Great Tohoku earthquake and tsunami devastated the supply chain network of Toyota, Nissan, Honda, and other manufacturers. Immediately they stopped the production in Japan and shifted the production orders to their EU and US based production plants. Networked manufacturing helps them not only in uncertain situation but also heavy fluctuation of material availability, heavy demand, shout fall of electrical power, labor issues and so on. Harley Davidson, Falcon are some the examples using networked plant due to trade war.

14.4.3   Humanitarian Supply Chain Network

Since 1974, nearly 7,200 natural disasters have happened worldwide. Due to these disaster consequences, millions of people were injured, death and homeless. Humanitarian supply chain focused on quick relief to disasters affected people as shown in Figure 14.12. Demand and supply of essential goods are abnormal conditions after disaster happened. Supply of foods, cloth, medical devices, drugs, temporary shelters are shared by volunteers, government, international societies after some time delay with limited quantities at the starting period.

There is no record of supplied items to the affected people and no record for local NGOs volunteers contributed to distribution channels. This leads to chances of oversupply and nil supply of essential goods to the affected people. On the other side demand of wanted quantity of essential goods are uncertain. Humanitarian workers are facing with these unknown

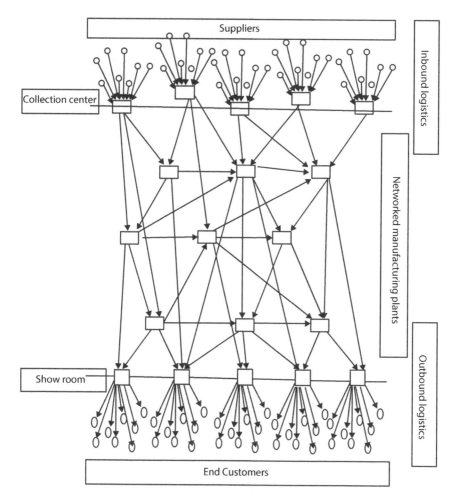

Figure 14.11 Networked manufacturing of supply chain network.

challenges, when, where, what, how much, where from and how many times short falls.

Recently researchers are focused on AI based tools to predict the affected zones, number of affected people for contact tracing and centralized information sharing centers or help-lines, channelized government or volunteers for recovery works, medical volunteers, medicines & emergency ambulance services, collection centers of essential goods from volunteers, distribution network of essential goods to be distributed to required places in time.

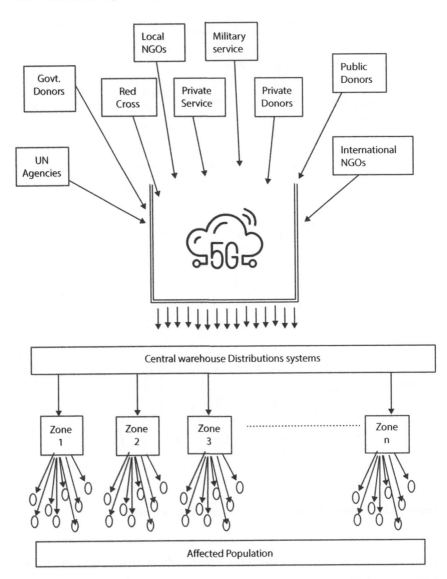

Figure 14.12 Humanitarian supply chain network.

Conclusion

Logistics and supply chain is an inevitable source of activities in any white product manufacturing and service industries. Competition between developed countries, between fortune international companies, between second and third level manufacturing sectors, between local retailers, impact of technology advancement, impact of globalization and impact of global warming and carbon footprint issues are again pressurizing this sector into complex. Next upcoming decades this logistics and supply chain network will be going more complex due to pandemic situations, natural disasters, increasing population and other side entities which are working over smart strategies. As of now the only solution to resolve these unbounded NP-hard problems will be overcome by only AI based tools.

References

1. Stanton, D., *et al.*, *Supply Chain Management for Dummies*, John Wiley & Sons, USA, 2017. https:/ww.wiley.com/en-us/An+Introduction+to+Commu nication+and+Artificial+Intelligence-p-978509533176

2. Etraj, P. and Jayaprakash, J., Analytic Hierarchy Process to select environmentally conscious suppliers for sustainable supply chain management: A case study in a public sector transport corporation. *Appl. Mech. Mater.*, 813, 1133–1139, 2015.

3. Agumas, M., Jayaprakash, J., Teshome, M., Simulation Study of Inventory Performance Improvement in Consumer Products Trade Business Unit Using System Dynamic Approach. *Lect. Notes Inst. Comput. Sci. Soc. Inform. Telecommun. Eng.*, 274, 401–409, 2018.

4. Negussie, R. and Jayaprakash, J., Inbound Multi-echelon Inventory Supply Network Model in Ethiopian Leather Industry: A Simulation Study. *Lect. Notes Inst. Comput. Sci. Soc. Inform. Telecommun. Eng.*, 274, 418–428, 2018.

5. Govindan, K., Mina, H., Esmaeili, A., Gholami-Zanjani, S.M., An integrated hybrid approach for circular supplier selection and closed loop supply chain network design under uncertainty. *J. Cleaner Prod.*, 242, 118317, 2020.

6. Sathish, T. and Jayaprakash, J., Multi period disassembly-to-order of end-of-life product based on scheduling to maximize the profit in reverse logistic operation. *Int. J. Logist. Syst. Manage.*, 26, 3, 402–419, 2017.

7. Hasani, A., Mokhtari, H., Fattahi, M., A multi-objective optimization approach for green and resilient supply chain network design: A real-life case study. *J. Cleaner Prod.*, 278, 123199, 2020.

8. Mueller, J.P. and Massaron, L., *Artificial Intelligence for Dummies*, Wiley Publishing, USA, 2018. https://www.wileyindia.com/artificial-intelligence-for-dummies.html

9. Pache, G., Covid-19: The two sides of healthcare supply chain management. *Eur. J. Manage.*, 20, 1, 79–84, 2020.

10. Snyder, L.V. and Shen, Z.-J.M., *Fundamentals of Supply Chain Theory*, 2nd Edition, Wiley Publishing, USA, 2019. https://www.wiley.com/en-us/Funda mentals+of+Supply+Chain+Theory%2C+2nd+Edition-p-9781119024842

11. Birhanu, D., Lanka, K., Rao, A.N., A survey of classifications in supply chain strategies. *Proc. Eng.*, 97, 1, 2289–2297, 2014.

12. Hugos, M.H., *et al.*, *Essentials of Supply Chain Management*, 4th Edition, Wiley Publishing, USA, 2018. https://www.wiley.com/en-us/Essentials+of+ Supply+Chain+Management,+4th+Edition-p-9781119461104

13. Jayaprakash, J. and Teshome, M.M., Improving operational efficiency of bank sector using simulation techniques. *AIP Conf. Proc.*, 2283, 1, 020014, 2020.

14. Farahani, R.Z., Rezapour, S., Drezner, T., Fallah, S., Competitive supply chain network design: An overview of classifications models solution techniques and applications. *Omega*, 45, 92–118, 2014.

15. Dagne, T.B., Jayaprakash, J., Haile, B., Geremew, S., Optimization of green logistic distribution routing problem with multi depot using improved simulated annealing. *Lect. Notes Inst. Comput. Sci. Soc. Inform. Telecommun. Eng.*, 274, 183–197, 2018.

16. Thinakaran, N., Jayaprakash, J., Elanchezhian, C., Greedy algorithm for inventory Routing Problem in a Supply Chain—A Review. *Mater. Today: Proc.*, 16, 1055–1060, 2019.

17. Etraj, P. and Jayaprakash, J., An Integrated DEMATEL and AHP approach multi criteria green supplier selection process for public procurement. *Int. J. Eng. Technol.*, 9, 1, 113–124, 2017.

18. Dagne, T.B., Jayaprkash, J., Geremew Gebeyehu, S., Design of Supply Chain Network Model for Perishable Products with Stochastic Demand: An Optimized Model. *J. Optim. Ind. Eng.*, 13, 1, 29–37, 2020.

19. Pryke, S., *et al.*, *Successful Construction Supply Chain Management: Concepts and Case Studies*, 2nd Edition, Wiley Publishing, USA, 2020. https://www.wiley. com/en-us/Successful+Construction+Supply+Chain+Management%3A+ Concepts+ Case+Studies %2C+2nd+Edition-p-9781119450542

20. Jayaprakash, J., Thinakaran, N., Sathish, T., JADE implementation of multi-agent based inventory routing problem. *Int. J. Appl. Eng. Res.*, 9, 24, 28785–28792, 2014.

21. Sathish, T., Jayaprakash, J., Thinakaran, N., Multi-agent based disassembly sequencing and planning for end-of-life products. *Appl. Mech. Mater.*, 813, 1193–1197, 2015.

22. Sathish, T., Jayaprakash, J., Senthil, P.V., Saravanan, R., Multi period disassembly-to-order of end-of-life product based on scheduling to maximize the profit in reverse logistic operation. *FME Trans.*, 45, 1, 172–180, 2017.

23. Nasr, N., *et al.*, *Remanufacturing in the Circular Economy: Operations, Engineering and Logistics*, Wiley Publishing, USA, 2019. https://www.wiley. com/en-ie/Remanufacturing+in+the+Circular+Economy:+Operations,+ Engineering+ and+Logistics-p-9781118414101

24. Gunkel, D.J., *et al., An Introduction to Communication and Artificial Intelligence*, Wiley-Scrivener, USA, 2015. https://www.wiley.com/en-us/An+Introduction+to+Communication+and+Artificial+Intelligence-p-9781509533176

25. Shahbazbegian, V., Hosseini-Motlagh, S.M., Haeri, A., Integrated forward/reverse logistics thin-film photovoltaic power plant supply chain network design with uncertain data. *Appl. Energy*, 277, 115538, 2020.

26. Mozafari, M. and Zabihi, A., Robust water supply chain network design under uncertainty in capacity. *Water Resour. Manage.*, 34, 13, 4093–4112, 2020.

27. Alotaibi, S., Mehmood, R., Katib, I., The role of big data and twitter data analytics in healthcare supply chain management, in: *Smart Infrastructure and Applications*, pp. 267–279, 2020.

28. Srivastava, S. and Singh, R.K., Exploring integrated supply chain performance in healthcare: A service provider perspective. *Benchmarking: An International Journal*, 28, 1, 106–130, 2020.

29. Davis, R.A., *et al., Demand-Driven Inventory Optimization and Replenishment: Creating a More Efficient Supply Chain*, 2nd Edition, Wiley Publishing, USA, 2015. https://www.wiley.com/en-us/Demand+Driven+Inventory+Optimization+and+Replenishment%3A+Creating+a+More+Efficient+Supply+Chain%2C+2nd+Edition-p-9781119174028

15

Hereditary Factor-Based Multi-Featured Algorithm for Early Diabetes Detection Using Machine Learning

S. Deepajothi[1], R. Juliana[2], S.K. Aruna[3] and R. Thiagarajan[4*]

[1]Dept. of CSE, Gurunanak Institute of Technology, Hyderabad, India
[2]Dept. of IT, Loyola ICAM College of Engineering & Technology, Chennai, India
[3]Dept. of CSE, Christ (Deemed to be University) School of Engineering &
Technology, Bangalore, India
[4]Dept. of CSE, Prathyusha Engineering College, Thiruvallur, India

Abstract

Today's advent in the medical industry have given numerous chances to improve the quality of detection and reporting the diseases at the early stages for a better diagnosis. Modern day datasets generate fruitful information for timely and periodic monitoring of patients' health conditions. Such information is hidden to a naked eye or hidden in multiple track records of highly affected population. Diabetes mellitus is one such disease which is predominant among a global population which ultimately leads to blindness and death in some cases. The model proposed in this system attempts to design and deliver an intelligent solution for predicting diabetes in the early stages and address the problem of late detection and diagnosis. Intensive research is carried out in many tropical countries for automating this process through a machine learning model. The accuracy of machine learning algorithms is more than satisfactory in the detection of Type 2 diabetes from the dataset of PIMA Indians Diabetes Dataset. An additional feature of hereditary factor is implemented to the existing multiple objective fuzzy classifiers. The proposed model has improved the accuracy to 83% in the training and tested datasets when compared to NGSA model of prediction.

Keywords: Diabetes detection, multi-featured algorithm, decision trees, classification algorithm, prediction

[*]Corresponding author: rthiyagarajantpt@gmail.com

R. Kanthavel, K. Ananthajothi, S. Balamurugan and R. Karthik Ganesh (eds.) *Artificial Intelligent Techniques for Wireless Communication and Networking,* (235–254) © 2022 Scrivener Publishing LLC

15.1   Introduction

Diabetes mellitus is known as a pancreatic disease. Hormone insulin is produced by the pancreas. The body consumes its diet for energy through insulin, and those with diabetes are dying to harvest sufficient insulin. To deliver glucose into the cells to be burned up as energy, the insulin works. If glucose cannot enter the body's cells then there is an insufficient level of insulin. Diabetes is also called as hypoglycemia. There are three types of diabetes: Type1, Type2, and gestational diabetes. When the immune system in pancreas destroys the data cells Type1 occurs. They are then unable to produce insulin for the cells. With unhealthy lifestyle habits, Type2 diabetes occurs and is most common. Gestational diabetes occurs only during pregnancy. If the mother's pancreas cannot produce more insulin it leads to this form. Normally it is temporary. Diabetes mellitus includes complications like eye damage, heart problems and heart stroke, kidney failure, and nerve damage. There is a need for diabetes prediction because of the following:

1) Heart problems and heart stroke:
In people with diabetes this disease is common. There is a coincidental rise of weight of plaque tiled up in artery walls because of high blood glucose levels. It makes it difficult for blood flow for arteries and even a chance of heart problems and heart stroke by blocking it.

2) Blindness:
Another common problem in diabetic patients is eye damage. The blood vessels around the eye weaken because of high blood glucose levels for a long period of time. By forming new blood vessels when your body peels itself it can affect (like swelling and bleeding) inside eyes.

3) Kidney Failure:
Damage of blood vessels inside kidneys by high BGL causes them to leak. Inurine proteins and nutrients are lost and in blood stream toxins buildup which can lead to failure complications.

4) Nerve Damage:
Nerve damage is also caused by high BGL over a long period of time. When a high GL blood passes through blood vessels it can damage them averting nutrients from reaching a nerve. There is a feel of twinkling or burning in that part of body when the nerve is damaged. There is a complete loss of feeling in body when that nerve dies.

15.1.1   Role of Data Mining Tools in Healthcare for Predicting Various Diseases

The healthcare industry is one of the fastest developing arenas. The massive amount of data set groups about patient particulars, diagnosis and prescriptions is handled by healthcare industries. To maintain this data carefully for further usage and to predict the upcoming trends the healthcare industries use data mining approaches. A massive amount of data is collected by the healthcare industry which are not mined to find out hidden data. Day by day the medical industries emanate across with new cures and medication. Better diagnosis and therapy should be provided by the medical industry to patients to acquire virtuous quality of service. Good decision making of this data mining provides different techniques. These techniques play different roles in predicting various diseases. A few of these prediction-based data mining techniques are:

1) Neural network
2) Classifiers
3) Decision Tree
4) Support Vector Machine.

Data mining tools are also used in predicting the results of data verified on healthcare problems. In different healthcare problems to analyze the different accurateness the data mining tools are used. The following are the list of some data mining tools:

1) Artificial Neural Networks
2) Rough Set Theory
3) Statistical Package.

The accuracy levels of various diseases by using different data mining techniques and tools are shown in Table 15.1.

15.2   Literature Review

For Type 2 Diabetes Mellitus (T2DM) it is important to guess the long period difficulties risk for medical assessment process. There are guidelines for T2DM patient to stop Cardiovascular Disease (CVD) possibility by inducting proper treatment. The investigation of use of MLT'S in an improvement direction of revised replicas to envisage T2DM patient from

Table 15.1 Tools and techniques in healthcare.

S. no.	Disease type	Tools of data mining	Data mining techniques	Algorithm	Accuracy level %
1.	Heart Disease	ODND, NCC 2	Classification	Naïve	60
2.	Cancer	WEKA	Classification	Rules Decision Table	97.77
3.	HIV/AIDS	WEKA3.6	Classification and Association Rule Mining	J 48	81.88
4.	Blood Bank Sector	WEKA	Classification	J 48	89.9
5.	Diabetes Mellitus	ANN	Classification	C 4.5 algorithm	875.9
6.	Kidney Dialysis	RST	Classification	Decision Making	72.6
7.	*In Vitro* Fertilization (IVF)	ANN ANN, RST	Classification		91
8.	Brain Cancer	K-means clustering	Clustering	MAFI A	85
9.	Hepatitis C	SNP	Information Gain	Decision Rule	73.20
10.	Dengue SPSS	SPSS Modeler		C 5.0	80
11.	Tuberculosis	WEKA	Naïve Bayes Classifier	KNN	78

CVD occurrence is the main goal of this study. By applying unusual cooperative schemes, the essential task of managing unstable environment of open dataset is addressed. By following a sub-sampling technique HWNNs and SOMs create the primary schemes for constructing troupes. By applying various models, the results of primary schemes are pooled and evaluated. For progress and estimating purpose the five-year recorded data of more than 550 patients with T2DM is used. The best results are achieved in terms of AUC by considering primary schemes outputs which based on HWNNs and SOMs. BLR model i used to validate the requirements to apply sophisticated methods in satisfactory way to provide unfailing CVD possibility marks. The future models are higher than the BLR model [1].

In medical research field the prevalent and significant approach is machine learning. Using medical registers of cardiorespiratory fitness for expecting diabetes the performance of various machine learning methods like Logistic Model Tree, Decision tree and Random Forests are examined in this study. To expose possible clairvoyants of diabetes the author also applied some other techniques. This study used 5 years follow-up of more than 32,000 patients who are not having heart problems and who undertook the treadmill stress test at the Henry Ford Health Systems. At the end of the 5th year 5,000 patients had diabetes. The collection of data had 62 characteristics which divided into four types. Those are history of medication used, history of disease, characteristics of demographic, and signs of stress test. Using 13 of those characteristics the author established an ensembling-based analytical method. The established model had a negative outcome which was controlled by SMOTE (Synthetic Minority Oversampling Technique). The analytical model complete performance was enhanced by the decision trees of Ensemble machine learning approach and accomplished great prediction accurateness as 0.92 AUC. For guessing diabetes by using cardiorespiratory fitness data, the capacity of ensembling and SMOTE approaches was shown in this study. Even though a large number of researches have been collected to design models to guess the diabetes, the machine learning approach has gained continuous attention of the healthcare society. In the prediction of incident diabetes, the SMOTE approach showed the major development [2].

Diabetes is a metabolic disorder. There are Type1 diabetes and Type2 diabetes. In Type1 diabetes the body's immune system kills a level of insulin generating beta cells. Type2 diabetes is a condition where your blood sugar levels or glucose levels are too high. This occurs when your body cannot use glucose you get from food as a consequence glucose forms in the body. Insulin cannot respond to the body. Finally, the body does not generate insulin completely. Because of this the body undergoes different complications.

This can damage the arteries to make two to three times a likely heart attack, stroke or develop vascular dementia, blindness, kidney failure, or nerve damage. Providing some valuable information to the patients for predicting some significant complications in Type2 diabetes is the aim of this study. A set of known algorithms have been accomplished and tested over 1,000 patients' dataset to know the best algorithm to predict the complications in Type2 diabetes. The Random Forest algorithm and the Naïve Bayes classifier algorithms are resulted as the best and worst algorithms respectively. Maximum previous research done to find the finest algorithm to predict the complications of Type2 diabetes and few attempts were made by increasing the dataset to reduce the error rate of the prediction whereas the future techniques attempts to follow mutual aspects. For supporting physicians to take decisions based on the health information system this study presents a method with the observation of complications of diabetes patients, family history of patients and BMI index and so on [3].

One of the most distressing health problems around the world is Diabetes Mellitus (DM) which causes domestic financial problem and short life period. Because of this there is a necessity to prevent and detect diabetes which should improve the diabetes treatment and control. The performance of assessment of recent glucose prediction methods are the aim of this study. To implement data analytics in a wireless body area network system, based on the evaluation a best fit method is suggested. The recommended glucose prediction algorithm is established on ARX model which considered BP, LDL, CGM data, TC and HDL as inputs. To estimate the performance of the recommended algorithm over MAE, R2, RMSE above 440 diabetic patients' dataset was used. The tentative results determine that the estimated accurateness of glucose can be improved by recommended prediction algorithm. For next level improvement of prediction algorithm methods probable research work and dares are listed out. The patient's data which include medication, way of life and common information handled by self-observation and leads a large dataset which demands well prediction, prevention, detection and treatment of diabetes system. For further work this research can be protracted to examine and enhance the glucose prediction algorithm performance [4].

Diabetes-associated characteristics of complications have been analyzed with the main objective of successfully preventing dangerous complications. More than 49,000 non-diabetic patients and nearly 8,000 related diseases of diabetic patients were examined. Hypertension, hyperlipidemia, heart disease and cerebral infarction were four major complications. Based on the associated relationship between these complications the characteristics of these four complications in male, female and different age groups were examined. Statistical analysis was performed over 599 medical exposure indices in diabetic patients who were having and not having these four complications. It showed that there was frequent occurrence of these complications in diabetic women having age between 65 and 70 years. Women before reaching this age should change their diet and life style by doing exercise and food control to prevent these complications. This study showed that cerebral infarction was 2.5% in diabetic patients. In other cases cerebral infarction extended to 10% if the diabetic patient had huge heart diseases. Compared to women heart diseases occurred frequently in men having diabetes [5].

T2DM is a metabolic disease which develops several complications. A significant clinical value is the primary identification of a personal at menace for complications after being identified with T2DM. In this study, the author presents an extrapolative method to envisage the above significant clinical value. To ideal the time-to-event of T2DM complications the author proposes a novel survival analysis method calculated to concurrently achieve two significant metrics: 1) accurate estimation of event times, and 2) respectable level of the comparative risks of two patients. In additional a multi-task version of the survival model is developed to well capture the associations of time-to-events of the numerous complications. The author executes general experimentations on patient data mined from a large electronic health record claims database, to measure the presentation of these approaches. The outcomes showed efficiency of the multi-task framework above demonstrating every complication individually. A quantity of upcoming research guidelines is available. International Classification of Diseases ciphers and primary demographic data were used in evaluation. An expectation performance of complication can improve by integrating new types. It is essential to detect the significant related risk features long with the obstacle measures. In conclusion the author also fascinated to get used these methods to other kinds of electronic health record data and other metabolic diseases [6].

There are many patients who are suffering from comorbidity like T2D, heart diseases, cancer, infectious diseases, BP and dementia, eating disorders, anxiety disorders, and substance abuse. Most of the medical expenditures in the US is for management of patients with these several parallel disorders. The promotion of Pre-emptive caring and cost reduction of a single patient can be achieved by Guessing prospective comorbid conditions of that patient. Because of the restricted access to Electronic Health Records by secrecy laws determining the comorbidity relationships is difficult and challenging. In this study the author used a trajectory prediction diagram model to disclose evolution pathways of comorbid conditions and to envisage probable comorbid conditions for different patient's common comorbidity prediction method also presented. Patients' reports made by the SHR (Social Health Records) are used for prediction methods of this study. Based on the SHR Foundation the results showed that this approach is able to predict upcoming comorbid conditions of a patient and also the method is able to make known each possible development trajectory among any two conditions. From the medicinal fiction the expected trajectories are validated with existing comorbidity relations and the variance of trajectory outcomes crosswise patient's sex. The author guided that for future work the tree-based trajectory model can be improved, however the present trajectories are having high prevalent conditions and also possible that sieving trajectories with low confidence ranks. For assessing the excellence of projected trajectories more tests will be considered and executed. Also, the trajectory result is used in the evaluation of whether here any significant sex or age particular changes in trajectories. The advance trajectory one hand expects the possible prevalence on the other hand it expects the intermediary situations, so it can be considered as a standard form of a cooperative expectation model. The author planned to apply helpful expectation time series features in the upcoming and also planned to combine the two models into one single model [7].

This study shows usefulness of a mobiab system for patients and also show topographies of the system generally used. Few users who used mobiab systems are selected of which the data collected for this study was chosen from a one year period. The users who were involved in this study was the users of mobiab system who was suffering with diabetes mellitus and also non-diabetic users. The outcomes showed that the mobiab system is convenient for 70% of the users and they used maximum components of the system. Approximately 30% of the users used limited components of the system only. A user used mobiab system in daily rehearsal. As example, a specific diabetic user in a 6-month period recorded entries of food, activities, glycaemia, and insulin values. Quantity of users were augmented by publicity and non-diabetic users were motivated by maximum rewards to escalate continuing observance. In the forthcoming compulsory remodeled system, mobile applications are expected to appear as system design to attract users. The grouping of many functionalities and survival of inspiration and gasification components is the main benefit of the mobiab system [8].

Now a Diabetes is treated as worse than cancer and HIV. It causes blindness, kidney failure, and heart disease. In the healthcare community the avoidance of the disease is a warm topic. To find the cause of the disease and antidote it several investigations have taken place. In this study the author discussed that diabetes is likely to happen based on the persons' lifestyle events. It includes eating and sleeping ways, bodily movement along with other indicators like BMI, waist circumference, etc. For an extremely unqualified dataset CART estimate model has been applied with one third precision in this effort. As a major factor of producing diabetes, blood pressure is known. Other causes are street food eating, late-night sleeping, heredity, rice intake and bodily events made by a person in a day. So it can be said that anyone can enjoy each part of his life but a petite attention in ones' daily routine does not hurt [9].

It is needed to estimate the tool to determine a diabetic patient. The back propagation neural network is among one of the different prediction methods which produces accurate result at present. In this paper the author discussed about this tool. To make tool user friendly the GUI is developed to get perfect results in the absence of doctor. This project helps doctors to get the results of patient in a second so that he can save the time for next treatment of the patient. This study shows tool implementation and progress in MATLAB. In the case of identifying whether a patient is diabetic or not his BPNN performance of 80% is compared to previous work which is an improvement and is better for patients instead of the finger stick which painful. This tool shows the results in binary format i.e. 0 or 1. The number 0 means non-diabetic and number 1 means diabetic [10].

Based on bodily and biochemical tests numerous techniques are presented for analyzing diabetes. For diabetic protection the procedures toughly built on the data mining techniques can be successfully applied. Via five different data mining methods the author discovers the primary prediction of diabetes in this study. These include GMM, SVM, ELM, ANN, LR. Among these five ANN shows more accuracy compared to other methods proved by experimental results. Even though ANN shows efficient accuracy it has some limitations also though this paper simply demonstrates a possible use of the data mining techniques. The feature used in this study can integrate other medicinal features. It can also deliberately use additional data mining methods, like Time Series, Clustering and Association Rules [11].

Non-invasive diabetes prediction has been achieving importance since the last decade. In this paper the author searches the use of a 1D modified CNN algorithm which associates feature extraction and classification methods. In this paper the methodology projected is shown to knowingly decrease the restrictions related with using these methods and further improving the classifier's performance. The carrying out tests and the performance of the system is accepted out and assessed A non-invasive technique of identifying diabetes has been discussed and evaluated in this paper. To yield a set of attribute maps the CNN algorithm convolutes the new data sign with a kernel-based filter. It is noticed that this algorithm diminishes the computational cost and the essential for best feature section methods [12].

To predict the levels of diabetic mellitus development of sample type-2 diabetes adult patients the author used computational imitation inside a tele-consult scheme and estimates the section of patients which would procure diabetic mellitus complications which the author used as computational algorithms [14, 15]. To this end the author generated a function G which shows the behavior of glucose in time but it based on parameter. As a result few patients upturn their possibilities to permit to the consequent diabetes such diabetic kidney failure. To find maximum risk of kidney failure the author schemed up to four scenarios. A patient may start to develop kidney failure around in 120 days as shown by the initial sample collected. In order to anticipate upcoming cases where kidney disease come to be irrevocable, in an upcoming study the author enlarges the data to make this analysis more accurate [13].

To show people that find high risk personalities is a significant task, fasting blood sugar analysis is the accurate test for diabetes, but it is intrusive and expensive so there is a need for predicting risk in advance with a reliable non-intrusive and costless test. In this paper the author used a classification to coalmine a wide dataset. The author used Decision Tree and Naive Bayes classifiers to predict the menace and the results of this compared with the existing hand-computed diabetes menace counting machineries. The comparison results showed that classification can improve the prediction performance [14].

15.3   Objectives of the Proposed System

Machine learning involves the prediction of parameters for evolution of desired results. Applications with medical results will include numerous datasets with immense and diverse range of parameters. Proper selection of parameters for applying within the algorithms will drive the solution in a faster pace. Redundant features present in the datasets will also lead to unnecessary computations, noise and dependence of multiple features. An algorithm will demand a neat and clean dataset with minimal dependency among features for errorless and reliant production of results. The parameters are expected to belong within a given class and becomes a predictive variable. Accounting to the fact of reducing dependability, feature selection plays a significant role in promising quality results. Selection of features delivers a final set of parameters to be utilized by the algorithm, feature extraction process enhances the quality of features through refinement processes. The proposed model defines a novel method of introducing new features and extracting useful features for processing with the modified algorithm. The classification accuracy of the proposed algorithm over the standard datasets available in the Pima Indians Diabetes datasets is guaranteed. The same results sets are compared with existing systems in the literature survey and documented in the following sections.

15.4   Proposed System

The dataset utilized for testing the proposed algorithm is retrieved from the Pima Indian Diabetes Database from National Institute of Diabetes, Digestive and Kidney Diseases. This database comprises of diabetes patients, documented by Vincent Sigillito after analysis of 768 medical reports from patients of Phoenix, Arizona in the United States of America. The standard set of features available in the datasets are eight and for this study an additional parameter is selected namely heredity factor. Two outcomes are expected from the proposed algorithm in the form of positive and negative presence of diabetes. The results are numbered to be 1 for being positive and 0 for testing negative. The novel method is tested with Hive and R programming logics.

The architecture of the proposed model is illustrated in the above Figure 15.1. The database is loaded into the database of the system and controlled by HiveSQL. The input data is in the form of a CSV file consisting all the attributes: a) Number of times pregnant, b) Plasma glucose concentration, c) Diastolic blood pressure mm Hg, d) Triceps skin fold thickness (mm), e) 2-Hour serum insulin (mu U/ml), f) Body mass index kgm^{-2},

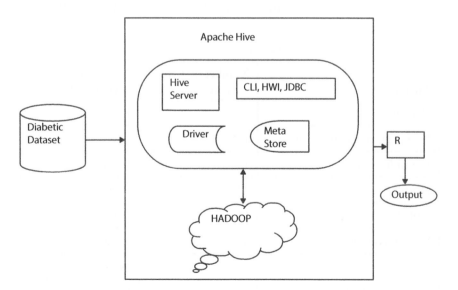

Figure 15.1 Architecture of the proposed system.

g) Diabetes pedigree function, h) Age in years, i) Binary Class variable and j) Heredity Factor. The important addition to the existing attributes is the hereditary parameter that denotes 0 or 1. The addition helps the segregation of information not related to pregnancy alone but also derives a better decision tree.

The input information is categorized according to the range of values present in the given CSV file. Hive carefully segregates the information and delivers a well formatted output for easier understanding. The output of Hive is forwarded as input into the R. R programming has been used for deriving a meaningful statistical information from various websites. YouTube is one such example where R programming is implemented and generating graphs as results.

15.5   HIVE and R as Evaluation Tools

The research methodology has implemented Hive and R for analyzing the dataset and predict the presence of diabetic conditions or not. HIVE is a data mining and data warehousing working model implemented along with Hadoop. The model works like a SQL database and can be accessed with a number of SQL like queries in a HiveQL syntax. The tables are registered as a Hadoop Distributed File System (HDFS). The queries assist in producing efficient map like structures or decision trees through logistic regression techniques. Since the outcome of these trees are to predict a continuous

Table 15.2 Attributes and distinct values.

Attribute	Number of distinct values	Time taken in HiveQL (s)
Hereditary Factor	2	1
Plasma glucose concentration	136	20.039
Serum Insulin	186	19.088
Diastolic BP	47	19.06
Diabetes pedigree	517	19.056
Body Mass Index	358	19.12
Age	52	19.191
Triceps skin fold thickness	51	21.551

variable, the present information is recursively split into smaller segments with different combinations to derive different decision trees. The traditional list of attributes for decision tree derivation is tabulated in Table 15.2.

15.6   Decision Trees

The actual decision tree is formed with the conventional parameters and will derive a decision tree in the following Figure 15.2. With the information in the given dataset, the figure demonstrates how the decision tree produces different color of leaves which indicates the binary value of being positive or negative. Decision trees produces successful results with minimal features obtained from the given dataset. The significance of glucose ranges in the blood, body mass index of individual, age and other constraints is evident from the produced tree. The proposed method is to include yet another important parameter to the existing dataset to yield a better decision tree. Apart from the blood glucose level, impact of hereditary factor influences the decision trees with better precisions.

This technique is a model under supervised learning methodologies, primarily used for simplifying the classification problems. The given set of input conditions are split into smaller capsules recursively until the nodes cannot be split further. For every node value, the branch is divided into two smaller and narrowed down segments. The objective of this model is to narrow

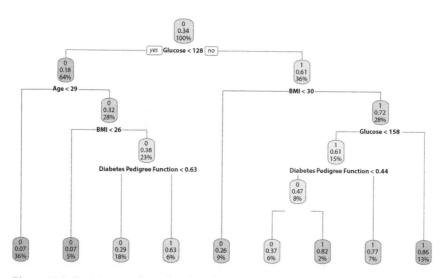

Figure 15.2 Decision tree derived with updated attributes.

down to the possible value or name of the classification when the decision trees reach the leave nodes. The decision trees are constructed in two possible means, one to derive in a binary form or a continuous form. Final stages of the trees would lead a way to find the class of unknown variables.

A decision tree is supposed to derive the root node with highest entropy values. The selection of optimal features for a decision tree will ensure the advantage of an algorithm. Dataset with other normal attributes are added with the family history of having type 2 diabetes and normal list of constraints include a splitting attribute, pruning and truncating, stopping criterion, sample information, quality and quantity of information, diverse range of parameters, splitting orders and much more. The following figure illustrates how a decision tree will be constructed with a decision node and leaves. A decision tree is segmented according to the initially selected parameter. This decision is usually the tough criteria for every algorithm. But in the proposed methodology, even before the high levels of glucose in blood are considered, the hereditary factor is computed. This value gives better precision and improved results when compared to existing techniques. A decision tree will always be divided into two branches. In this proposal, the root node which starts the process is either 0 or 1, representing the presence of type 2 diabetes in the history of family members.

The objective of this proposed method is to examine the dataset and identify the presence of diabetes with a classification technique as illustrated in Figure 15.3. This research work intends to minimize the complications caused due to diabetes mellitus and improve the lifestyle of affected people with faster and reliable predications. The common reasons for an individual to be affected with diabetes are hereditary, blood glucose levels, ages, obesity and sometimes of multiple factors. The model in the research work intends to facilitate the right selection of features for a large dataset, completely based on sensitivity of individuals. Selection of right attributes also include the elimination of unwanted and irrelevant dataset attributes. For diabetes, the normal attribute selected for analysis is the plasma glucose level and finding the correlation with other attributes given in the datasets. The formula for finding the correlation values between attributes is given by the following Equation 15.1.

$$\text{Correlation Value of Attribute} = (\text{Max}_{\text{attribute}} - \text{Attribute}_{\text{I to N}}) - 1 \quad (15.1)$$

The process is continued with all existing attributes to find the difference values between one attribute and the other. If the difference is less significant, its value is comparatively lesser than other difference values of other attributes. This process is regulated by the procedures mentioned in Figure 15.4 and decision tree in Figure 15.5.

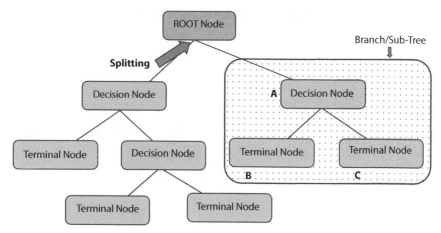

Note:- A is parent node of B and C.

Figure 15.3 Formation of decision trees.

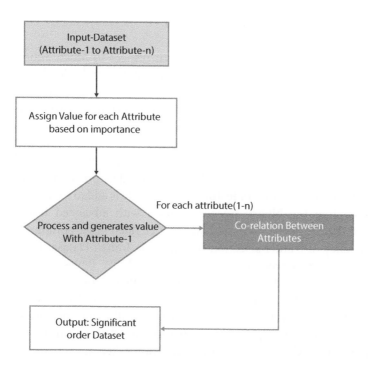

Figure 15.4 Significant order dataset formation.

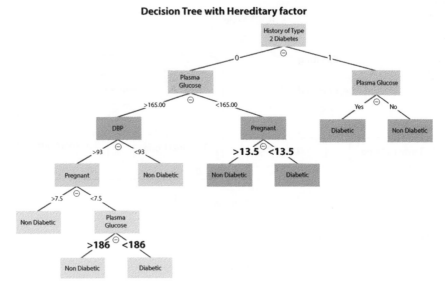

Figure 15.5 Decision tree with hereditary factor.

15.7   Results and Discussions

The results are evaluated and stated with respect to Mean Square Error values of different classification algorithms. When multiple objectives are considered for features selection in an algorithm, it yields accurate results but takes a higher computational time to produce the decision trees. The number of features plays a pivotal role in producing decision trees and thus classifying the result sets. Hence this proposal worked on a better feature selection and has resulted in prominent five features namely hereditary factor, plasma glucose level, body mass index, pregnancy and age in years. For every selection of features, a cost value is added to the algorithm. Implementing the binary trees derivation with advanced features had reduced the dataset to a compact size that enabled faster computations.

Efficiency of feature selection on the Pima Indian Dataset is evaluated with a number of renowned algorithms like Naïve Bayes, Decision Tree Graft J48, Enora and NGSA. A normal ENORA algorithm identifies the result set with 80% accuracy level. With the new set of features and correlation levels the performance level of the algorithm has increased to 83%. The accuracy of the proposed model before and after determination of correlation values exhibited a better classification schema.

The consistency of the proposed model is better than that of ENORA strategy which produces a faster classifier rate in Figure 15.6(a). This efficiency is promised even when the number of training samples increment exponentially. The proposed model delivers a standard result of over 80% consistently for new datasets and increased features. Every machine learning algorithm is expected to produce reduced amount of Root Mean Square Error Values in Figure 15.6(b). From the following results, it is evident that the proposed selective features method with hereditary factor generates a lesser RMSE value in all stages of training and test datasets. This proves that the proposed model outperforms ENORA in all aspects.

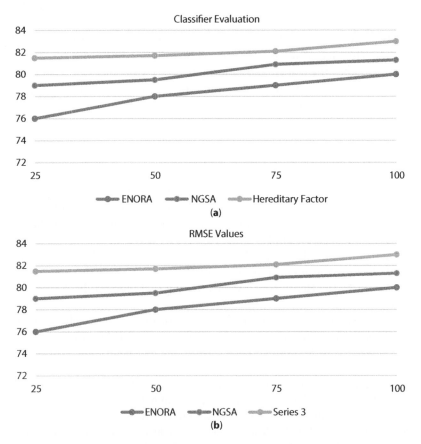

Figure 15.6 (a) Comparison of classifiers on proposed method vs ENORA vs NGSA. (b) Comparison of RMSE on proposed method vs ENORA vs NGSA.

15.8   Conclusion

Data Mining techniques implemented in medical industry is a sensitive and a sector which demands utmost accuracy before a decision is attained by a medical practitioner. Association rule mining or rule-based classifiers will not support a critical decision system and thus the machine learning algorithms are implemented after intensive series of testing and training. The proposed model includes an additional feature that guarantees the prediction to a higher range. Many classifier algorithms have been proved to be a slow performing solution. Attempts to simplify the further processes of prediction includes the clever preprocessing methodologies like feature selections. Irrelevance and redundancy are major problems that affects the performance of existing systems. Genetic feature selection is adapted in multiple research areas and is thus adapted with additional hereditary feature in this proposed scheme. As a result of this new inclusion, the model has outperformed other state of the art techniques and produced a better prediction rate. The feature reduction rate is 0.6 which became a successful result as the added feature incremented the chances of predicting diabetes with a better accuracy.

References

1. Zarkogianni, K., Athanasiou, M., Thanopoulou, A.C., Nikita, K.S., Comparison of machine learning approaches toward assessing the risk of developing cardiovascular disease as a long-term diabetes complication. *IEEE J. Biomed. Health Inf.*, 22, 5, 1637–1647, 2017.
2. Alghamdi, M., Al-Mallah, M., Keteyian, S., Brawner, C., Ehrman, J., Sakr, S., Predicting diabetes mellitus using SMOTE and ensemble machine learning approach: The Henry Ford ExercIse Testing (FIT) project. *PLoS One*, 12, 7, e0179805, 2017.
3. Farzi, S., Kianian, S., Rastkhadive, I., Predicting serious diabetic complications using hidden pattern detection, in: *2017 IEEE 4th International Conference on Knowledge-Based Engineering and Innovation (KBEI)*, 2017, December, IEEE, pp. 0063–0068.
4. Thiagarajan, R. and Moorthi, M., Energy consumption and network connectivity based on Novel-LEACH-POS protocol networks. *Comput. Commun.*, Elsevier, (0140-3664), 149, 90–98, November 2019.
5. Huzooree, G., Khedo, K.K., Joonas, N., Glucose prediction data analytics for diabetic patients monitoring, in: *2017 1st International Conference on Next Generation Computing Applications (NextComp)*, 2017, July, IEEE, pp. 188–195.

6. Chen, P. and Pan, C., Evaluation of the relationship between diabetes and large blood vessel disease, in: *2017 13th IASTED International Conference on Biomedical Engineering (BioMed)*, 2017, February, IEEE, pp. 200–207.

7. Liu, B., Li, Y., Sun, Z., Ghosh, S., Ng, K., Early prediction of diabetes complications from electronic health records: A multi-task survival analysis approach, in: *Thirty-Second AAAI Conference on Artificial Intelligence*, 2018, April.

8. Ji, X., Chun, S.A., Geller, J., Predicting comorbid conditions and trajectories using social health records. *IEEE Trans. Nanobiosci.*, 15, 4, 371–379, 2016.

9. Burda, V., Novák, D., Schneider, J., Evaluation of diabetes mellitus compensation after one year of using Mobiab system, in: *2016 38th Annual International Conference of the IEEE Engineering in Medicine and Biology Society (EMBC)*, 2016, August, IEEE, pp. 6002–6005.

10. Anand, A. and Shakti, D., Prediction of diabetes based on personal lifestyle indicators, in: *2015 1st International Conference on Next Generation Computing Technologies (NGCT)*, 2015, September, IEEE, pp. 673–676.

11. Joshi, S. and Borse, M., Detection and prediction of diabetes mellitus using Back-propagation neural network, in: *2016 International Conference on Micro-Electronics and Telecommunication Engineering (ICMETE)*, 2016, September, IEEE, pp. 110–113.

12. Thiagarajan, R. and Moorthi, M., Efficient Routing protocols for Mobile Ad Hoc Networks. *International conference on AEEICB* (978-1-5090-5434-3), August 2017, IEEE SJR 1.2.

13. Komi, M., Li, J., Zhai, Y., Zhang, X., Application of data mining methods in diabetes prediction, in: *2017 2nd International Conference on Image, Vision and Computing (ICIVC)*, 2017, June, IEEE, pp. 1006–1010.

14. Lekha, S. and Suchetha, M., Real-time non-invasive detection and classification of diabetes using modified convolution neural network. *IEEE J. Biomed. Health Inf.*, 22, 5, 1630–1636, 2017.

15. Nieto-Chaupis, H. and Matta, H., Evaluation of type-2 diabetes progress in adult patients by using predictive algorithms, in: *2016 IEEE Ecuador Technical Chapters Meeting (ETCM)*, 2016, October, IEEE, pp. 1–5. https://doi.org/10.1109/ETCM.2016.7750811

16. Songthung, P. and Sripanidkulchai, K., Improving type 2 diabetes mellitus risk prediction using classification, in: *2016 13th International Joint Conference on Computer Science and Software Engineering (JCSSE)*, 2016, July, IEEE, pp. 1–6. https://doi.org/10.1109/JCSSE.2016.7748866

16

Adaptive and Intelligent Opportunistic Routing Using Enhanced Feedback Mechanism

V. Sharmila*, K. Mandal†, Shankar Shalani‡ and P. Ezhumalai§

Department of Computer Science and Engineering, R.M.D. Engineering College, Kavarapettai, India

Abstract

Opportunistic routing reveals intercepted packets provide an effective wireless mesh network but did not fulfill any of the high-speed requirements. Traditional opportunistic routing algorithms, to provide high speed, use batching of packets which is a complex task. Therefore an enhanced opportunistic feedback-based algorithm is proposed. Individual packet forwarding uses a new route calculation in the proposed work that takes into consideration the cost of transmitting feedback and the capacity of the nodes to choose appropriate rates for monitoring operating conditions. The packets are not forwarded if the recipient has already obtained the feedback given. Results from simulation show that the proposed feedback based opportunistic routing algorithm will achieve better performance than the comparative algorithms.

Keywords: Feedback mechanism, opportunistic routing, packet forwarding, routing protocol, TCP

16.1 Introduction

In recent decades, wireless mesh systems have emerged as a promising technology to provide large Internet connectivity to communities. The

---
Corresponding author: sharmilavaradhan@gmail.com
†*Corresponding author*: kuppanmandal@gmail.com
‡*Corresponding author*: shalinishankar022@gmail.com
§*Corresponding author*: ezhumalai.es@gmail.com

R. Kanthavel, K. Ananthajothi, S. Balamurugan and R. Karthik Ganesh (eds.) Artificial Intelligent Techniques for Wireless Communication and Networking, (255–268) © 2022 Scrivener Publishing LLC

mesh routers can be connected via wireless links in a wireless mesh network. However, the problem is improving network efficiency as a result of distortion, intrusion and fading, wireless links are much less reliable than wired connections. Typically a transmission over a wireless mesh network traverses multiple nodes before it encounters a wired internet connectivity gateway node. The biggest advantage of mesh networks is that they can have the same spectrum as point-based single-hop wireless communication at considerably lower fixed costs [5]. For these obvious benefits, a variety of research and commercial mesh networks have been implemented with the goal of delivering fast and cheap internet access [10]. Typical architecture of wireless mesh networks is shown in Figure 16.1.

Typically the mobile nodes are computers, cell phones, and other associated networks. Wireless routers include serving consumers within a distributed structure, and help with the routing of the packets. Wireless mesh networks offer additional routing methods that differ significantly from wired network routing. Wireless channels are unpredictable, in fact, and can cause significant deviations in signal strength. Furthermore the communications between nodes are intermittent. Second, a wireless network may depend on multiple network criteria such as unwanted packet transmission proportions for the same device, limited bandwidth, communication

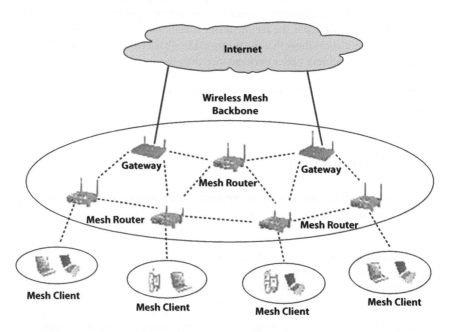

Figure 16.1 Typical architecture of wireless mesh networks.

cost, etc. Third, wireless communication is usually enabled by these and the one-channel contact would interfere with the transmissions on other neighboring channels [7].

Within the consulting firm of wireless networks, routing methods over multihop wireless networks has been a significant topic for many years. Much of the past studies focused on providing versatile node connectivity using batteries in the sense of mobile nodes, and continually developing topologies or power consumption constraints. The architecture of wireless mesh network connectivity frames and routing algorithm is a successful area of research, and a large portion of approaches have been discussed. Opportunistic routing has been shown to be efficient for wireless mesh networks, and has become increasingly common over the years. The opportunistic routing routers, and plenty of packet exchanges. While portable to many networks, the method is considered more effective than all existing methods [9].

The major challenge for the opportunistic routing design is to maximize the routing progress of every data transference to the destination without generating redundant transmissions or incoming systems. To achieve the positive advantages of opportunity routing and avoiding the above-mentioned problems, a successful protocol should implement the following tasks in a distributed way: All nodes in the network must be running an algorithm for filtering and sorting the set of neighboring nodes (candidate list), which can best support the specific goal to a specific destination. The candidates are referred to as this algorithm. The objective of the selection algorithm is to ensure that the only eligible nodes are candidates and to establish the nominee selection lists. In order to correctly create the candidate list, OR protocols require certain metrics to assess network and classify network nodes.

Forwarder selection offers a scheme to pick only one node that actually forwards the packet, from all the candidates that have successfully obtained the packet. The forwarder selection process is achieved by the collaboration of several applicants since there is no central controlling node. Coordination involves signaling among candidates, and duplicate packet transmissions can be caused by imperfect coordination. Forwarding obligation transfer helps the nodes participating in the forwarding process to become aware of the winner of the selection—the real forwarder plus the candidates. The transition of accountability is the distinctive aspect that separates opportunistic routing from flooding. In reality, multiple nodes can obtain the broadcast transmission from a packet sender in both opportunistic routing and flooding. Opportunistic routing, however, allows only one node at a time to be in control of packet forwarding, unlike the flooding algorithm.

Only in the case of an incomplete transfer of authority, duplicate transmission prevention is required. Where a forwarding obligation is passed properly to the winning forwarder, the packet is forwarded by only one node at any time. There are multiple packet communications by comparison, although only one packet is groundbreaking, that is, the winning forwarder. The duplication avoidance mechanism is more powerful and less network resources would be expended. With all the consideration of these limitations, the main contributions of this work are to include a routing scheme that prefers a viable route by analyzing both the forward cost of reviewing the information and the reversed cost of receiving information, and the capacity of the nodes pick suitable data rates to handle network parameters [8, 12].

16.2   Related Study

Network devices in wireless mesh networks with short wave transmitters act similarly as a wireless link to transfer data. A route is the collection of nodes which a packet travels from transmitter to the receiver. Defining and choosing the route through routing algorithms are used depends entirely on when the routes are discovered, identified wireless mesh routing protocols may be categorized as traditional routing and opportunistic routing [3]. Traditional wireless communication routing adopted the pattern similar to those used in wireless connections by handling the wireless links as wired links.

Routing is achieved until the packet is used by the minimal hop count, the minimum cost or the channel capacity between transmitter and receiver. For network devices, therefore, conventional routing networks are needed to get the cost of the communications that the nodes will use to decide the shortest path to identify the best routes for connection. Such trade costs might include the likelihood of delivery, the number of links, the expected delay along the route, etc. [14]. Performed routinely (proactive protocols), on demand (reactive protocols), or on both (hybrid protocols), routing criteria are used to measure track's characteristics, such as the lowest, least expensive, or optimum route throughput. Metrics are focused primarily on applying the routing method correctly. Standard existing methods conclude the link metrics defined during the steady route discovery process, and select route before transmission. Conventional routing methods therefore concentrate on the consistent and stable operations of the individual links. However, the rapid development of wireless communication with traditional routing algorithms can lead to poor performance, such as low likelihood of data packets and high overhead power [2].

Opportunistic routing allows for the transmission of the same packet by two aspects of multi-hop wireless network which are hierarchical connectivity and which transmits multiple attractions to different nodes. The major benefit is the increased likelihood of failure. Opportunistic routing spreads packets via multiple links instead of one single connection. There is therefore a high risk of loss of packets. Wireless mesh networks are ideal for regular routing. An opportunistic routing will connect a packet of data to a candidate's forwarders collection rather than selecting a designated carrier on each connection. Relay then candidates with the data packet perform the coordinating task to choose the best relay for the packet transmission [6].

Opportunistic routing is a modern wireless sensor network routing paradigm that chooses the node closest to the target node to forward the data. It utilizes the existence of wireless sensor networks to broadcast. The performance, throughput and reliability of sensor networks have been improved by opportunistic routing. In order to maximize the network lifespan, several energy-saving strategies have been implemented using opportunistic routing in wireless sensor networks. The basic concept of opportunistic routing, various areas in which it has been claimed to be useful, some protocols, their metrics and their disadvantages have been elaborated in this article [7].

Multi-hop wireless platforms have a special feature apart from point-to-point wireless communication while broadcasting. Nodes of their adjacent nodes will overhear several suitable packets and partial packets. Thus, it creates a pool of shared durability and possibility in that group. Routing and packet forwarding systems would benefit from this shared efficiency and the ability to transfer packets to the required packet and prevent retransmission of a whole packet for each portion packet [11]. Therefore an efficient feedback mechanism per packet is needed to avoid redundant records from being sent. Here we create an algorithm to choose the best path for forwarding packets based on cost metric and the capacity of nodes to select acceptable levels to monitor operating conditions [1, 4] .

16.3   System Model

We regard a centralized wireless network consisting of N nodes distributed randomly in two-dimensional areas, with each node stagnating and fitted with a single omnidirectional antenna (like an intelligent surveillance system and security alarm system). A packet is transferred to an organized node list by means of an imported opportunistic routing algorithm. This investigation provides the categorized source routing in the non-High Workload Packet Header and the usual low path length in a wireless network.

The network as a whole is defined as the connected undirected graph G= (V, N), where N is the node set and $|V|=N$ is the number of nodes. P denotes the set of all connections between pairs of nodes for bi-directional wireless communication. In the case where a node $i \in V$ transmits a data packet X with the full power Pt, and another node $j \in V$ has the ability to decode X effectively without the assistance of any other nodes, we say that a connection exits Pi, $j \in P$. The signal that was obtained from node i at node j can be expressed as

$$y^j = h^{i,j}w^iX + z^j \qquad (16.1)$$

Where zj is a zero-mean,
X is the unit of data packet
wi is the power control coefficient

The packet in the proposed routing is separated into blocks and the checksum is transmitted along with the packet to recognize whether or not a block received is compromised [13]. Since none of its down-stream endpoints have acquired those blocks, a node may move ahead to transmit blocks in a message; it will not continue to spread the blocks it gets. A node declares the interpretation of the data of a packet in a feedback frame; a node does not probably send a packet until it receives its response from its down-stream endpoint, or until it has a timeout.

16.3.1   Dividing Packets Into Blocks

The node divides a packet into blocks and calculates the checksum for blocks. In addition to the message, control sums are assigned in the frame header. Every checksum frame in our current condition is 50 bytes; obviously less could be the last frame depending on the packet size. In an incomplete packet, checksum were used to distinguish the handled blocks. If you pass the checksum test of the received packet and do not have to check each row for the Hash value. If not, then it will be limited to packages. Therefore the node uses incomplete packet checksum to recognize the manipulated blocks. Instead of using prevalent 32-bit CRCs that have greater capabilities for error handling, we use a 16-bit CRC represented by

$$X^{16} + X^{15} + X^2 + 1$$

Because of its greater trade between overhead and detection capacity.

16.3.2   Packet Transmission

Once a node frame is received on the route it contributes the packet's identical frames to its queue. The node does not instantaneously transmit the packet as its message might have been adequately received by one of its downstream nodes, or even by a few frames inside. It would then inspect for feedback from the message for a timeout that is addressed at 15 ms in our initial configuration until the packet frame is distributed. Normally, a route in a wireless network alone has no more than five bumps and therefore the latency of the network does not greatly improve with a 15-ms packet; but, 15 ms should enable downstream entities to receive feedback. If the recipient uses the feedback from the backend endpoints, and if the recipient instructs it to have all the frames that the downstream nodes need, then the frames that are missing from the downstream endpoints are assigned for transmission. If no feedback has been obtained until transmission is finished, an attenuation will be arranged for the entire packet if it is received appropriately. The full messages are being sent in single frames within our current iteration; transmission of data blocks received considerably at the consolidated downstream endpoints, then sent to a single frame. Since the maximum data rates are suitable for different flows, only frames which make a significant contribution to the same flow can be integrated. The node may resend a packet or frames in a packet if it is not contacted by the backend endpoints that it has adequately received the packet or frames. Data transfer partitioned by at least 15 ms, and distributed up to five times a packet, after which it is lost.

16.3.3   Feedback

Under the following characteristics a device may coordinate a feedback for a packet in the implemented routing:

1) When this is the next origin hop and has an incomplete packet size with not only about 50% of the appropriate block.
2) If the sender is downstream but not the next hop, and has received at least 50% of the appropriate frames in the message;

Feedback from a packet is 8 bytes consisting of the packet ID and the bitmap of the blocks obtained similar to that of an ACK. Feedback is a network layer component, differentiate from the means of communication of ACKs, and often sent in a frame to the previous hop node. Feedback is sent in a single frame and not integrated with data packets, as a feedback block may be sent to secure way at a lower data rate. The feedback rate on the correlation to the prior hop node is selected in our current iteration as the highest rate with obtaining ratio of messages no less than 0.6.

Feedback may not be forwarded promptly and may be collated with feedback to error code for several other frames; only feedback may be integrated for the same flow compared to the data packets. For instance, if a node has not accepted a packet but recognizes that the packet has been obtained from a message from one of its downstream entities, it will notify its upstream entities so that they will no longer need to submit the packet. More explicitly, if the host distributes a feedback from its endpoint downstream, with its own bitmap and use the new bitmap as the information. When the node detects a downstream node that communicates those frames of a packet, this is a huge indicator that these downstream entities have certain blocks accurately, it will do the identical bitmap of this packet.

Feedback may not be sent instantly and may be collated with feedback for other communications to minimize errors; only feedback for nearly the same flow compared to data packets can be combined which can trigger the two major limitations into a consolidated feedback framework:

- 15 ms scheduled since feedback.
- eight new feedbacks scheduled.

When an entity analyzes a packet that contains no less than five right frames more upstream nodes when the ACK packet is not acquired from its instantaneous node to upstream as shows in Figure 16.2.

- First, feedback header.
- Input loop accompanied by input numeric pattern. The amount of feedback information is the optimum number of packets that contains information within the current point of reference, both in limited packets as well as in the correct messages.
- CRC1 is the header for MAC checksum, and the header for the data frame. If this feedback message is an incomplete packet, the receiver will discard a feedback frame which appears to lack this CRC, it could not decode the header information.
- The packet control messages field, in the Input data field, comprises the packet hash value obtained by the input nodes.

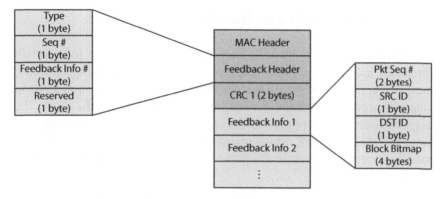

Figure 16.2 Feedback frame format.

Upstream nodes use the source ID and destination ID to assess which data flows are part of that packet.

• The block bitmap attribute governs which packet blocks the current node is appropriately receiving.

Routing Algorithm

A-> { X}
$P_1 (\delta)$ -> (δ, X) for all 1<=δ<N. Candidate paths are set as empty
While A belongs to all entities do
Let Vu be the best candidate path.
A->AU {a}
For all V_j do
For k = 1 to w do
P-> [$P_k (a)$, ß]
Let P_t (ß) be the candidate path ß.
End For
End For
End While

First, path computations are executed by origin only for each flow; second, each node on a predetermined route will implement rate evaluation. Second, path measurement can be very difficult and can include the shifted topology and traffic circumstance of the overall infrastructure; hence the route is only infrequently computed. But at the other hand, the wireless channel can vary substantially at a very high velocity, and can only be regulated by a detector for speedy rate preference.

16.4   Experiments and Results

Every simulation runs 50s. The network was originally set to a certain threshold, and each endpoint is set to run at the acceptable speed under these available bandwidths. Then we randomly pick the starting steps to take into account the channel situation for the duration of the study. The suggested method is opposed to the standard, opportunistic routing protocol (MORE) and SPP, which stands for shortest path routing without handling overheard packets and partial packets. The standard protocol for shortest path routing.

Until forwarding, MORE mixes packets randomly, which means that the routers that overhear the same transmission do not forward the same packets. For the synchronization of routers, MORE does not need a special scheduler. You can directly run MORE on top of 802.11. It applies network coding to the OR in this manner. Unicasting and multicasting are provided by MPRE. Unlike ExOR, which is an unreasonable scheme to use the nodes based on their priorities, the use of ETX in MORE is not acceptable since MORE is a rational method. ETX does not demand that candidate nodes with priorities be chosen and handled on the basis of various priorities. Moreover, it does not implement schemes to manage errors and rate control.

An opportunistic routing protocol built for wireless mesh networks is MORE, which stands for MAC independent Opportunistic Routing. MORE, like other opportunistic routing protocols such as ExOR and SOAR, eliminates reliance on the MAC layer. A scheduler to manage transmission between the nodes is used by both ExOR and SOAR. At a given time, only one node is transmitting, and all the other nodes are listening. This transmission node deletes the packets that they have queued for retransmission upon listening. This ensures that separate nodes do not redundantly retransmit the same packet.

In each test, we distribute Data packets from an origin to destination, called a flow. The results of 100 track flows with not less than two track lengths are received according to this routing; the proportion of track lengths 2 to 7 is 42, 33, 19, 7, 5 and 2 respectively. We operate SPP, MORE and proposed occasional routing based on feedback in our test bed. Increasing experiment required to finish 60 s. The packet size of all three configurations is 1,000 bytes. We gather readings before running an experiment to assess the probability distribution of delivering link packets, which are then fed into SPP and MORE. Similar calculations are used through scheduled route selection routing as shown in Figure 16.3. For each source-destination pair, we track the average by scheme throughput.

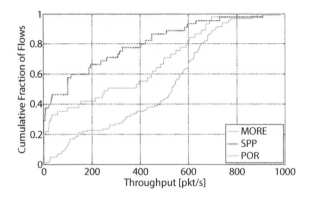

Figure 16.3 Throughput comparison POR Vs conventional opportunistic routing protocols.

Each point represents the output of a specific source—target set; points just above single direction indicate a rise with the proposed routing. We can see that the proposed routing in most streams is equal to or better than SPP. MORE may exceed proposed routing on certain flows; Nonetheless, the proposed routing benefit over MORE on other flows is significantly greater, which is why the implemented routing accomplishes a better overall effectiveness. We can see that the proposed routing scale and proportion across the whole spectrum of throughputs; the advantages for poor quality routes are higher and for great quality routes are smaller.

The links between the lost ratio of the packet and the path cost in Figure 16.4 are shown when the path hop count is 4. The results suggest that when the cost of the route is significant the loss ratio of the packs is increased, because if the route value is low, the route may require some

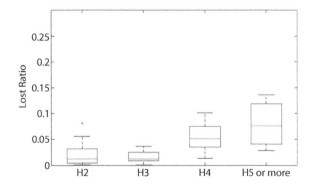

Figure 16.4 Packet loss ratio.

very weak points and loss in some way is inevitable. We can see that the proposed routing results in a low end-to-end packet loss ratio: if the hop count is less than 3, the incomplete ratio is less than 1%, and the hop count is even below 5%. We mention the fact that trails of greater than 4 are unusual for precise wireless mesh networks since such paths cannot keep large bandwidth.

The average transmitting power of POR is shown in Figure 16.5. Opportunity routing proposed for the integration of large flows. The test node bed appears in Figure 16.6. In addition to testing the one-flow IP packets, we operate POR with numerous flows. Due to the lack of a specific concomitant flows in the MORE code which we only test with SPP POR. By selecting source and destination combinations at random, we conduct 40 inter-flow experiments, resetting the number of specific active flows in the network. Various flow outputs are heavily dependent on many problems well beyond this task, including network-wide load balance. But we can see that POR is better than SPP.

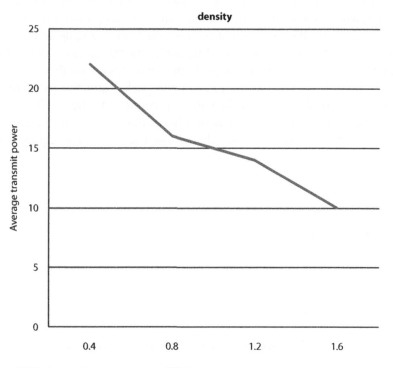

Figure 16.5 Average transmit power—POR.

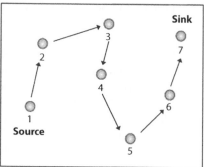

Figure 16.6 Node test bed.

16.5 Conclusion

The proposed opportunistic routing protocol for high-speed, multi-rate wireless mesh networks that do not require packet batching, has high efficiency and is full of great-performance, partial packets. We conclude that the proposed routing solution has these important characteristics and is therefore more reasonable and efficient than the current opportunistic routing algorithms for wireless mesh networks. We develop a packet transmission system for the forwarding of individual packets. We design an integrated per-packet feedback mechanism so that duplicate data is not sent out. The method chooses the appropriate path for forwarding packets based on a new path cost metric which takes into consideration both the cost of sending feedback and the capacity of nodes to select appropriate levels to measure the channel condition.

References

1. Kashani, Azimi, A., Ghanbari, M. and Rahmani, A., Improving the performance of Opportunistic Routing Protocol using the Evidence theory for VANETs in Highways. *IET Commun.*, 13, 20, 3360–3368, 2019.
2. Baek, K., Seo, D., Chung, Y., an Improved Opportunistic Routing Protocol Based on Context Information of Mobile Nodes. *Appl. Sci.*, 8, 1344, 2018.
3. Boukerche, A. and Darehshoori Zadeh, A., Opportunistic Routing in Wireless Networks: Models, Algorithms, and Classifications. *ACM Comput. Surv.*, 47, 1–36, 2014.

4. Hajer, H. and Bouallegue, R., *Comparative Analysis of Opportunistic Routing Protocol Algorithms in Wireless Sensor Network*, pp. 158–163, 2018.
5. Hsu, C.-J., Liu, H.-I., Seah, W., Opportunistic routing—A review and the challenges ahead. *Comput. Networks*, 55, 3592–3603, 2011.
6. Ismail, N. and Mohamad, M., Review on energy efficient opportunistic routing protocol for underwater wireless sensor networks. *KSII Trans. Internet Inf. Syst.*, 12, 3064–3094, 2018.
7. Jadhav, P. and Satao, R., A Survey on Opportunistic Routing Protocols for Wireless Sensor Networks. *Proc. Comput. Sci.*, 79, 603–609, 2016.
8. Lee, G. and Zygmunt, H., Simple, Practical, and Effective Opportunistic Routing for Short-Haul Multi-Hop Wireless Networks. *IEEE Trans. Wireless Commun.*, 10, 3583–3588, 2011.
9. Lu, M. and Wu, J., *Opportunistic Routing Algebra and its Applications*, pp. 2374–2382, 2009.
10. Mazumdar, Prokash, A. and Sairam, A., Opportunistic routing: opportunities and challenges. *International Journal of Information and Electronics Engineering*, 2, 2, 247, 2012.
11. Minamiguchi, C., Kawabata, N., Nakamura, R., Ohsaki, H., *A Study on Comparative Analysis of End-to-End Routing and Opportunistic Routing*, pp. 955–958, 2018.
12. Rahman, Z., Hashim, F., Rasid, M., Othman, M., Totally opportunistic routing algorithm (TORA) for underwater wireless sensor network. *PLoS One*, 13, 6, e0197087, 2018.
13. Saidi, H., Driss, G., Addaim, A., Opportunistic Routing In Wireless Sensors Networks. *In Proceedings of the 2nd international conference on computing and wireless communication systems*, pp. 1–5, 2017.
14. Triviño-Cabrera, A. and Cañadas-Hurtado, S., Survey on Opportunistic Routing in Multihop Wireless Networks. *Int. J. Commun. Netw. Inf. Secur.*, 3, 170–177, 2011.

17

Enabling Artificial Intelligence and Cyber Security in Smart Manufacturing

R. Satheesh Kumar[1]*, G. Keerthana[2], L. Murali[3], S. Chidambaranathan[4], C.D. Premkumar[5] and R. Mahaveerakannan[5]

[1]*Department of CSE, Sahrdaya College of Engineering and Technology, Thrissur, India*
[2]*Anna University, Chennai, India*
[3]*Department of ECE, P.A. College of Engineering and Technology, Pollachi, Tamil Nadu, India*
[4]*St. Xavier's College (Autonomous), Palayamkottai, India*
[5]*Department of IT, Hindusthan College of Engineering and Technology, Coimbatore, India*

Abstract

SM (Smart Manufacturing) is a broad category of manufacturing that employs a computer-based integrated manufacturing system, with a higher end of new adaptability and quick change in design structure, along with digitalization and effective workforce training. It is necessary to incorporate new techniques in the SM system to adapt to the changes in the present system. Smart factories increase the output of the unit, quality, and consistency maintenance by satisfaction for the customers. Smarter technology helps to get information with the help of computed technology in the organization through which the information/data will be recorded periodically. The Smart Manufacturing system [5] which is very safer for the environment is known to us as Green Manufacturing (GM). Green-tech or Green Manufacturing [1] is an umbrella term which comes under the same branch in one way or another which is used in several technologies or the field of science in order to bring up with products which are eco-friendly for the environment. Usage of circular manufacturing in industries [2] to save energy and reduce waste by which GM is incorporated in industries/factories etc. GM is the most needed one which may lead to a higher level of development in the aspect of the economy. Moreover, the confidentiality of the information and the vulnerabilities they come with SM systems is also needs to be solved when it comes to Cyber security. Hence,

---

*Corresponding author: satheeshpkd@gmail.com

R. Kanthavel, K. Ananthajothi, S. Balamurugan and R. Karthik Ganesh (eds.) *Artificial Intelligent Techniques for Wireless Communication and Networking*, (269–286) © 2022 Scrivener Publishing LLC

we have proposed an efficient green manufacturing approach in SM systems with the aid of Artificial Intelligence (AI) and cyber security frameworks. The proposed work employs a Dual stage ANN to find the design configuration of SM systems in industries. Then, for maintaining the data confidentiality while communication, the data are encrypted by using 3DES approach.

Keywords: Intelligent manufacturing, artificial intelligence, cyber security, green manufacturing, artificial neural network, data analytics, IoT, deep learning

17.1   Introduction

The advanced technological revolution and revolution in industries [3] are gaining more attention. The new era is getting enhanced with the usage of the internet along with the integration of AI in it which is responsible for bringing in more changes in the upcoming time in several fields. The other technologies rapped up with the internet and AI in their application will bring advancement in that particular field and will definitely be a game-changer of that corresponding place. When compared to other industries manufacturing sectors are capable of providing a livelihood for many. The fusion of several technologies like communication, intelligent-based, product-based technology in manufacturing industries is considered a game-changer in that sector in terms of a new approach in manufacturing and its entire system. Figure 17.1 illustrates the characteristics, design principles and enabling technology defining smart manufacturing.

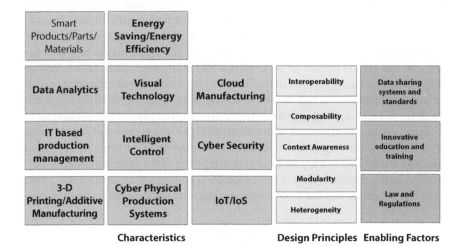

Figure 17.1 Characteristics, design principles and enabling technology defining smart manufacturing.

17.2 New Development of Artificial Intelligence

AI has proved its advancement in several applications like sensors, big data management, e-commerce, development of information technology, space, cybersecurity, the structure and pattern of AI have brought in advancement in its system itself known as Artificial Intelligence 2.0. AI 2.0 is the new stage of artificial intelligence research [10] which is highly different from that of the past 60 years older one. The newer version of AI known as the AI 2.0 helps in intensive deep learning (DL) with the obtained data, swarm intelligence, hybrid-based augmented reality, cross-media engagement, etc. The evolution in Smart city, medical field, transportation, logistics, robotics, smart vehicles, smartphones, toys, etc. with the help of artificial intelligence creates a huge demand in market space [6] which drives the value and need of the products more than before.

17.3 Artificial Intelligence Facilitates the Development of Intelligent Manufacturing

Intelligent manufacturing [8] is considered as the new manufacturing technique which has given scope for development in information technology, communication, advanced science, manufacturing sector, engineering, product manufacturing technology, which are also integrated by the means of the entire network with a new development from the base level.

Intelligent manufacturing is a wider range of innovation in manufacturing with the purpose of increased production, and transaction of products with the aim of utilizing advanced information in the manufacturing sector. The benefit of adapting intelligent manufacturing helps in detecting the activity and response to information, which same time helps in increasing the yield, quality, reduction in downtime, and also leads to improved overall equipment effectiveness. Through which competitive structure in the market improves by which particular industries with intelligent manufacturing will be able to show its capability as a stronger competitor in that firm among other competitors.

According to Li et al., AI technology has brought in development in the model in all aspects from the basic level of the system up to the end of the system. This new adaption of techniques in the system helps in providing better production and a better service system to the users.

The new means of adaption in technology involves smart manufacturing with digitalization, IoT, virtual reality, a collaboration of technology,

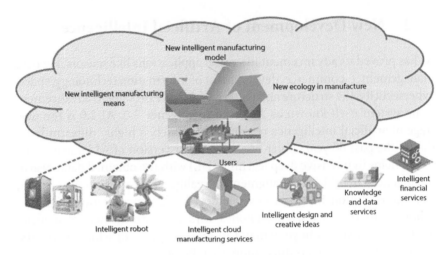

Figure 17.2 New models, means, and forms of intelligent manufacturing.

flexibility, and intelligent-system. The new forms of adaption in technology involve intelligent manufacturing with interconnection, data-driving, cross-sector integration, innovation, and an autonomy-based intelligent system. The deep integration in this new model is about the usage of all new means, and form in the advanced intelligent system. Figure 17.2 illustrates this structure in detail as follows.

17.4   Current Status and Problems of Green Manufacturing

17.4.1   Green Manufacturing

It is a well-known fact that the manufacturing industry [7] has faced three major revolutions in this sector and ongoing is the 4th revolution which is illustrated in Figure 17.3. The first three revolutions helped in bringing change in the production and development of the economy. The present 4th revolution is described as SMART MANUFACTURING which is expected to bring in changes with the help of utilizing a more advanced technological system [12].

Chemicals and petroleum were considered as an important component for the process industry [13]. The petrochemical industry has brought a big change for the development of the economy of the country but it has brought an equal amount of negative aspects in health and environmental

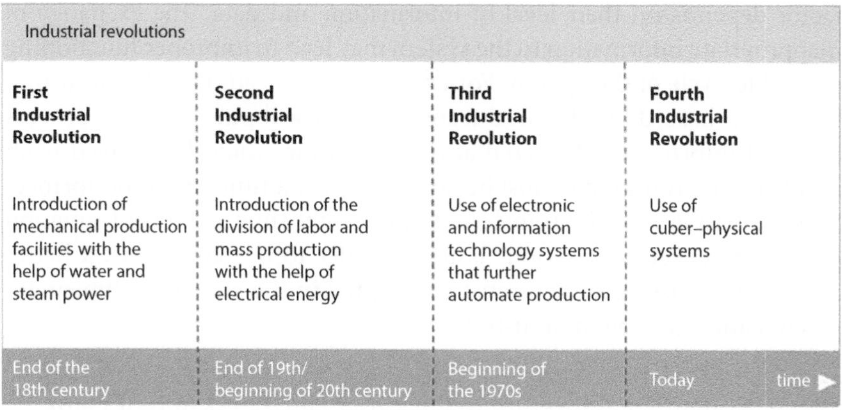

Industrial revolutions			
First Industrial Revolution	**Second Industrial Revolution**	**Third Industrial Revolution**	**Fourth Industrial Revolution**
Introduction of mechanical production facilities with the help of water and steam power	Introduction of the division of labor and mass production with the help of electrical energy	Use of electronic and information technology systems that further automate production	Use of cuber–physical systems
End of the 18th century	End of 19th/ beginning of 20th century	Beginning of the 1970s	Today time ▶

Figure 17.3 Four industrial revolutions.

damage [4] for people by the means of a frequent accident and raise in pollution level [14]. In this present era accidents in industries gain more attention because of widespread information through news, and social media. This makes the government more careful by providing a standard set of rules and regulations for industries/factories. This creates more demand for Green Manufacturing [16]. The cause of environmental damage [9] because of the petrochemical industry will have more impact on the surrounding system. When considering the demand for the process industry that is gained in India, there is an immediate need for addressing the issue of energy consumption and emission by that industry need for immediate environmental protection [17, 18]. Green Manufacturing is the only solution to achieve safety, lesser consumption of energy, and lesser-level of emission from industries. It tries to track the issue with the help of process life-cycle through smart monitoring, beforehand warning, effective decision making, and pollution reduction. It can improve the efficiency and safety of process industries, and it is highly demanded the means of economic development.

17.4.2   Current Status and Major Problems

The problems faced by industries due to green manufacturing have been discussed as follows in the sections below.

17.4.2.1   Isolation of Information Among Multiple Fields

In the process industry, some factors like storage, production, and transportation, waste management are interrelated to one and another. But each factor depends on their level of information and data. The exchange of inappropriate information to the system may lead to improper functioning of the life-cycle of the system. For example, if misleading or late information about hazardous chemical transportation will put the entire process at risk if information delivered at the right time would have saved from accidents and things that must be done at the right time will be performed. So information must be transferred at the right time lack of information passing may lead to a serious issue. In order to overcome this, a better information passing system must be adopted in the system to implement green manufacturing in industries.

17.4.2.2 Diverse Information Types and Different Kinds of Data

The different levels of knowledge will be preferred for the different processes such as transportation, manufacturing, and storage have their own level of information system and working system. The information about pressure, temperature level is important to overcome the unexpected situation and other issues. In the aspect of transportation, the information about the destination, status of a vehicle, information about drivers is considered to be important. The above-mentioned information will sometime be stored in a different system in such a situation it will be difficult to process the information to one and another due to format in data, and information collecting method [36]. When proper information is not obtained at right time may lead to a lack of a process of the life-cycle of the system. There are different methods involved during the process of collecting information and computing all those collected information in the system may require more time and be considered a challenging task.

17.4.2.3 Lack of a Process-Safety-Oriented Decision-Making System

The utilization of Geometric magnification in the process industry and petrochemical industry will help in reducing the cost and helps in gaining more benefits in the firm, which enables larger production and supply in the market space. The industry will be seen as one within a single city, individual province, but the result of support will be seen as a whole across the nation. Industries in the aspect of production and supply need help national-wide for the purpose of transport, storing materials, in order to satisfy the needs of the customer who live in areas populated in a different region. The bulk storage of hazardous material may lead to risk in storage for nearby communities.

In production, the scale-up process needs full control of the system, perfect operation by a human, and good condition mechanical integrity. If problems are not handled properly in the initial stage may lead to a bigger error in the system in the future. Risk management technique has been taken into consideration while developing petrochemical plants with the support of tackling the problem during dangerous situation by identifying and managing it some risk management analysis may help in a typical situation they are HAZOP (hazard and operability analysis), LOPA (layer of protection analysis), SIL (system integrity level).

The problem must be analyzed from the base level so that the error from the beginning stage will be eradicated but maintaining risk management information is considered a challenging task.

The operator behavior is highly dependent on provided training and management skills to him [19, 20]. The accident which occurred in a chemical factory in Germany known as BASF leads to economic loss and casualties. This accident was due to the operation failure of one part of the tools/machine. A proper decision must be taken before operating a system in order to overcome operation failure. In such a situation an intelligent system is needed to handle the issue and suggest proper steps to overcome it.

This kind of system will help with the progress of the system when compared to human capacity. One of the important factors for practicing safety is to have a system with no error or mistake so that hazardous situation will never occur in real-time.

17.4.2.4   Lack of Early Warning and Risk Tracing Systems

The accidents in the process industry are very severe due to lack of an efficient warning [21]. The operation petrochemical industry is based on its own level of restriction in each sector and they are capable of addressing it. But the small effect will sometimes lead to a bigger instance and the system will face downstream because of critical issues.

The accidents will be addressed with the experience of dealing with the same kind of instance which would have happened before. To overcome these problems the system must be capable of understanding the abnormalities as soon as possible so that the problem will be addressed in the initial stage itself.

The diagnosing function must provide a solution for the present real-time problem and must have the potential for handling it and to overturn the situation to the normal one. A decision-making system is needed to deal with the issue. But due to several reasons, a smart system for dealing with accidental situations is still not available at the present time.

17.5   Artificial Intelligence for Green Manufacturing

Machine Intelligence is the branch of automation and CS (Computer Science) [22]. With Artificial intelligence, machine intelligence will interact with machines or the environment intelligently. Artificial intelligence combines with other branches like CS, Engineering, mathematics, automation, and psychology to obtain knowledge from that branch. The issues/problems faced by artificial intelligence are illustrated in Figure 17.4.

The problems of Green Manufacturing can be categorized into four groups based on their characteristics:

- Integration of information
- Risk management
- Help during decision making
- Early warming.

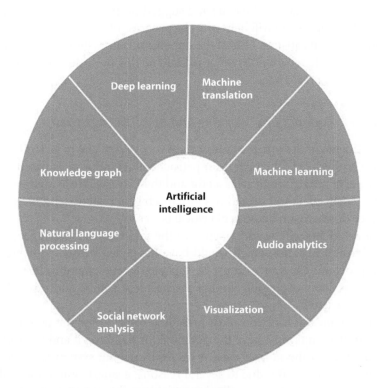

Figure 17.4 Several sub-problems in Artificial intelligence.

Many techniques and solutions can address the problems faced by Green Manufacturing. Some of the problem-solving factors will be discussed in detail in the following section.

17.5.1   Information Integration via Knowledge Graphs

Knowledge Graph is the best-known technique involved in addressing linked data management in Artificial Intelligence. This graph is a semantic structure that helps in describing the concept and the relationship within the system. This graph will provide reasoning and advanced rules based on the concept of deep learning (DL) [11].

Knowledge Graphs are highly preferred in internet-based applications like social networking, internet-based financial system, social security, and encyclopedia [23, 24].

The process industry needs more specific information in the areas of specialization in the fields of chemical engineering, safety, control, automation system, and mechanical side. The knowledge graph can only be implemented in the industry with a complete idea about the working structure of the graph.

Implementation of the knowledge graph needs more understanding of the required field [25]. Figure 17.5 illustrates the model for building a knowledge graph the implementation of the knowledge graph is categorized into three stages are discussed in the sections below.

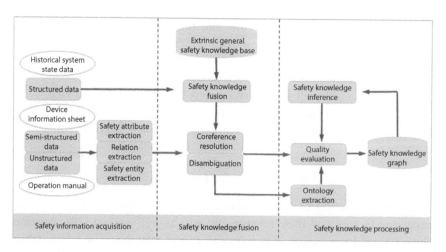

Figure 17.5 Technical architecture of a typical knowledge graph [25].

17.5.1.1   Process-Safety Information Extraction

[26] The Knowledge graph will be constructed with relevant information about certain factors like safety, chemicals, documents, controlling system, information, risk management factors, etc. [26]. To collect the above-mentioned data diversity of information, coverage of information by the means of all aspects like tables, graphs, charts, texts, and diagrams, etc. must be obtained [27, 28]. The main aim of the knowledge graph is to address linked data and to generate the information of individual entities and their relationship between information from various sources. This process of gathering information is known as the extraction of an entity, extraction of relationship, and extraction of an attribute.

- *Extraction of entity*: This refers to the identification of entity from text automatically. It is the most beginning part of information extraction. In the process, factor information extraction depends on ontology schema [37] in order to obtain factors that cause risk. The data extraction is done through manual operation or through maintaining sheets, P & IDs (piping and instrumentation diagrams), and PFD (process flow diagram).
- *Extraction of Relationship*: It is the 2nd step in the process of extracting information in this step the relationship between the extracted entities will be identified. These steps will take place through semantic information or charts, tables, and diagrams. In the petrochemical industry, the information related to safety measures will be generated through documents. In order to know the relationship about factors causes risk will require a deep understanding of the factors reason for this kind of hazardous situation.
- *Extraction of Attribute*: Each factor reason for accidents may have a different section of reasons to point out. In this step, all the attributes which are reasonable for creating an issue must be addressed and qualified to overcome the problem.

17.5.1.2   Process-Safety Knowledge Fusion

With the extraction of safety information the complete reason for risk involving factors and their relationship will be well-known [29]. Anyone the obtained information may have errors and mistakes. The relationship obtained will be flat, improper connecting point, and logical. With the implementation of knowledge fusion, this kind of mistake or errors will be eliminated.

17.5.1.3   Process-Safety Knowledge Processing

After the implementation of knowledge fusion, the errors will be eliminated. Then a set of factual articulations will be expressed. The analysis regarding safety is important in the process safety step. The reason for the main hazard and reason for the incident must be identified and avoided completely. Safety-related knowledge is needed for understanding the issue completely especially about the processing of chemicals, equipment, operation, and other mechanisms. The other smaller factors reason for issue must also be addressed gradually to identify the error in the beginning stage and the factor which is responsible for downstream must also be diagnosed with the help of predefined rules and knowledge. The knowledge processing involves 3 most important aspects which will be discussed in detail in the following section.

Safety ontology reconstruction: The term Ontology refers to a set of models and factors reason for describing the concept to the objective world. This term refers to the concept of knowledge and its relationship. This process can be developed through brainstorming with present knowledge.

Reason for risk in obtained relationship: Reasoning helps in identifying the key relationship between the present entity based on a set of rules [30, 31]. Reasoning can be classified into reasoning based on logic-term, and reasoning based on the graphical method.

Assessment of quality: It is also one of the important aspects of developing a process safety knowledge graph. The obtained data will still have errors and mistakes even through obtained through the state-of-the-art method. Before the process of merging the newly obtained data and data obtained from the knowledge graph, a quality assessment is essential for evaluating the process. The knowledge graph provides a proper method for integrating information into the process industry. The problems like divergence in data, information gap, and representation of complex relationships will be addressed with the help of a knowledge graph.

17.5.2   Risk Assessment and Decision-Making Using Bayesian Networks

Bayesian networks are a type of Probabilistic Graphical Model that can be used to build models from data/and expert opinion [32, 33]. In the processing factory, the reason for abnormalities may be due to several probabilistic relationships.

The important five parameters must be addressed while analyzing hazardous reactions. Those five parameters include temperature, hot-material flow rate, heated material flow rate, and coking degree in furnace tubes. These mentioned parameters will have different probabilistic deviations.

The Bayesian network will address the complex probabilistic relationships between the above-mentioned parameter and the runaway reaction. This process can be used for other kinds of accidents and other factors involving risk. In order to obtain accurate performance, the parameters of the Bayesian network must be handled carefully to achieve better performance.

The Bayesian network can track the risk factors more accurately. And it can also provide a solution for an emergency situation depending on the abnormalities involved in it.

17.5.3   Incident Early Warning Based on Deep Learning

Deep learning (DL) is an artificial intelligence-based function that mimics the working of the human brain in processing data for the purpose of detecting objects, recognizing speech, language translation, and decision making, which helps to learn without human intervention and supervision [34]. In the process industry, the chances for accidents are mainly due to fluctuation in data. Composition change in the system may lead to more generation of heat which may narrow the working of the system.

DL helps in recognizing the reason for the accident and other factors involved in the occurrence of this accident [15] will also be found. If clear information regarding data, equipment, and human operation was present in such a case the reason behind the accident will be found and steps to rectify it will be found.

Labeling of big data is an important step in DL and other related techniques and identification of risk and its evaluation [35]. But in reality, obtained big data may have mistakes and errors. So the present data are inadequate and with zero percent accuracy. Moreover, the industries will highly depend on expert advice and alarm from the system.

17.6   Detailed Description of Common Encryption Algorithms

The Encryption algorithm helps in generating, modifying, and transporting key data. The encryption algorithm is also termed as a cryptographic algorithm. The power of the encryption algorithm is based on a Computer system which is utilized for generating keys. In this research paper, Triple-DES is used for encrypting data in order to maintain data confidentiality during the process of communication.

17.6.1   Triple DES (3DES)—(Triple Data Encryption Standard)

The 3DES may also be referred to as TDEA (Triple Data Encryption Algorithm) which was developed by IBM during 1998. This was found to be a replacement of DES because of the improved structure and DES was applied three times in the data block. The DES with 56 bit was enough in the initial time during the early designing process but in a later period due to an increase in power of computing the attack realizable.

3DES is a simplistic method while considering the design pattern of the whole block cipher and its capacity against forceful attack. The forceful attack tries to attack harder until getting the original message. The DES is embedded with a 56-bit key size and 3DES with 138 bit. The length of the key for 3DES is 112 and 168 bits respectively for 48 rounds and the size of the block is 64.

The main aim of this algorithm is to maximize security with a longer length key. The Ks—size of the key, Nk—number of keys, Tr 1 D—time needed for one decryption, and Tr 106 D—time needed for 106 decryption.

The advantage of 3DES is considered as thrice the size of the key (2,168) when compared to the key size (256) of DES. This is the main reason for 3DES to be preferred over DES. It gives an adequate amount of security for the information but at the same time, it requires more time for encryption when compared to DES. The 3DES algorithm is represented as follows:

C = EncryptK3(DecryptK2(EncryptK1(P)

(3) and decryption algorithm of 3DES is given as follows:

P = DecryptK3(EncryptK2(DecryptK1(C)

(4) Where C represented the ciphertext, P represented the plaintext and K1, K2, K3 represent the keys.

[9] The 3DES in the following years shall be defined as

- To overcome the forceful attack of the DES with the utilization of 168 bits size of the key.
- The 3DES is almost similar to that of the DES in many ways.

The 3DES algorithm for the purpose of security will be the best choice for a standard encryption algorithm in the future. The main disadvantage of 3DES was considered to be the slower set of software systems because

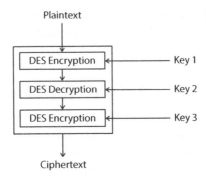

Figure 17.6 3DES structure.

it was developed in the early 1970s and the software is not efficient for the present time. The reason for the slow software structure is because it involves 3 more additional rounds.

The 2nd drawback in DES and 3DES is that the size of the block is 64 bit which is used and in the aspect of security the larger block size is preferred. The 3DES structure is illustrated in Figure 17.6.

17.7   Current and Future Works

To understand green manufacturing through Artificial Intelligence studies have been initiated relating to processing safety knowledge in delaying the coking process. The outcomes of this present paper are illustrated in Figure 17.7. The figure describes the entire method involved in this present research.

In the aspect of the knowledge graph, all the elements related to safety are observed including all the upper and lower factors involved in the parameter, the up and downstream in a relationship the reason for another parameter for the cause of the accident was also considered.

The visualization process and question answering was conducted to enhance the interaction between machine and human, which is an important factor for SM (Smart Manufacturing).

The cause and effect relationship between arbitrary deviation and their involvement downstream will be given more importance in the future study.

The downstream at the initial level will be analyzed with the help of decision making. The main aim is to address the current abnormal situation through the process monitoring method and to permit logical analysis to address the simple fault and events automatically. With the involvement

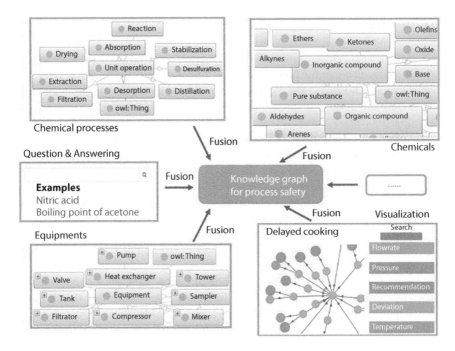

Figure 17.7 Framework of current and future works.

of more detailed data the knowledge graph, tracking of risk, and the process of decision making will be attained in future research proposals with the help of deep learning (DL) and Bayesian network.

17.8 Conclusion

This present research paper addressed the significance, present status, and other problems involved in Green Manufacturing in the terms of the process industry. Various techniques with the usage of Artificial Intelligence have been reviewed which includes the Bayesian network, knowledge graph, and DL. These factors helped in solving a significant problem faced by Green Manufacturing. The technical challenges in process safety were also discussed. Some of the challenges involved are the acquisition of knowledge and reasoning regarding error and mistakes in obtained data, beforehand warning regarding error/accident, and effective decision making. The possible factors for addressing the above-mentioned challenges were proposed and other achievements were detailed.

References

1. Mao, S. *et al.*, Opportunities and challenges of artificial intelligence for green manufacturing in the process industry. *Engineering*, 5, 6, 995–1002, 2019.
2. Qian, F., Zhong, W., Du, W., Fundamental theories and key technologies for smart and optimal manufacturing in the process industry. *Engineering*, 3, 2, 154–160, 2017.
3. Giffi, C.A., Rodriguez, M.D., Gangula, B., Roth, A.V., Hanley, T., *Global manufacturing competitiveness index*, Deloitte Touche Tohmatsu Limited Global Consumer & Industrial Products Industry Group and the Council on Competitiveness, London, 2016.
4. Williams, E., Environmental effects of information and communications technologies. *Nature*, 479, 7373, 354–358, 2011.
5. Smart Manufacturing Leadership Coalition, *Implementing 21st century smart manufacturing: Workshop summary report*, Smart Manufacturing Leadership Coalition, Washington, 2011.
6. State Council of the People's Republic of China, *New generation of artificial intelligence development plan* [Internet], State Council of the People's Republic of China, Beijing, 2017 Jul 8 [cited 2019 May 8].
7. Yuan, Z., Qin, W., Zhao, J., Smart manufacturing for the oil refining and petrochemical industry. *Engineering*, 3, 2, 179–182, 2017.
8. Zhou, J., Li, P., Zhou, Y., Wang, B., Zang, J., Meng, L., Toward new-generation intelligent manufacturing. *Engineering*, 4, 1, 11–20, 2018.
9. Cernansky, R., Chemistry: Green refill. *Nature*, 519, 7543, 379–380, 2015.
10. Russell, S.J. and Norvig, P., *Artificial intelligence: A modern approach*, Pearson Education Limited, Kuala Lumpur, 2016.
11. Silver, D., Huang, A., Maddison, C.J., Guez, A., Sifre, L., van den Driessche, G. *et al.*, Mastering the game of Go with deep neural networks and tree search. *Nature*, 529, 7587, 484–489, 2016.
12. Bogle, I.D.L., A perspective on smart process manufacturing research challenges for process systems engineers. *Engineering*, 3, 2, 161–165, 2017.
13. Chai, T., Industrial process control systems: research status and development direction. *Sci. Sin. Inf.*, 46, 8, 1003–1015, 2016 (Chinese).
14. Tauseef, S.M., Abbasi, T., Abbasi, S.A., Development of a new chemical process-industry accident database to assist in past accident analysis. *J. Loss Prev. Process Ind.*, 24, 4, 426–431, 2011.
15. Huang, P. and Zhang, J., Facts related to August 12, 2015 explosion accident in Tianjin, China. *Process Saf. Prog.*, 34, 4, 313–314, 2015.
16. Wang, B., Wu, C., Reniers, G., Huang, L., Kang, L., Zhang, L., The future of hazardous chemical safety in China: Opportunities, problems, challenges and tasks. *Sci. Total Environ.*, 643, 1–11, 2018.
17. Bond, J., Professional ethics and corporate social responsibility. *Process Saf. Environ. Prot.*, 87, 3, 184–190, 2009.

18. Dornfeld, D.A., *Green manufacturing: Fundamentals and applications*, Springer, New York, 2013.
19. Clark, J.H., Green chemistry: Challenges and opportunities. *Green Chem.*, 1, 1, 1–8, 1999.
20. BASF Corporation, *Fire at the North Harbor in Ludwigshafen* [Internet], BASF Corporation, Ludwigshafen, 2016 Oct 27 [cited 2019 May 8].
21. BASF Corporation, *German firefighter dies 11 months after BASF explosion* [Internet], Haarlem, Expatica, 2017 Sep 5 [cited 2019 May 8].
22. Qu, Z., Feng, H., Zeng, Z., Zhuge, J., Jin, S.A., SVM-based pipeline leakage detection and pre-warning system. *Measurement*, 43, 4, 513–519, 2010.
23. Paulheim, H., Knowledge graph refinement: A survey of approaches and evaluation methods. *Semant. Web*, 8, 3, 489–508, 2017.
24. Färber, M., Bartscherer, F., Menne, C., Rettinger, A., Linked data quality of DBpedia, Freebase, OpenCyc, Wikidata, and YAGO. *Semant. Web*, 9, 1, 77–129, 2018.
25. Ehrlinger, L. and Wöß, W., Towards a definition of knowledge graphs, in: *Proceedings of SEMANTICS 2016: Posters and Demos Track*, Leipzig, Germany, 2016 Sep 13–14, 2016.
26. Liu, Q., Li, Y., Duan, H., Liu, Y., Qin, Z., Knowledge graph construction techniques. *J. Comput. Res. Dev.*, 53, 3, 582–600, 2016.
27. Gordon, S.E., Schmierer, K.A., Gill, R.T., Conceptual graph analysis: Knowledge acquisition for instructional system design. *Hum. Factors*, 35, 3, 459–481, 1993.
28. Miwa, M. and Sasaki, Y., Modeling joint entity and relation extraction with table representation, in: *Proceedings of the 2014 Conference on Empirical Methods in Natural Language Processing*, Doha, Qatar, 2014 Oct 25–29, pp. 1858–69, 2014.
29. Paliouras, G., Spyropoulos, C.D., Tsatsaronis, G., *Knowledge-driven multimedia information extraction and ontology evolution: bridging the semantic gap*, Springer, Heidelberg, 2011.
30. Dong, X.L., Gabrilovich, E., Heitz, G., Horn, W., Murphy, K., Sun, S. *et al.*, From data fusion to knowledge fusion. *Proc. VLDB Endow.*, 7, 10, 881–892, 2014.
31. Wang, X., Gu, T., Zhang, D., Pung, H.K., Ontology based context modeling and reasoning using OWL. *Proceedings of the 2nd IEEE Annual Conference on Pervasive Computing and Communications Workshops*, Washington, DC, USA, 2004 Mar 14–17, IEEE, New York, pp. 18–22, 2004.
32. Kamsu-Foguem, B. and Noyes, D., Graph-based reasoning in collaborative knowledge management for industrial maintenance. *Comput. Ind.*, 64, 8, 998–1013, 2013.
33. Zhu, J., Ge, Z., Song, Z., Zhou, L., Chen, G., Large-scale plant-wide process modeling and hierarchical monitoring: A distributed Bayesian network approach. *J. Process Control*, 65, 91–106, 2018.

34. Larrañaga, P., Karshenas, H., Bielza, C., Santana, R., A review on evolution-ary algorithms in Bayesian network learning and inference tasks. *Inf. Sci.*, 233, 109–125, 2013.

35. LeCun, Y., Bengio, Y., Hinton, G., Deep learning. *Nature*, 521, 7553, 436–444, 2015.

36. Zhu, J., Ge, Z., Song, Z., Gao, F., Review and big data perspectives on robust data mining approaches for industrial process modeling with outliers and missing data. *Annu. Rev. Control*, 46, 107–133, 2018.

37. Zhou, Z., Qi, G., Glimm, B., Exploring parallel tractability of ontology materialization. *Proceedings of the 22nd European Conference on Artificial Intelligence*, 2016 Aug 29–Sep 2, Amsterdam, the Netherlands, IOS Press, Amsterdam, pp. 73–81, 2016.

18

Deep Learning in 5G Networks

G. Kavitha[1], P. Rupa Ezhil Arasi[1*] and G. Kalaimani[2†]

Muthayammal Engineering College, Namakkal, India
Sadhan Women's College of Engineering and Technology, Hydrabed, India

Abstract

In the era of 5G networks, traffic management is an essential task. Machine Learning techniques can be utilized to provide solution for traffic management in 5G networks. The traffic data can be maintained in a database and analyzed using various machine learning techniques. In this work, 3D CNN model is combined with RNN model for analyzing and classifying the network traffic into three various classes such as Maximum, Average and Minimum traffic. The result proves that the combined 3D CNN and RNN model provides better classification of network traffic.

Keywords: 5G Networks, Artificial intelligence, machine learning, deep learning, recurrent neural network, convolution neural network, traffic prediction, traffic loads

18.1 5G Networks

5G is a new global wireless standard for mobile network. 5G networks connect machines, objects and devices virtually together. The major advantages of 5G networks are high reliability, more network capacity, increased availability, low latency, higher performance, improved efficiency, etc. 5G networks also provide users with new experience and the networks establishes connections with new industries.

Figure 18.1 shows the first generation (1G) mobile network supported analog device for communication. Communication through Digital voice was bought into existence in Second Generation (2G) network through

---

Corresponding author: rupasharan@gmail.com
†*Corresponding author*: kalaimaniphd@gmail.com

R. Kanthavel, K. Ananthajothi, S. Balamurugan and R. Karthik Ganesh (eds.) *Artificial Intelligent Techniques for Wireless Communication and Networking*, (287–298) © 2022 Scrivener Publishing LLC

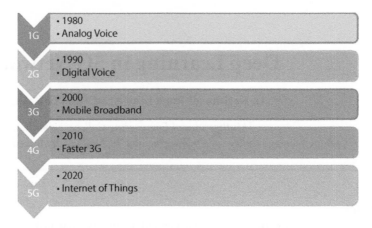

Figure 18.1 Evolution of 5G networks.

the usage of Code Division Multiple Access (CDMA) technology. Mobile data was introduced in third Generation (3G) and the Fourth Generation (4G) mobile network paved way for mobile broadband service. The 5G Technology provides more connectivity than the existing mobile networks. The technologies such as Mobile broadband, Mission Critical Services, and Internet of Things contributed for the evolution of 5G Technology.

A. 5G Network Architecture

The 5G network employed Radio Access Networks (RAN) in its architecture (Figure 18.2) [1]. Hence, 5G network is not complex and has an intelligent

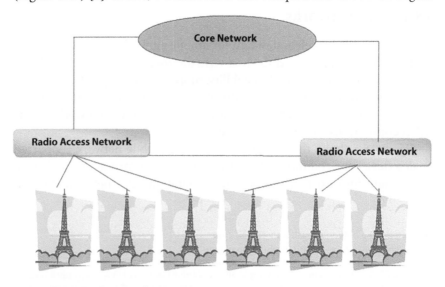

Figure 18.2 5G network architecture.

infrastructure. The intelligent network is updated with functional architecture, new host interfaces, protocols. The main transformations in the 5G network are Radio access network, new core and operations with massive MIMO antenna systems. The frequency range will be from 450 MHz to approximately 50 GHz.

The Radio Access Network (RAN) is formed by connecting various cells, mobile towers, systems, etc. The RAN then establishes the connection with the core network. The main responsibility of Core Network is to supervise the connections that exist among data, voice, etc. The Core Network provides faster response time by integrating itself with various cloud based services. The functionalities of Core Network include Network virtualization, Network Application slicing and so on.

B. Need for 5G Network

The world today is a cellular world and there is always a need for data management, network management and so on. Industries and Organizations are in need of fastest network and this leads to the evolution of 5G. 5G extends the reach of mobile broadband and hence it supports virtual reality, autonomous vehicle technology and it also provides improved data and network security.

C. Benefits of 5G Network

a) Internet of things connects billions of devices and 5G paves way for Machine to Machine communication in the interconnected network. This advancement laid the foundations for revolutions in various fields such as agriculture, education, healthcare, etc.

b) 5G provides Ultra reliable low latency communications. This is advantageous for remote medical care, treatments, robotics and automation and various safety systems.

c) 5G networks provide increased broadband than any other network. Hence the data are transferred at faster rate.

d) The 5G Network enables downloading and streaming contents with high speed hence it provides faster speeds in data access.

e) Increased Computing Power—5G provides spontaneous interconnections between the devices and hence offers enhanced computing power.

f) Increased Spectrum—With new 5G technology the mobile spectrum shows the radio frequency range above 6 Ghz.

g) Greater Capacity—The 5G network covers wide range of devices.

D) 5G Applications
The 5G networks play a vital role in various applications such as healthcare, transport, industrial automation, virtual and augmented reality, etc. (Figure 18.3).

E) 5G Requirements
5G Network architecture transfers data at 10 Gbps data rate in 1 ms latency. The Network covers more number of devices and provides battery life more than 10 years (Figure 18.4).

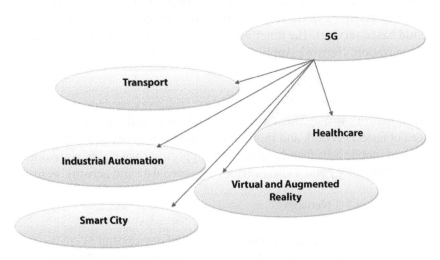

Figure 18.3 Applications of 5G.

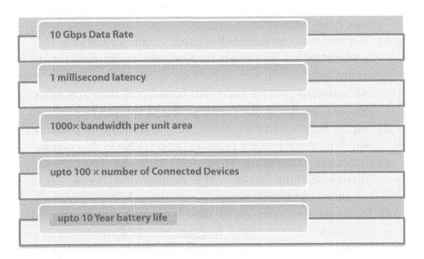

Figure 18.4 Requirements of 5G.

18.2   Artificial Intelligence and 5G Networks

Artificial intelligence (AI) enables machines to think and act like human beings. In recent times 5G and AI are the most innovative technologies. Employing AI to improve the performance of mobile networks also solves the existing issues in the wireless technology which cannot be solved using traditional methods.

AI has a strong effect on 5G network management. AI improves the quality, of service, simplifies deployment, provides higher network efficiency, and improves Network Security [2]. AI also detects various issues in the network infrastructure (Figure 18.5).

The objective of 5G networks is to provide low latency, high speed network that connects massive number of devices. AI and Machine Learning (ML) complement 5G networks with autonomous operations that transform 5G into a scalable real-time network. AI and ML can be used in all the layers of 5G Network, from Radio Access Layer, to Integrated access backhaul (IAB) and then to the distributed Cloud (Core) Layer. Hence, AI and ML complement 5G Technology in Network planning, Automating Network operations, Network Slicing, Reducing Operating Costs, etc.

A. AI in Radio Access Network Layer
AI and ML when implemented in RAN, improve the network's performance in three domains such as Network design, Network Optimization, and RAN algorithms (Figure 18.6). The RAN performance optimization depends upon the parameters utilized, the type and number of network

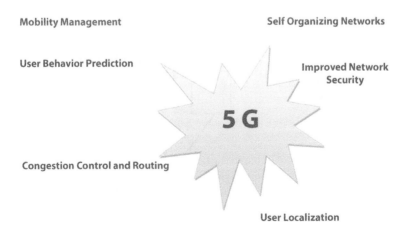

Figure 18.5 AI and 5G technology.

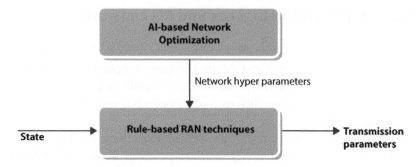

Figure 18.6 AI for RAN optimization.

objects involved, and the frequency at which network is updated. The performance optimization is obtained when RAN algorithms are replaced by AI controller.

B. AI in Integrated Access Backhaul (IAB) Layer
The objective of IAB network layer is to provide 5G networks at millimeter wave frequencies (mmWave) and AI can be utilized for improving the performance of IAB network layer (Figure 18.7).

C. AI in Core Layer
In the core layer, AI and ML can be utilized for System Resource Optimization, Autoscaling, Anomaly Detection, Predictive Analysis, Prescriptive Policies, etc.

In general, AI and ML when integrated with 5G Networks help in Network resource management, Network Security Optimization, Traffic management, Fault Prediction, and System Monitoring. Machine Learning

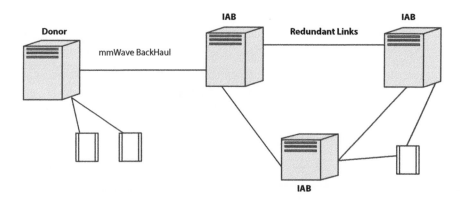

Figure 18.7 Integrated Access Backhaul (IAB).

algorithms consist of Representation, Evaluation and Optimization techniques to enhance the performance of 5G networks.

18.3 Deep Learning in 5G Networks

Deep Learning (DL) subset of Machine Learning Techniques extracts features automatically from the given data set. The extracted features are utilized by DNN (Deep Neural Network) in classifying the mobile data and in decision making. In 5G networks, DL is utilized for predicting and classifying the mobile applications, generating network slices, making routing decisions, providing network security and so on.

Convolution Neural Network (CNN) is a special type of Deep Neural Network (DNN) capable of handling large volume of data [3]. CNN is based upon the mathematical models such as convolutions and linear operations. CNN is mainly utilized for traffic flow prediction in 5G networks and object classification.

Recurrent Neural Network (RNN) [3] uses have long-short term memory to recollect the information learned in the previous steps in addition to the inputs. RNN provides a solution for mobility issues and helps in traffic prediction in 5G networks.

A. Research Challenges
Deep Learning is utilized to detect the issues in 5G network at various levels. At physical level, DL addresses channel state information (CSI) estimation, fault detection, device location prediction, coding/decoding scheme representation, radio frequency characterization, multi user detection, self interference and radio parameter definition, beam forming definition. DL at the Network level can be utilized for Traffic prediction and Anomaly detection. Finally, at the Application Level, DL techniques can be utilized for characterization of applications. But, there are various issues and challenges in integrating DL with 5G Networks (Figure 18.8).

The challenges in integrating DL and 5G Networks are [4]:

    a. Designing and Developing Mathematical models using DL is very difficult.

    b. DL models are capable of processing large variety of data but the solutions proposed offers only low computational complexity.

    c. Inclusion of new parameters might have an effect on Network Performance

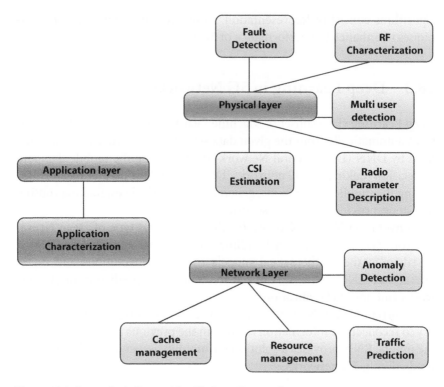

Figure 18.8 Research challenges identified in 5G network.

    d. Deep Learning techniques can be utilized only for networks with massive connections and the processing power of the devices might influence the utilization.

B. Deep Learning Based Traffic Prediction in 5G Networks
Evolution of modern communication media and 5G Networks had lead to the growth of traffic data. Managing Internet Traffic is the challenge to be faced by the researchers in the near future.

Traditional network traffic prediction methods are ineffective in handling the huge volume of network traffic data [5]. Hence, the solution is to design a network architecture that optimizes available network resources by employing appropriate scheduling techniques thereby minimizing energy consumption and avoiding the issues in the underlying network structure.

From the literatures, it is evident that a pro active network slice technique integrated with Deep Learning can be utilized for network traffic prediction [6]. Deep learning model based on spatial and temporal dependencies can also be utilized to predict the traffic [7]. Hence, a mobile traffic dataset when investigated using Deep Learning Neural Network [8] can classify the traffic as low, medium or high. CNN and RNN can be merged and utilized to extract geographical and temporal traffic features and predict the type of traffic (Figure 18.9).

The RNN [9] model comprises of Regression stage and Feature extraction stage. This RNN model accepts traffic data predicted at the final hour as its inputs. Then, various DL models can be utilized for feature extraction from the inputs. The features thus extracted are passed to the Regression Layer. The upper layer provides the output values.

The 3D-CNN model [10] along with the spatial, temporal information also utilizes the time for Traffic Prediction. The CNN model consists of three Pooling Layers and three Convolution Layers. The kernel size parameters and number of kernels vary in each convolution layers similar to stride size and pooling policy (Figure 18.10).

The 3D CNN model [11, 12] suits spatial domain and the RNN model suits time domain. The combined RNN and 3D CNN model description is given as Figure 18.11.

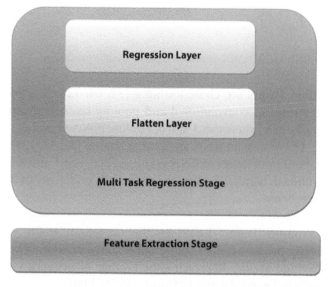

Figure 18.9 Recurrent neural network (RNN) model for traffic prediction.

Figure 18.10 3D CNN model for traffic prediction.

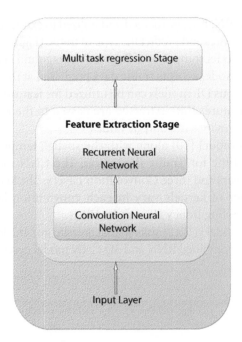

Figure 18.11 RNN and 3D CNN combined model for traffic prediction.

Convolution Layers are chosen among {32, 64, 128, 256, 512, 1024}. Kernel and strides in convolutional and pooling layers is given as {k,k}, where the value of k is between 1 and 6. Pooling policy is average poling or max poling. LSTM cells in RNN are chosen among {32, 64, 128, 256, 512, 1024}. The number of layers in RNN is chosen between 1 and 4.

At the multitask regression stage the traffic falls under any of the following three categories

- Maximum Traffic: Refers to the maximum traffic value among the six network traffic values in the upcoming hour.
- Average Traffic: Represents the average of network values predicted every 10 min in the upcoming hour
- Minimum Traffic: Refers to the minimum traffic value among the six network traffic values in the upcoming hour.

Conclusion

In the 5G network, each layer offers various functionalities but still there are some challenges that are to be addressed. The challenges at network

Recurrent Neural Network	Layer	Cells	Cell Type	Steps
	Layer 1	256	LSTM	6
	Layer 2	256	LSTM	6

Convolution Neural Network	Layer	No. of kernels	Kernel Size	Stride size	Pooling Policy
	Convolution 1	64	5,5	1,1	
	Pooling 1		2,2	2,2	Maximum
	Convolution 2	128	5,5	1,1	
	Pooling 2		2,2	2,2	Average
	Convolution 3	64	5,5	1,1	
	Pooling 3		2,2	1,1	Average

Figure 18.12 The hyper parameters for RNN and 3D-CNN.

layer are Anomaly detection, Cache management, Resource management, Traffic prediction, etc. In this work, network traffic in 5G networks is predicted and classified using a combined 3D CNN and RNN model (Figure 18.12). The employed machine learning techniques accurately predict and classify the network traffic from the traffic data stored. Thus by using combined RNN and 3D CNN for Traffic Prediction, the traffic loads can be predicted and classified as Maximum or Minimum or Average.

References

1. Ozturk, M., Gogate, M., Imran, M.A., Onireti, O., Adeel, A., Hussain, A., A novel deep learning driven, low-cost mobility prediction approach for 5G cellular networks: The case of the Control/Data Separation Architecture (CDSA). *Neurocomputing*, 358, 479–489, 2019.
2. Meng, H., Shafik, W., Matinkhah, S.M., Ahmad, Z., A 5G Beam Selection Machine Learning Algorithm for Unmanned Aerial Vehicle Applications. *Wireless Commun. Mobile Comput.*, 2020, 1–16, 2020.

3. McClellan, M., Cervelló-Pastor, C., Sallent, S., Deep Learning at the Mobile Edge: Opportunities for 5G Networks. *J. Appl. Sci.*, 10, 1–27, 2020.

4. Li, M. and Li, H., Application of deep neural network and deep reinforcement learning in wireless communication. *PLoS One*, 2020, 1–15, 2020.

5. Abbasi, M., Shahraki, A., Taherkordi, A., Deep Learning for Network Traffic Monitoring and Analysis (NTMA): A Survey. *Comput. Commun.*, 170, 19–41, 2021.

6. Mozo, A., Ordozgoiti, B., Gómez-Canaval, S., Forecasting short-term data center network traffic load with convolutional neural networks, 13, 1–31, February 6, 2018, https://doi.org/10.1371/journal.pone.0191939.

7. Liu, L., Lin, J., Wang, P., Liu, L., Zhou, R., Deep Learning-Based Network Security Data Sampling and Anomaly Prediction in Future Network. *Discrete Dyn. Nat. Soc.*, 2020, Article ID 4163825, 9 pages, 2020, https://doi.org/10.1155/2020/4163825.

8. Alawe, I., Ksentini, A., Hadjadj-Aoul, Y., Bertin, P., Improving traffic forecasting for 5G core network scalability: A Machine Learning approach. *IEEE Netw. Mag., IEEE*, 2018, 1–10, 2018, ffhal-01933966f.

9. Huang, C.-W., Chiang, C.-T., Li, Q., A Study of Deep Learning Networks on Mobile Traffic Forecasting. *IEEE Conference Proceedings*, pp. 1–6, 2017.

10. Sadok, D., Leoni Santos, G., Endo, P.T., Kelner, J., When 5G Meets Deep Learning: A Systematic Review. *J. Algorithms*, 1–34, 2020.

11. Huang, C., Chiang, C., Li, Q., A study of deep learning networks on mobile traffic forecasting. *2017 IEEE 28th Annual International Symposium on Personal, Indoor, and Mobile Radio Communications (PIMRC)*, Montreal, QC, Canada, pp. 1–6, 2017.

12. Mejia, J., Ochoa-Zezzati, A., Cruz-Mejía, O., Traffic Forecasting on Mobile Networks Using 3D Convolutional Layers. *Mobile Netw. Appl.*, 25, 2134–2140, 2020.

EIDR Umpiring Security Models for Wireless Sensor Networks

A. Kathirvel[1*], S. Navaneethan[2] and M. Subramaniam[3]

[1]Department of Computer Science and Engineering, Karunya Institute of
Technology and Sciences, Karunya Nagar, Coimbatore, Tamilnadu, India
[2]Department of CSE, SRM Institute of Science and Technology, Chennai, India
[3]Department of Information Technology, Sree Vidyanikethan Engineering College,
Sree Sainath Nagar, Tirupati, Andhra Pradesh, India

Abstract

WSN (Wireless Sensor Network) is an infrastructure-less network that is used temporarily in a number of wireless sensors to monitor computer, physical, or environmental conditions like earth climatic temperature, environmental noise and environmental pollution levels, sound, humidity, wind, enemy crossing in the country border, etc. IEEE 802.15.4 WSN is organizing the collected data at a centralized server in the secured location. Various routing algorithms are used to find the most efficient route in WSN based on distance, network traffic, etc. Routing protocols should be used for path maintenance as sensor nodes are low resources such as battery power, communication range. In this study we have provided an overview of WSNs with its classification, as well as comparisons between different routing algorithms with our proposed EIDR (Enhanced Intrusion Detection and Response). Soundness of proposed EIDR tested using Qualnet 5.0.

Keywords: WSN, IEEE 802.15.4, routing protocols, EIDR

19.1 Introduction

In recent times sensor network plays a vital role in all the areas in today's life style. The basic idea and objective of WSN is to empower an end client to communicate estimated information in the remote connections in

Corresponding author: ayyakathir@gmail.com

R. Kanthavel, K. Ananthajothi, S. Balamurugan and R. Karthik Ganesh (eds.) *Artificial Intelligent Techniques for Wireless Communication and Networking,* (299–316) © 2022 Scrivener Publishing LLC the presence of unified controller. The term "sensor network" refers to a collection of sensors, plugged for some dedicated application to keeping track of and recording physical conditions of the natural environment. IEEE 802.15.4 WSN is organizing the collected data at a centralized server in the secured location [1]. It will measure environmental conditions like earth climatic temperature, environmental noise and environmental pollution levels, sound, humidity, wind, enemy crossing in the country border, etc.

For mainstream web, a devoted network router constrained by the ISPs exists. Anyway in remote organizations hubs should act both as ordinary sensor hub such as source or sink and also as transitional switches nodes for other sensor nodes [2, 3]. In the presence of centralized switches, providing network authorization becomes a more difficult task in the networks. Conventional heritage directing conventions for remote organizations neglect to give the necessary security instrument.

Noticeable existing remote sensor directing conventions, such as AODV (Ad hoc On Demand Distance Vector) routing protocol, DSR (Dynamic Source Routing) protocol and Low Energy Adaptive Clustering Hierarchy (LEACH) commonly expect an organization trusted and steady circumstance [32]. Thus, a vindictive hub assailant can promptly turn into a moderate switch and interfere with network activities by purposely defying the organization convention terms [4].

It is found that the performance of a typical on demand routing protocol sharply decrease in the percentage of mitigating malicious nodes increases. The objective of the researcher's work is to provide security and obtain improved performance when malicious nodes are present [5]. The researcher focuses on civilian situations and assume overheads is to be kept as minimum as possible [42, 44].

The paper studies an important security and power issue in wireless sensor networks, i.e. the protecting operations at the network layer being harmed [6]. Malicious nodes can cause routing algorithms to malfunction by transmitting out an invalid or wrong hop count, such as a lower hop count or no route; they may eliminate information parcels, network course the information bundles through unintended courses, etc. Three studies are presented.

The first study deals with the behavior of ETUS routing protocol in the face of different types of generic attacks. We have led reproduction studies to survey the improved exhibition of Generic ETUS over ETUS routing protocol. In this investigation we have done these studies using AODV protocol and modified AODV protocol called as Generic ETUS. Generic attack incorporates Black posting assault, Black opening assault, Byzantine assault, Changing course tables assault, Gray opening assault, Jelly fish assaults, Network sticking sign, Masquerading information assault, Man in the center assault, Replay assault, Rushing assault, Sybil assault, Selfish hub assault, Sink opening assault and Worm opening attack. The results of simulation studies show that Generic ETUS routing protocol enhances ETUS [39] routing protocol performance substantially as compared to plain AODV protocol, with only minor overheads.

The second study presents a new model to the extension of the protecting the network layer from the pernicious assaults, by characterizing a token-based IDS method [64, 65] is suggested, where each hub needs a token to take an interest in the organization and the adjoining hubs go about as umpire. The Intrusion Detection Scheme for Mitigating Attacks (IDSM) Using Energy Monitoring (IDSEM) protocol is proposed, in which each node requires a token and good energy forces, and only nodes are allowed to participate in the organization, with neighboring hubs serving as umpires. This proposed IDSEM has been found to be highly successful, with a shorter discovery period and lower overhead. The security examination and trial output generated in that IDSEM is practical for upgrading the security and organization execution of genuine applications.

The sensor nodeID and sensor status bits are two significant fields in the token; sensor nodeID is assumed to be absolute. All participating nodes' sensor status bits are initially "green flagged" with free, and they must engage in all network operations, including routing and forwarding. When a nearby umpiring hub learns its subsequent hub is unloading, it sends an Error message to the source hub S, and the status bit of the moderating hub is modified using a Flag message ("red flag"). The culprit node is barred from engaging in all other network operations with a "red flag" on it. On the routing and packet forwarding, IDSEM does not use any cryptographic techniques. The system concentrates only on two types of malicious attacks: giving false hop count/sequence number and dropping of the packets.

The last study is on the extension of the IDS. Intrusion Detection System (IDS) of network security is not enough for these networks. We introduce an enhanced intrusion detection and response (EIDR) system using two tire processes. The first contribution of proposed EIDR system is optimal cluster formation and performed by the chaotic ant optimization (CAO) algorithm. The second contribution is to use the multi objective differential evolution (MODE) algorithm to measure the trust value of each sensor node. The computed trust value is used to design the intrusion response action (IRA) system, which offers additional functions and exhibit multiple characteristics of response to mitigate intrusion impacts.

We propose a frame work enhanced intrusion detection and response (EIDR) system that gives security to directing and information sending tasks. In our framework, every hub's conduct from source to objective is firmly observed by a bunch of three nearby nodes are called umpires. On the off chance that any bad conduct is seen, EIDR banner off the liable hub from the wireless network. We have suggested three upgrades to ETUS, for example, Link status, Token status and Battery status. Conventions have need of right data of the connection status between adjoining portable hubs. In the symbolic status getting out of hand hubs, node token status is changed from green to red. The Battery Life status will help you choose hubs with excellent battery power. EIDR is the name of the model that integrates these three enhancements. We used the LEACH convention to implement EIDR. Broad examination contemplates utilizing test system build up the adequacy and heartiness of the proposition [64, 65]. The output shows that EIDR, significantly improves the execution of IDSEM and Generic ETUS altogether measurements, parcel conveyance proportion. The number of packets received by Destination Node divided by the observation time.

Extensive simulation studies have been performed using NS 2, a simulation that can be scaled environment for wireless network system. The four studies on the NS 2 simulator [49] experimental results validate the soundness of the proposal.

19.2 A Review of Various Routing Protocols

19.2.1 Trust-Based Routing Protocols

Trust the board assumes a significant part in IoT for solid information combination and mining, qualified administrations with setting mindfulness, and upgraded client protection and data security [7]. It assists individuals with defeating impression of vulnerability and hazard and takes part in client acknowledgment and utilization on IoT administrations and applications [8–10]. Nonetheless, current writing actually does not have a far reaching concentrate on trust the board in IoT [11]. Verified key arrangement convention is a valuable cryptographic crude [12].

Based upon shrewd directing and arbitrary straight organization coding, Code Pipe works on transmission coordination between hubs as well as enhanced the message to group and throughput essentially by misusing both intra-cluster and inter batch coding openings [13]. Specifically, four key procedures, in particular LP-based pioneering steering structure [14] crafty taking care of, quick cluster moving, and entomb bunch coding, are proposed to offer significant improves the fast, energy proficiency, and reasonableness [15].

In the paper, [16] introduces a multi-constrained QoS multicast routing method using the genetic algorithm. The proposition will flood restrict

[17] utilizing the accessible assets and least calculation time in a unique climate. By choosing the suitable qualities for boundaries like hybrid, change, and populace size, the hereditary calculation improves and attempts to advance the courses.

For the creator of this paper [18], they consider the task technique with geography safeguarding by getting sorted out the cross section hubs with accessible channels and target limiting the co-direct obstruction in the organization.

The channel problem with geography conservation has become NP-hard, and finding an improved arrangement in polynomial time is impossible. They devised the DPSO-CA channel task estimation, which is based on discrete molecule swarm progression [19].

All the above plans just attempt to shield the framework from the assailant, however not worry about isolating aggressors [20–22]. TBUT frameworks identify the devilish hubs as well as forestall their further interest in the organization [23], however are more far reaching, as in parcel dropping as well as different mischievous activities like giving incorrectly jump tally are covered [24]. Several other surveys papers on secure protocols for networks [25–35].

19.2.2 Intrusion Detection System

Many researchers have given a variety of solution for IDS solutions in the papers [1–5, 36–40].

In paper [37] have proposed rules based on Neighborhood data against sinkhole attack. The proposed calculation incorporates the accompanying three stages: Identifying presumed hubs, perceiving sinkhole hubs and killing sinkhole hubs. In the primary stage, Identifying speculated hubs; two kinds of directing ways are characterized to recognize dubious hubs as per the quantity of sensor hubs on a steering way. In the subsequent stage, perceiving sinkhole hubs the sinkhole hubs between two correspondence sensor nodes are detected from the suspicious nodes based on the number of interaction times and acknowledgments (ACKs). The last stage is to remove sinkhole nodes.

In paper [41] have developed a completely novel globoid model to affirm at each and every directional recognition quality though saving the organization POWER viably, that separates the detecting space into external shell and inside area. An external shell inclusion calculation used to confirmation the acknowledgment nature of intruding on occasions. Based on the intruder's previous trajectory, a Markov forecast model is used to estimate the probability of motion in the surrounding area. Based on the predicted results and using SDR technology, covered nodes will be allocated different working frequencies [42]. The distinctive working frequencies will be distributed to the covered hubs by a direction revision methodology to migrate the missing gatecrashers during the activity [44].

In paper [46] have proposed a new speculation of specialists based frameworks to determine an intricate issue in wireless sensor networks, i.e., Denial Jamming Attacks. The algorithm is motivated by organic pests, ants and their behavior, which uses stigmergic round about correspondence. There are different components like the affectability of fake specialists, the boundary used to apply direct and indirect communication also used. Agents are grouped on the basis of their sensitivity level. Agents "group work together to solve agents" communications and problems. The presented algorithm increases the responses of specialists in the organization, sending the data when a sticking assault is exist in the remote sensor organization.

In paper [47] proposed using a HSOM (Hierarchical Self-Organizing Map) neural network to detect intrusions. It's used to analyze traffic dynamics and detect intrusions, as well as a complex learning tool for dealing with vast volumes of useless training data. A traffic model is created to explain the complex features of network traffic. Using this traffic model, the size of the training set worn for traffic pattern learning can be consciously reduced.

IDSHT (Intrusion detection using dynamic state context and hierarchical trust), proposed by Zhang et al. [66], is adaptable and appropriate for regularly changing sensor nodes classified by perceptual environment deviations, node state changes, and variations in trust value. They created a multidimensional two-level hierarchical trust mechanism at the sensor node level. They considered intelligent trust, trustworthiness trust and substance trust, which consolidates direct assessment and criticism based assessment in the fixed bounce range [48–52]. This implies that the trust is assessed by neighbor and base station, the intricacy of assessment is diminished. A self-versatile powerful trust based interruption discovery system is depicted to improve the adaptability and pertinence and is ideal for bunch based WSNs.

In paper [47] have proposed the automated attack generation system using genetic programming (GP) and the accreditations can be attempted sensibly. The GP passed on aggressors concentrated on publish–purchase in trades inside a WSNs that was guaranteed by a faker safe IDS. The GP aggressors alluringly secured more clear messages than the hand-coded get used at first to test the IDS, while diminishing the likelihood of area. It was possible to reconfigure the IDS to animate its execution. A proof-of-control as opposed to a turnkey hypothesis, they show that GP-influenced aggressors to can connect with the endorsement of structures with clearing strike surfaces.

In paper [57] have proposed an ids and ejection framework against lethal attacks, which sees savage ambushes with a high accuracy before they hurt the structure while thinking about the shocking position preventions of different obsession centers. The security redirection issue is controlled by a Bayesian beguilement plot. It other than made by the IDS and attackers with the outline of impedance release structure (IES) and suspicious obsessions, where each and every one of them finishes particular approaches to help their own particular settlements.

Multi-protocol oriented middleware-level intrusion detection has proposed by [43]. MP-MID, passes on all known catch makes for any controlling custom. The managing custom with the framework Algebra for remote work structures (AWN) tongue, and used the beginning of catch centers to find all catch shapes. Working up hit centers with formalized tradition in AWN to complete the co-sentences which address the catch joins into the custom. With program cutting change, all known trap makes can be found in light of co-sentences.

In paper [56] have proposed hybrid network intrusion detection systems (NIDS) using Dempster-Shafer (DS) theory to sympathetically watch mastermind allocator vector (NAV) ambushes. The high certification rate execution have made by signature-based NIDSs close to the noticeable strikes gave by the assortment from the standard based NIDSs. The zone justification ties the mix of evaluations from different estimations over various layers of learning with a particular monster focus to settle on a total decision on whether a NAV get happens or not [57].

In paper [58] have proposed ETS (energy trust system) to successfully detect sybil attacks, which uses multilevel clear insistence in setting of character and position bolster. A trust figuring is connected in setting of the centrality of each sensor center point. To reduce correspondence overhead and increase centrality, data indicate is used. The execution of this structure is poor down the degree that security and resource use using theoretical and redirection based procedures.

In paper [33] have proposed the novel sensor hub catch assault identification and protection (SCADD) convention. SCADD gives a savvy arrangement against the hub bargain and catch assaults in WSNs, improving the in general WSN security for security-touchy applications. This convention comprises of two structure blocks: hub assault location square and safeguard supporting measure block. The previous gives key based assault location to dispose of the chance of misconception and the last uses an implosion safeguard measure against hub catch assault, without really obliterating the hub's radio assistance, to maintain a strategic distance from a significant security penetrate.

Riecke and colleagues [45] developed three decentralized, lightweight data anomaly detection mechanisms that can be run directly on sensor nodes. These algorithms are put to the test on a specific dataset with plausible attacks.

Xie *et al.* [43] have proposed another method for taking care of information in a fragment based way. Zhou *et al.* [50] have been proposed advancement strategies to limit the energy cost of guard dog deployment, while keeping the framework's security in an adequate level. Their commitments comprise of hypothetical examinations and commonsense calculations, which can proficiently and adequately plan the guard dog errands relying upon the sensor hubs' areas and the objective hubs' dependability.

Han *et al.* [20] have proposed IDS dependent on energy expectation in group based sensor nodes. Shafiei *et al.* [58] have proposed two ways to deal with distinguish and alleviate such assault in WSNs. That gives a concentrated way to deal with recognize dubious districts in the organization utilizing geostatistical danger model.

19.2.3   The Network Layer Routing Protocols

The network layer unicast protocols for MANETs can be grouped into as discussed in *Section 2.1*. In this section some of the prominent unicast routing protocols for network layer are detailed [2]. The routing protocols are: Wireless Routing Protocol, FSR (Fisheye State Routing), DSR protocol, AODV routing protocol [51–63] and ZRP (Zone Routing Protocol).

19.2.3.1   WRP

Wireless Routing Protocol is a DV routing protocol for data packet radio networks. Network topology changes [1] and it relies on communicating the changes to its nearby neighboring nodes, which propagate all the way through the complete network [2].

19.2.3.2   AODV

Ad hoc on-demand distance vector is a reactive routing protocol. It will utilize objective arrangement number (DestSeqNum) as course newness to decide a cutting-edge way to the objective hub D. Hub refreshes its directing way data if the DestSeqNum got is more prominent that the last DestSeqNum put away in the hub steering table. In the event that any hub have a course towards the objective hub D with a more prominent grouping number than the RREQ parcel, it unicasts a course answer (RREP) back to source hub S. All transitional hubs N having substantial course to the objective hub D, or the actual objective are permitted to send course answer (RREP) to the source hub.

ZigBee is a critical advancement for Wireless Sensor Networks [54], focusing on radio-recurrence (RF) [55]. It's an on-demand calculation, which means it assembles routes between hubs based on what source hubs want [32]. It continues to offer these courses as long as the sources demand it. This paper investigates the presentation of improved AODV in ZigBee-based remote sensor networks [54].

WSN [56] is used to lower power utilization, quick geography, great constant, etc. Most importantly, low force utilization endures the worst part. To improve the presentation of the organization and increment the lifetime of the organization, we need to bring down the force utilization of sensor hub in the remote sensor organization [57]. In this paper, an improved AODV steering convention dependent on insignificant course cost is introduced, and OPNET is utilized to reproduce the throughput, start to finish delay and different boundaries for assessing the presentation of the remote sensor network with the improved convention, the mimicked results show the approval of the introduced improved AODV.

19.2.3.3   LEACH Protocols

Low Energy Adaptive Clustering Hierarchy protocol proposed by Heinemann *et al.* [39, 60], is a prominent energy efficiency protocol for sensor node. LEACH consists of two levels: Cluster heads and member nodes. LEACH works on two phases: construction and communication. During construction phase cluster heads form a group. Cluster head is choose based on threshold T (n) value. Other than cluster head node is join with good signal strength. The cluster head allocates the packet communication time slot for each node members based on TDMA mechanism. In the communication phase sensor nodes can send their data via cluster head. Reserved slots are used to save energy.

19.3   Scope of Chapter

19.3.1   Objective

The researcher focuses on civilian situations and assume overheads are to be kept as minimum as possible. Thus the model does not correspond to the situation where heavily jacketed, steel helmeted and fully armed commandos are trying to protect nuclear installations, but rather corresponds to a scenario where a team of local policemen, each armed with no more additional components such as a whistle and a stick control the traffic flow. Based on the above motivations security features are to be incorporated to the popular AODV protocol while limiting overheads. The following situations involving malicious nodes are to be taken care of:

- Reporting false hop count and false sequence number.
- Deliberate dropping of data packets.

With this perspective enhanced triple umpiring system ETUS is proposed. Researchers extended a solution ETUS to conventional assault, for example, Black posting assault, Black opening assault, Byzantine assault, Changing course tables assault, Gray opening assault, Jelly fish assaults, Network sticking sign, Masquerading information assault, Man in the center assault, Replay assault, Rushing assault, Sybil assault, Selfish hub assault, Sink opening attack and Worm hole attack. In second work, IDSM Using Energy Monitoring (IDSEM) protocol is proposed, where each hub needs a token and great energy power then just hubs are permit to take part in the organization and the adjoining hubs go about as umpire. Final work, solution for malicious node problem using the frame work approach. The conventional security frame work mechanisms like intrusion detection system (IDS) of network security are not enough for these networks. The first contribution of proposed EIDR system is optimal cluster formation and performed by the chaotic ant optimization (CAO) algorithm. The second contribution is multi objective differential evolution (MODE) algorithm. The computed trust value is used to design the intrusion response action (IRA) system, which offers additional functions and exhibit multiple characteristics of response to mitigate intrusion impacts. Broad recreation contemplates utilizing. Network Simulator assists with considering the proposed arrangement sufficiency and demonstrates the vigor of the framework.

19.3.2 Contributions

The paper studies an important security and power issue in wireless sensor networks, i.e. the protection of the network layer undertakings from easing attacks. Harmful center points may disturb coordinating computations by sending a fake hop consider such lesser bob check or no course; they may drop data packs, network course the data bundles through unintended courses, and so forth. Three examinations are presented.

The first study deals with the behavior of ETUS routing protocol in the presence of various types of generic attacks. We have directed reproduction studies to survey the improved exhibition of Generic ETUS over ETUS routing protocol. In this investigation we have done these studies using AODV protocol and modified AODV protocol called as Generic ETUS. Generic attack includes Boycotting assault, Black opening assault, Byzantine assault, Changing course tables assault, Gray opening assault, Jelly fish assaults, Network sticking sign, Masquerading information assault, Man in the center assault, Replay assault, Rushing assault, Sybil assault, Selfish hub assault, Sink opening assault and Worm opening assault.

The second study presents a new model to the extension of the protecting the network layer from the malicious attacks, by defining a token. IDSEM convention is proposed, where each hub needs token and great energy controls then just hubs are permit to take part in the organization and the adjoining hubs go about as umpire. The symbolic comprises two significant fields like sensor_nodeID and sensor_status bit; sensor_nodeID is viewed as total. At first the sensor_status cycle of all partaking hubs are "green banner" with freedom of thought to take an interest taking all things together organization activities incorporates steering and sending tasks.

Last study is on the extension of the IDS. Intrusion Detection System (IDS) of network security are not enough for these networks. We introduce an enhanced intrusion detection and response (EIDR) system using two tire processes. The first contribution of proposed EIDR system is optimal cluster formation and performed by the chaotic ant optimization (CAO) algorithm. The second contribution is multi objective differential evolution (MODE) algorithm. The computed trust value is used to design the intrusion response action (IRA) system, which offers additional functions and exhibit multiple characteristics of response to mitigate intrusion impacts.

We propose a frame work enhanced intrusion detection and response (EIDR) system that offers security to coordinating and data sending undertakings. In our system, each center's lead from source to objective is solidly checked by a lot of three nearby center points are called umpires. Expansive assessment considers using test framework develop the adequacy and fortitude of the recommendation. The results show that EIDR, by and large improves the presentation of IDSEM and Generic ETUS taking everything together estimations, group movement extent, communication overhead and delay. Studies on the NS 2 simulator [49] experimental results validate the soundness of the proposal.

19.3.3   Performance Evaluations

We use a simulation model based on NS2 in our evaluation. Our performance evaluations are based on the simulations of 200 in 1,000 m × 1,000 m, 600 s. We present an assessment of bundle transport extents of GETUS, plain AODV, ETUS, IDSEM and EIDR examines in Table 19.1.

We find that EIDR yields significantly higher pack transport extent diverged from GETUS, ETUS, IDSEM and plain AODV inside seeing 40% noxious center point in Table 19.1. It is found that with EIDR, there is a higher bundle movement extent going from 15.37% (ETUS with 200 center thickness) to 10.21% (ETUS with 50 center thickness).

It is discovered that with EIDR there is an abatement the correspondence overhead going from 18.08% (ETUS with 50 hubs) to 35.75% (ETUS with

Table 19.1 Rate of production for GETUS, plain AODV, ETUS, IDSEM and EIDR.

| Node density | Throughput for malicious node = 40% | | | | |
	GETUS	Plain AODV	ETUS	IDSEM	EIDR
50	87.83	50.44	83.10	89.16	92.55
75	81.83	42.18	78.12	83.36	85.94
100	76.81	30.89	70.65	78.52	80.42
150	70.72	28.55	64.12	72.75	74.63
200	63.78	26.07	57.98	65.71	68.51

Table 19.2 Communication overhead for GETUS, plain AODV, ETUS, IDSEM and EIDR.

| Node density | Communication overhead for malicious node = 40% | | | | |
	GETUS	Plain AODV	ETUS	IDSEM	EIDR
50	25,089	13,136	26,184	23,184	22,174
75	26,678	13,603	26,978	23,849	22,889
100	27,367	14,082	28,868	24,868	23,898
150	29,561	14,580	29,998	25,869	24,889
200	30,678	15,082	35,440	26,521	25,541

200 hubs). Anyway plain AODV correspondence overhead is a lot higher when contrasted with IDSEM and EIDR. For instance versatility of 20 m/s, ETUS has 134.98% correspondence overhead when contrasted with plain AODV. We find that our proposed EIDR yield a lot higher yield when contrasted with any remaining frameworks. Table 19.2 Communication overhead for GETUS, plain AODV, ETUS, IDSEM and EIDR within the sight of 40% pernicious hubs.

19.4   Conclusions and Future Work

The first study introduced the GETUS mechanism in the On-demand Distance Vector routing protocol; the second study presented a new approach to the extension of the protecting the organization layer from the pernicious assaults, by characterizing an IDSEM for Security; the third examination is on the augmentation of the IDSEM system another methodology called EIDR mechanism. Simulation studies have been performed on the NS2 network simulation tool, and the results are found to be promising.

Our future work will zero in on displaying all nonexclusive organization layer assaults. As a conscious approach to keep the framework exceptionally straightforward, and not dealing with keys. On the off chance that need be, in circumstances requesting such safety efforts they can be joined in the fundamental model to the ideal degree of security. Endeavors are on additionally toward this path.

References

1. Abduvaliyev, A., Pathan, A., Jianying, Z., Roman, R., Wong, W.-C., On the Vital Areas of Intrusion Detection Systems in Wireless Sensor Networks. *IEEE Commun. Surv. Tutorials*, 15, 3, 1223–1237, 2013.
2. Kathirvel, A., Subramaniam, M., Navaneethan, S., and Sabarinath, C., Improved IDR Response System for Sensor Network, *Journal of Web Engineering*, 20, 1, 53–88, 2021.
3. Amicarelli, A., Leuzzi, G., Monti, P., Lagrangian micromixing models for concentration fluctuations: An overview. *Am. J. Environ. Sci.*, 8, 577–590, 2012.
4. Arockiasamy, Performance evaluation of multicrypt encryption mechanism. *Am. J. Appl. Sci.*, 9, 1849–1861, 2012.
5. Arya, M. and Jain, Y.K., Grayhole attack and prevention in mobile ad hoc network. *Int. J. Comput. Appl.*, 27, 21–26, 2011.

6. Alsaedi, N., Hashim, F., Sali, A., Rokhani, F., Detecting sybil attacks in clustered wireless sensor networks based on energy trust system (ETS). *Comput. Commun.*, 110, 75–82, 2017.

7. Bleda, A., Fernandez-Luque, F., Rosa, A., Zapata, J., Maestre, R., Smart Sensory Furniture Based on WSN for Ambient Assisted Living. *IEEE Sens. J.*, 17, 17, 5626–5636, 2017.

8. Briesemeister, L. and Hommel, G., Role Based Multicast in Highly Mobile But Sparsely Connected Ad hoc Networks. *Proceedings of First Annual Workshop on Mobile and Ad hoc Networking and Computer (MOBIHOC)*, Boston, MA, USA, pp. 45–50, 2000.

9. Broch, J., Maltz, D., Johnson, D., Ou, Y.C., Jetcheva, J., A performance comparison of multihop wireless ad hoc network routing protocols. *Proceedings of ACM/IEEE International Conference on Mobile Computing and Networking (MOBICOM 98)*, Dallas, TX, USA, pp. 85–97, 1998.

10. Bu, S., Yu, F., Liu, X., Tang, H., Structural Results for Combined Continuous User Authentication and Intrusion Detection in High Security Mobile Ad hoc Networks. *IEEE Trans. Wireless Commun.*, 10, 9, 3064–3073, 2011.

11. Charles Perkins, E., Elizabeth Royer, M., Das, S., Ad hoc on demand distance vector (AODV) routing. Internet Draft, Available, in: *tools.ietf.org/html/draft-ietf-manet- aodv-10.txt*, 2002.

12. Charles Perkins, E. and Elizabeth Royer, M., Ad hoc On-demand Distance Vector (AODV) Routing. *Proceedings of the Second IEEE Workshop on Mobile Computing Systems and Applications*, pp. 90–100, 1999.

13. Chen, J., Li, J., Lai, T., Energy-Efficient Intrusion Detection with a Barrier of Probabilistic Sensors: Global and Local. *IEEE Trans. Wireless Commun.*, 12, 9, 4742–4755, 2013.

14. Chen, T.W. and Gerla, M., Global State Routing: A New Routing Scheme for Ad hoc Wireless Networks. *Proceedings of IEEE International Conference on Communications*, Atlanta, GA, USA, pp. 171–175, 1998.

15. Chiang, C.C., Gerla, M., Zhang, L., Forward Group Multicasting Protocol for Multihop Mobile Wireless Networks. *ACM-Baltzer J. Clust. Comput.: Special Issue on Mobile Computing*, 1, 2, 187–196, 1998.

16. Chiang, C.C., Wu, H.K., Liu, W., Gerla, M., Routing in Clustered Multi-Hop Mobile Wireless Networks with Fading Channel. *Proceedings of IEEE Singapore International Conference on Networks (SICON 97)*, Singapore, pp. 197–211, 1997.

17. Deif, D. and Gadallah, Y., An Ant Colony Optimization Approach for the Deployment of Reliable Wireless Sensor Networks. *IEEE Access*, 5, 10744–16, 10756, 2017.

18. Elizabeth Royer, M. and Charles Perkins, E., Multicast Ad hoc On-Demand Distance Vector Routing Protocol. *Proceedings of Fifth Annual ACM/IEEE International Conference on Mobile Computing and Networking (MOBICOM 99)*, Seattle, Washington, USA, pp. 207–218, 1999.

19. Guo, G., Li, X., Xu, G., Feng, N., MP-MID: Multi-Protocol Oriented Middleware-level Intrusion Detection method for wireless sensor networks. *Future Gener. Comput. Syst.*, 70, 42–47, 2017.

20. Han, G., Jiang, J., Shen, W., Shu, L., Rodrigues, J., IDSEP: A novel intrusion detection scheme based on energy prediction in cluster-based wireless sensor networks. *IET Inf. Secur.*, 7, 2, 97–105, 2013.

21. Harno, H. and Petersen, I., Synthesis of Linear Coherent Quantum Control Systems Using A Differential Evolution Algorithm. *IEEE Trans. Autom. Control*, 60, 3, 799–805, 2015.

22. Han, G., Rodrigues, J., Jiang, J., Shu, L., Shen, W., IDSEP: A novel intrusion detection scheme based on energy prediction in cluster-based wireless sensor networks. *IET Inf. Secur.*, 7, 2, 97–105, 2013.

23. Han, G., Li, X., Jiang, J., Shu, L., Lloret, J., Intrusion Detection Algorithm Based on Neighbor Information Against Sinkhole Attack in Wireless Sensor Networks. *Comput. J.*, 58, 6, 1280–1292, 2014.

24. Kalkha, H., Satori, K., Satori, H., Performance Evaluation of AODV and LEACH Routing Protocol. *Advances in Information Technology: Theory and Application*, 1, 1, pp. 113–120, 2016.

25. Hamela, K. and Kathirvel, A., EIMO-ESOLSR: Energy Efficient and Security Based Model for OLSR Routing Protocol in Mobile Ad hoc Network. *IET Commun.*, 5, 2, 1–9, 2018.

26. Hoyle, B., Rau, M., Paech, K., Bonnett, C., Seitz, S., Weller, J., Anomaly detection for machine learning redshifts applied to SDSS galaxies. *Mon. Not. R. Astron. Soc.*, 452, 4, 4183–4194, 2015.

27. Huang, K., Zhang, Q., Zhou, C., Xiong, N., Qin, Y., An Efficient Intrusion Detection Approach for Visual Sensor Networks Based on Traffic Pattern Learning. *IEEE Trans. Syst. Man Cybern.: Syst.*, 47, 10, 2704–2713, 2017.

28. Tang, L., Jian, P., Jin, Y., Chunli, W., Energy-Efficient Prediction Clustering Algorithm for Multilevel Heterogeneous. Wireless Sensor Networks. *Int. J. Distrib. Sens. Netw.* 2013.

29. Jin, X., Liang, J., Tong, W., Lu, L., Li, Z., Multi-agent trust-based intrusion detection scheme for wireless sensor networks. *Comput. Electr. Eng.*, 59, 262–273, 2017.

30. Joa Ng, M. and Lu, I.T., A Peer-to-Peer Zone-Based Two-Level Link State Routing for Mobile Ad hoc Networks. *IEEE J. Sel. Areas Commun., Special issue Wireless Ad hoc Networks*, 17, 8, 1415–1425, 1999.

31. Johnson, D.B. and Maltz, D.A., Dynamic Source Routing in Ad hoc Wireless Networks, in: *Mobile Computing*, T. Imielinski and H. F. Korth (eds.), Springer, Boston, MA, 353, 153–181, 1996.

32. Jokhio, S., Jokhio, I., Kemp, A., Light-weight framework for security-sensitive wireless sensor networks applications. *IET Wireless Sens. Syst.*, 3, 4, 298–306, 2013.

33. Jokhio, S.H., Jokhio, I.A., Kemp, A.H., Node capture attack detection and defence in wireless sensor networks. *IET Wireless Sens. Syst.*, 2, 3, 161–169, 2011.

34. Kumar, J. and Kathirvel, A., Optimum Power Management In Mobile Ad hoc Networks. *J. Eng. Sci. Technol.*, Taylor's & Series Publisher, 13, 6, 1805–1815, 2018.

35. Kumar, J. and Kathirvel, A., A Unified Approach for Detecting and Eliminating Selfish Nodes in MANETs using TBUT. *Eurasip J. Wirel. Commun. Netw.*, 2015, 1–13, 2015.

36. Kathirvel, A. and Srinivasan, R., ETUS: An Enhanced Triple Umpiring System for Security and Performance Improvement of Mobile Ad hoc Networks. *Int. J. Netw. Manag.*, John Wiley & Sons, 21, 5, 341–359, September/October 2011.

37. Kathirvel, A. and Srinivasan, R., ETUS: An Enhanced Triple Umpiring System for Security and Robustness of Mobile Ad hoc Networks. *Int. J. Commun. Netw. Distrib. Syst.*, Inderscience, 7, 1/2, 2011, 153–187, 2011b.

38. Kathirvel, A. and Srinivasan, R., Double Umpiring System for Security of Mobile Ad hoc Network. *Int. J. Wirel. Netw. Appl.*, 1, 2, 151–162, 2011, 2011c.

39. Kathirvel, A., Single Umpiring System for Security and Performance Improvement in Mobile Ad hoc Networks. *IASMS J. Bus. Spectr.*, IV, 2, 30–41, July 2011.

40. Lin, K., Xu, T., Song, J., Qian, Y., Sun, Y., Node Scheduling for All-Directional Intrusion Detection in SDR-Based 3D WSNs. *IEEE Sens. J.*, 16, 20, 7332–7341, 2016.

41. Lei, F.-Y., Cui, G.-H., Liao, X.-D., Ad hoc Networks Security Mechanism Based on CPK. *Proceedings of IEEE International Conference on Computational Intelligence and Security Workshops (ICCISW 2007)*, Heilongjiang, pp. 522–525, 2007.

42. Li, J., Jannotti, J., De Couto, D.S.J., Karger, D.R., Morris, R., A Scalable Location Service for Geographic Ad hoc Routing. *Proceedings of ACM/IEEE International Conference on Mobile Computing and Networking (MOBICOM)*, Boston, MA, USA, pp. 120–130, 2000.

43. Xie, M., Hu, J., Guo, S., Segment-Based Anomaly Detection with Approximated Sample Covariance Matrix in Wireless Sensor Networks in *IEEE Trans. Parallel Distrib. Syst.*, 26, 2, 574–583, 2015.

44. Macker, J., Simplified Multicast Forwarding (SMF). *IETF MANET List*, 2010, http://datatracker.ietf.org/doc/draft-ietf-manet-smf-10.txt.

45. Riecker, M., Barroso, A., Hollick, M., Biedermann, S., On Data-centric Intrusion Detection in Wireless Sensor Networks. *Proceedings of IEEE International Conference on Green Computing and Communications, Conference on Internet of Things, and Conference on Cyber, Physical and Social Computing*, 2012.

46. Matyás, V. and Kur, J., Conflicts between Intrusion Detection and Privacy Mechanisms for Wireless Sensor Networks in *IEEE Secur. Privacy*, 11, 5, 73–76, Sept.-Oct. 2013.

47. Mrugala, K., Tuptuk, N., Hailes, S., Evolving attackers against wireless sensor networks using genetic programming. *IET Wireless Sens. Syst.*, 7, 4, 45, 113–122, 2017.

48. Murad, A.R., Anazida, Z., Maarof, M.A., Advancements of Data Anomaly Detection Research in Wireless Sensor Networks: A Survey and Open Issues. *Sensors*, 13, 8, 10087–10122, 2013.

49. Network Simulator, NS3, https://www.nsnam.org/, 2019.

50. Zhou, P., Jiang, S., Irissappane, A., Zhang, J., Zhou, J., Teo, J.C.M., Toward Energy-Efficient Trust System Through Watchdog Optimization for WSNs in: *IEEE Trans. Inf. Forensics Secur.*, 10, 3, 613–625, March 2015.

51. Perkins, C.E. and Royer, E.M., Ad hoc On Demand Distance Vector Routing. *Proceedings of Second IEEE Workshop on Mobile Computing Systems and Applications*, New Orleans, USA, pp. 90–100, 1999.

52. Pintea, C., Pop, P., Zelina, I., Denial jamming attacks on wireless sensor network using sensitive agents. *Log. J. IGPL*, 24, 1, 92–103, February 2016.

53. Raza, F., Bashir, S., Tauseefand, K., Shah, S.I., Optimizing nodes proportion for Intrusion Detection in Uniform and Gaussian distributed Heterogeneous WSN. *IEEE Proceedings of 12th International Bhurban Conference on Applied Science and Technology (IBCAST)*, 2015.

54. Bai, R. and Singhal, M., Salvaging Route Reply for On-Demand Routing Protocols in Mobile Ad hoc Networks. *Proceedings ACM International Workshop on Modeling Analysis and Simulation (MSWiM 2005)*, Montreal, Quebec, Canada, pp. 53–62, 2005.

55. Bai, R. and Singhal, M., DOA: DSR over AODV Routing for Mobile Ad hoc Networks. *IEEE Trans. Mob. Comput.*, 5, 10, 1403–53, 1416, 2006.

56. Santoro, D., Escudero-Andreu, G., Kyriakopoulos, K., Aparicio-Navarro, F., Parish, D., Vadursi, M., A hybrid intrusion detection system for virtual jamming attacks on wireless networks. *Measurement*, 109, 79–87, 2017.

57. Sedjelmaci, H., Senouci, S., Ansari, N., Intrusion Detection and Ejection Framework Against Lethal Attacks in UAV-Aided Networks: A Bayesian Game-Theoretic Methodology. *IEEE Trans. Intell. Transp. Syst.*, 18, 5, 1143–1153, 2017.

58. Shafiei, H., Khonsari, A., Derakhshi, H., Mousavi, P., Detection and mitigation of sinkhole attacks in wireless sensor networks. *J. Comput. Syst. Sci.*, 80, 3, 644–653, 2014.

59. Sun, B., Shan, X., Wu, K., Xiao, Y., Anomaly Detection Based Secure In-Network Aggregation for Wireless Sensor Networks. *IEEE Syst. J.*, 7, 1, 13–25, 2013.

60. Sundar, R. and Kathirvel, A., Enhanced Routing Algorithm to Reduce Number of Transmission in Manet. *Aust. J. Basic Appl. Sci.*, 9, 35, 142–146, 2015.

61. Sundar, R. and Kathirvel, A., Enhanced Trust Based Delegation for Load Balancing in Manets. *Int. J. Appl. Eng. Res.*, 10, 92, 104–109, 2015.

62. Varshney, S. and Kuma, R., Variants of LEACH Routing Protocol in WSN: A Comparative Analysis. *Proceedings of 8th International Conference on Cloud Computing, Data Science & Engineering (Confluence)*, IEEE, 2018.

63. Vinodh Kumar, A., Kaja Mohideen, S., Kathirvel, A., Performance Enhanced Reverse AODV Routing Protocol for MANETs. *Middle-East J. Sci. Res.*, 23, 8, 1720–1726, 2015.

64. Wei, M. and Kim, K., Intrusion detection scheme using traffic prediction for wireless industrial networks. *J. Commun. Networks*, 14, 3, 310–318, 2012.

65. Wu, J., Ota, K., Dong, M., Li, C., A Hierarchical Security Framework for Defending Against Sophisticated Attacks on Wireless Sensor Networks in Smart Cities. *IEEE Access*, 4, 416–424, 2016.

66. Zhang, Z., Zhu, H., Luo, S., Xin, Y., Liu, X., Intrusion Detection Based on State Context and Hierarchical Trust in Wireless Sensor Networks. *IEEE Access*, 5, 12088–12102, 2017.

Artificial Intelligence in Wireless Communication

Prashant Hemrajani, Vijaypal Singh Dhaka, Manoj Kumar Bohra* and Amisha Kirti Gupta

Department of Computer and Communication Engineering, Manipal University Jaipur, Jaipur, India

Abstract

Wireless communications and networking technology have developed rapidly in the past few years. As Artificial Intelligence (AI) technique is utilized, the network becomes more self-operational, self-configurational, and self-managed. Upcoming generations of wireless networks should be able to provide highly reliable and low-latency communication. Integrating fundamental concepts of artificial intelligence (AI) and machine learning into the wireless systems and user devices can become a big achievement. Artificial intelligence can help manage network systems more efficiently and make them autonomous as well, while significantly enhancing the performance. The current advances in machine learning and wireless communication technologies are a big breakthrough for future networks, which are expected to be reliable and intelligent.

Wireless communication infrastructure is an essential part of data transmission for the Internet of Things (IoT) also. 5G wireless systems and higher generation systems have the potential to provide services with high-range connectivity, ultra-high data speeds, low latency, high security, and extremely low energy consumption. To achieve this only AI can support the automation of the network systems. Applications of AI techniques in wireless communication technologies and networking can bring these changes through new research. AI has the potential to provide intelligent, smart, and quick solutions for the design, management, and optimization of wireless system resources. AI/ML techniques can improve the current state of network management, operations, and automation. They can support software-defined networking (SDN) and network function virtualization (NFV),

*Corresponding author: manojkumar.bohra@jaipur.manipal.edu

R. Kanthavel, K. Ananthajothi, S. Balamurugan and R. Karthik Ganesh (eds.) *Artificial Intelligent Techniques for Wireless Communication and Networking*, (317–334) © 2022 Scrivener Publishing LLC

which are considered important wireless communication technologies for the deployment of 5G and higher generation communication systems. The increase in complexity that might arise from heterogeneous network systems can be easily managed by AI techniques.

Keywords: Artificial Intelligence (AI), Machine Learning (ML), Internet of Things (IoT), Low-Latency, Software-Defined Networking (SDN), Network Function Virtualization (NFV)

20.1   Introduction

The world revolves around the common notion that miracles are objects of dreams and that what us humans have achieved are nothing but the products of our gradual advancements across centuries. But if we take a moment and reflect upon the occurrences in life today, much of the mechanisms come up on our countenance as some whimsical phenomenon, elements otherwise taken for granted, most of it so neatly integrated into our lives when it was thought to be impossible a few decades ago—machines with the ability to interact, to hear, make calculative decisions, and much more.

This global progress has been made possible with the help of Artificial Intelligence (AI), defined as "the ability of a digital computer or computer-controlled robot to perform tasks commonly associated with intelligent beings" [1]. In other words, attempts at artificial creation of human intelligence have successfully shed light upon possibilities wherein systems can make decisions and narrow down conclusions as per their environments. These factors would always continue to propel the question forward: would the day come when programming reaches a threshold of a new era, where machines replace human-oriented activities completely? How does this all play into the increasing user traffic of communication? As the population continues to grow globally, the demand for more efficient, smoother, faster and more effortless networking has made its place.

20.2   Artificial Intelligence: A Grand Jewel Mine

The world revolves around the common notion that miracles are objects of dreams and that what we humans have achieved is nothing but the products of our gradual advancements across centuries. But if we take a moment and reflect upon the occurrences in life today, much of the mechanisms comes up on our countenance as some whimsical phenomenon, elements otherwise taken for granted, most of it so neatly integrated into our lives when it was thought to be impossible a few decades ago— machines with the ability to interact, to hear, make calculative decisions, and much more.

The emergence of the concept of AI is difficult to trace, for many people have hinted towards the imagination of a futuristic setting in various periods. But it is safe to say, that the work of Isaac Asimov—a science fiction writer—called 'Three Laws Of Robotics' has impacted the idea of Artificial Intelligence to a large extent. Going even further back, in the 19th century, present in what we call 'modern fiction', thoughts about artificial beings were brought into existence, taking into account Mary Shelley's 'Frankenstein' which was written in the year, 1818.

However, the 'birth of AI' did not take place until 1956. Known as the 'Dartmouth Conference', involving Martin Minsky and John McCarthy, the result brought forward the coining of the term 'Artificial Intelligence' for the field dedicated to the study of stimulation of learning associated with the human mind [2].

The field has gone through many ups and downs since its founding. For nearly two decades, AI progressed at a wonderful speed, researchers claiming it to be the jewelled future of the world. But as every expectation demands a price, AI suffered financial losses, becoming the victim of its high optimistic hopes. The learning of extensive data was not an easy task; it was something that required many more years of study and the acceptance of its current shortcomings. But now, in present time, AI has advanced to a level wherein the vision of the 20th century seems somewhere near to the tip of our fingers. We have robots answering to our calls, mechanisms ready to read the weather to cater to agricultural needs, cars built with the ability to drive on their own and the list goes on.

With the beginning of the current century, following the demand of a dataset large enough to cater to the growing intelligence of systems from an economic perspective, 'Big Data' was introduced. The process of digitization—conversion of continuous, analog signals into discreet, digital signals—had gained popularity. It has become its different field devoted to the analysation of complex, huge amounts of information, otherwise being too hard to break down [3]. By the time the second decade rolled in, the market for AI-powered machinery exploded with further advances being made every day. The future of AI is indeed the jewelled mine the researchers had dreamt of in the past century.

20.3   Wireless Communication: An Overview

Long lines outside telephone booths, late-night endeavors to pick up calls for news from overseas, entertaining tales about somehow finding the way back home—these were commonplace until the late 1900s. Back then, contacting someone living far away was a privilege not everyone could afford. Even 'wired communication' was a rarity, the possession of telephones considered to be the sign of being well-off.

Wireless communication came into the picture in the late 19th century, 1880 to be precise, when photophone was invented by Alexander Graham Bell, a device that used sunlight to transmit information. Several wireless telegraphs were invented before the usage of radio waves came flying in1894 by Guglielmo Marconi, an Italian inventor. A patent was filed by him on June 2, 1896 [8].

20.4   Wireless Revolution

In the 1990s, the advent of the 'Wireless Revolution' saw the rapid increase in the growth rate of cellular radio systems. It was a dramatic shift from wired to wireless communication with growth rate being 33 to 50% till 1991 alone. National Aeronautics and Space Administration (NASA) had provided funding to the United States federal research for the mobile communication area [4].

It was the era of the shift from analog to digital radio frequency (RF) technology, a major driving force being MOSFET (metal-oxide-semiconductor field-effect transistor) [5]. It was created in 1959, by Mohamed M. Atalla and Dawon Kahng at Bell Labs [7]. MOSFETs were used to amplify the RF signals to enable long-distance communication on a level not previously ever imagined. By the 1990s, during the Wireless Revolution, it replaced BJT as a key element of RF technology [5] and would further go on to become the basic foundation of 2G, 3G, 4G and 5G [6].

The 'terms' radio and 'wireless' is, in fact, synonymous. They have both been used in place of the other from 1890 into the late 1900s. The whole concept of the 'wireless era' was to bring about a certain degree of proximity between places which would otherwise take days to travel to. And to remove wires gradually would have meant lowering costs for setting up complex circuits, ensuring increased efficiency and more possibilities of better connections [9].

20.5   The Present Times

The wireless revolution has paved the way to a new prosperous wireless communications industry. Because the world has now become a 'global village', methodologies of how businesses are managed have vastly changed [9]. For instance, people can now attend meetings with clients from anywhere in the world. In industries, important records in regards to the sales and the workings of the factories can now be accessed without visiting the site in person. Even in the 2020 pandemic, employees could carry on with their jobs by working at home.

Portable devices, like cell phones and personal digital assistants (PDA), make it possible for personal databases to be organized simultaneously and give access to online services related to networking like web browsing, social media, wireless e-mail and much more. This, furthermore, leads to a huge amount of savings [9] that would have otherwise been spent on travelling costs and wiring setups.

However, with every convenience comes greater risks to be catered to. Wireless communication leads to the insecurity of data as the process of sending and receiving can be attacked by outsiders with the intent of harming one's privacy and stealing confidential or personal information. These risks are not foreign to technologies in present times and as more and more progress continues to be made, the idea of security has remained to be a great concern and a matter of strong debate.

In this chapter, a concise study has been provided on how these two worlds—artificial intelligence and wireless communication—have merged to form a singular path towards rapid development. We would be looking at how Artificial Intelligence has propelled the industry of Wireless Communications forward, the challenges this fast-growing industry is facing and the current statistics of the reception and the response.

20.6   Artificial Intelligence in Wireless Communication

20.6.1   How the Two Worlds Collided

An enormous technical revolution has begun to impact the changes in industries and institutions across the world. Machine Learning (ML), a subset of

Artificial Intelligence known for providing learning capability to machines as they process data, gain experiences and improvise based on them, has ushered the past decade into the shining light of better performances than even humans themselves [10] in platforms such as speech and image recognition, conversational chatbots, legal translations, sentiment analysis and so on.

As we have entered into a global situation where numbers of users of wireless communication networking only keep increasing as the years go by, the fifth generation (5G) has neared its deployment and plans have already begun for development beyond. Artificial Intelligence can solve dilemmas involving even larger amounts of data and to fulfil the demands of higher data rates, better cost management, higher security, better flexibility, higher environment adaptation and better utilization of resources. Optimization of this huge amount of data would be a key component in the upcoming era of 5G and B5G wireless networks [11].

20.6.2   Cognitive Radios

Joseph Mitola coined the term 'Software Radio' in 1992 National Telesystems Conference. Although, there is a thin line of difference when the two are considered, often, the terminology 'Software-Defined Radios' (SDR) and 'Software Radios'(SR) are used in an exchangeable way. The differences arise when we think of their digitization processes. In SDRs, digitization takes place at a certain distance away from the antenna while in the case of SRs, it takes place near enough to the antenna. As technology is rapidly evolving, we can expect SDRs to get converted into SRs and the line to completely disappear [12].

Milton stated, that SDRs are said to hop instantaneous bandwidths over higher agility bandwidths, with the instantaneous waveform bandwidths limited. On the other hand, SRs digitize the bandwidth sand hence, the waveforms can be programmed to any bandwidth up to the higher agility bandwidths. He gave the model of Software Radio on which, he proposed, the model of 'Cognitive Radio' is based [13].

Cognitive Radios (CR) are built upon the idea of letting radios take intelligent decisions as to how they would manage spectrum and how they would carry out selections of waveform design, spatial diversity options, and time diversity [14]. In other words, rather than working in a fixed assigned band, they decide as to which band is appropriate to work in [19]. They can make appropriate changes at higher layers like changing route behavior, for instance, and work on observing their wireless connections and using algorithms and experiential learning for optimization [14].

More often than not, there is a debate over what can be called a CR and what cannot be but a conclusion has been drawn that those that have these following characteristic actions are taken under the umbrella term of CR:

A. *Cognizance or Discernment:* This means to sense information from the surroundings [15] which includes judging both the external constituents—such as, the status of the channel, needs of the user, etc.—and internal constituents (for instance, resources available for computing [14], available spectrum bands [15] remaining battery power, etc.) [14, 16].

B. *Reconfigurability:* Using this acquired information, the CR makes changes to help the adaptation mechanism for the

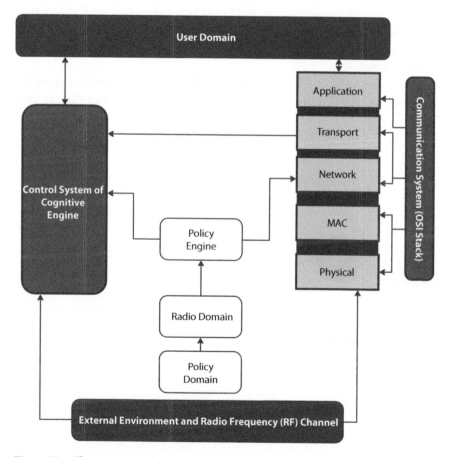

Figure 20.1 The cognitive radio concept architecture.

operation of the radio [14, 16] without any alteration in the hardware of the system [15].

C. *Cognitive Intelligence*: Based on the understanding of the environment and awareness of the radio, decisions are made, and perceiving the consequences of these decisions, the radio keeps on gaining a learning experience [16].

A diagram of the Cognitive Radio Concept Architecture is given in Figure 20.1.

20.7 Artificial Neural Network

Artificial Neural Network (ANN) was proposed by Warren McCulloch and Walter Pitts in 1943 [16] as a computing device designed to simulate the human brain for learning and processing information from its environment [17]. It is an integral part of artificial intelligence as we know it today.

ANNs are used in CRs wherein the artificial neurons form a complex interlinking web (Figure 20.2) to store information. They can discern and

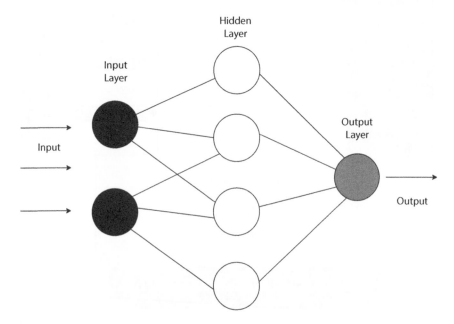

Figure 20.2 A simple Artificial Neural Network.

obtain learnings from patterns in the systems they are used in [16]. These artificial neurons are called processing units—input and output units. The input unit receives information and much like how the human brain functions, ANNs need a learning period called 'backward propagation of error' to come up with the best suitable output. This learning period consists of testing based on visuals, audio, and texts. There is a comparison made between the output produced and the output that it was supposed to produce. To adjust the difference between the outputs, 'backward propagation of error' is used which means going backward from the output to the input to adjust the input units until the correct output is obtained [17].

One of the major uses of ANN in CRs is spectrum sensing. According to the hypothesis model [18, 19], there are three spectrum sensing methods:

1. *Energy detection* is one of the most used methods where the energy of the received signal is measured to sense the spectrum in question. It helps the detection method if the noise power of the receiver is known beforehand, however, and the energy detector's performance can be affected significantly if this factor remains uncertain, leading to unreliability in detection [18, 19],

2. *Matched Filter Detection* is a method involving an optimum linear filter conceived in detail to increase the Signal-to-Noise Ratio (SNR) in the output received for an input signal [18, 19]. While the processing rate is highly efficient in the case of Matched Filter Detection, the prerequisite is prior knowledge about the user signal, that is, the information should be as accurate as possible to get the best result [19].

3. *Cyclostationary Feature Detection* has the mechanism of detecting features by analyzing a received signal and differentiating modulating signal energy from noise energy—noise energy being a stationary signal with no correlation while modulated signals being cyclostationary (meaning that their mean and autocorrelation showcases periodic behavior) with spectral correlation [19]. This can work better than others when it comes to differentiating noise energy but still needs prior knowledge like in the case of Matched Filter Detection [18] and a larger amount of observation time [19].

ANN and Cyclostationary Feature Detection have been combined for spectrum sensing, increasing reliability and efficiency as well as reducing the time for processing by executing a notable length of computational steps offline. This leads to the algorithm based on ANN accomplishing better performance as compared to the Bayesian-based algorithm [16] (The classification of techniques based on Bayes Theorem stating the assumption that features are independent of each other).

The following are the advantages of using Artificial Neural Network:

    a. Though prior knowledge is necessary in the case of Cyclostationary Feature Detection, usage of ANN along with it ensures that it can accommodate itself to the input user signal data accordingly.

    b. The model is non-linear and has several real-world applications.

    c. Accuracy in the approximation of any function is reliable.

Therefore, Artificial Neural Network is used to store the information of the user signal and helps in instruct 'the feature values of a signal' [20]. Also, the complexity of the solution adapting process is reduced as ANNs can be designed by using lesser instances even when the features of the system they are describing can be very nonlinear when it comes to input and output and highly numbered. So, they can be used to recognize spectrums and also for aiding in this process [16].

20.8   The Deployment of 5G

In 2019, the fifth generation of telecommunication began being deployed. Before that, the 4G cellular networks were having orthogonal frequency-division multiplexing (OFDM) as their sole base [21]. OFDM is a way of transmitting and encoding digital signals over several low rate carrier frequencies, carriers being orthogonal to each other [22]. It is used in both frequency-division duplex (FDD) and time-division duplex (TDD) formats and thus, TDD AND FDD 4G networks have a resembling framework [21].

But first and foremost, it is highly important to see the requirement of 5G in the current times. As the number of users of wireless networks is increasing exponentially, the Information and Communication Technologies (ICT) industry has been working on what would come next and with the plans being set into motion for quite a while, we see it finally becoming reality.

The following are some essential reasons for the need for the next step:

1. The explosive increase in the traffic of mobile data is one of the major driving factors for the dawn of the coming times of 5G.
2. Right now, the total roundtrip time or latency for 4g networks are of the order of about 15 ms. While this does not prove to have any inconveniences in most services, the expected 5G applications are said to have cloud-based technologies which may be a touchscreen and also having a total roundtrip time of an order of about 1 ms, that is considerably faster than 4G.
3. The main concern being the costs and the consumption of energy, the shift to 5G should lower them significantly. The per-link data rates being proposed will reach higher by about 100×. Accordingly, energy rates, that is, Joules per bit, and cost rates, that is, cost per bit should be brought down by 100× [23].
4. In terms of efficient use of spectrums, 5G will be able to utilize all three spectrums to the maximum potential [24].
5. 5G would break the limit of the previous generation's mobility, which was up to 350 km/h, and go up to 500 km/h to support the cellular devices using even higher data rates [24].

20.9   Looking Into the Features of 5G

A primary advantage of the current 5G network is that it has larger bandwidth, leading to increased download speed which has been achieved due to the higher-frequency radio wave as compared to its predecessors. However, for a higher outreach, since high-frequency radio waves cover small geographical areas, 5G networks operate on all ranges—low, medium, and high [25].

Speed of 5G largely depends on how wide the channels are which are being used to be operated. The low-band 5G works in frequencies well within 2 Ghz and even if they can cover wide distances, the channels aren't wide, and hence, the band is slow. Mid-band 5G works between 2 and 10 Ghz and has a fair range from their towers that had been set up. And lastly comes, the high-band 5G which comprises "millimeter waves" [29].

5G would use MIMO technology [26]—'Multiple-Input, Multiple-Output' which means how bandwidth is divided into parts and propelled forward to respective devices [27]. As already mentioned in this paper, the exponential increase in data users has resulted in the same bandwidth of radio-frequency spectrum being used in an amount unlike anything seen before. To tackle this issue, experiments have been made with introducing a whole new band of radio-frequency waves that haven't ever been used by cellular networks, one of them being bandwidth of "millimeter waves". These have broadcasting frequencies that work in the range of 30 to 300 GHz and comparably very high to the 6 GHz that was used before for mobile cellular networks using radio waves. One of the drawbacks, however, is that millimeter waves cannot travel between buildings, etc. easily [28].

20.10   AI and the Internet of Things (IoT)

The term 'Internet of Things' (IoT) came into existence in 1999 when a member of the Radio Frequency Identification (RFID) development community came up with it. It involves everyday objects (Figure 20.3) that are addressable through sensing devices and can be instructed by the Internet or some communication means be it RFID, wireless LAN, etc. Everyday objects refer to things we find around us be it electronic devices, vehicles, and also food, clothes, and much, much more [30].

Enormous amounts of data are collected via IoT devices and with the help of artificial intelligence, it becomes easier to study and analyze to learn

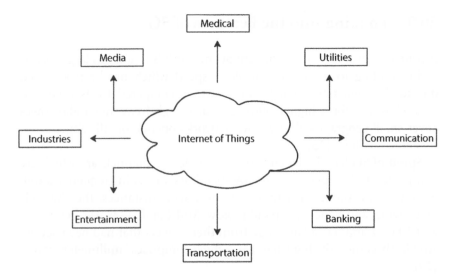

Figure 20.3 Some uses of the Internet of Things.

from the data collected. The increase in the usage of AI for data analytics has greatly boosted the utility of IoT. Two techniques are mostly used when it comes to AI in IoT: the artificial neural network and fuzzy logic [31].

Before we discussed the Artificial Neural Network, which is used with CRs, now following are some of the challenges faced by AI and IoT:

1. *Security:* As we are transitioning to a world where huge amounts of data are being handled simultaneously, a global concern for securing the privacy of users has risen. It is harder to secure data when it is being handled in bulk and this makes it sensitive and prone to hacking. Cloud attacks are said to become more frequent.
2. *Complexity:* IoT integrates technology from different places which increases the complexity of the system [32].

20.11 Artificial Intelligence in Software-Defined Networks (SDN)

Software-Defined Networks (SDN) are radio communication systems with the constituents that are software-based when earlier they were fit in by the means of hardware (detectors, amplifiers, etc., for instance) [37].

SDNs (Figure 20.4) are often having a Central Processing Unit (CPU) to carry out the functioning of the software embedded in it. These SDNs also have field-programmable gate arrays, which makes it hard to develop them faster, and hence, upgrades are slow to come by. Hence, there is a need for better SDN systems. Artificial Intelligence Radio Transceiver (AIR-T) was developed for the same, being the first artificially intelligent software-defined radio [38].

Problem-solving is an integral part of the development and artificial intelligence and machine learning is being used in great magnitude these days. The role of AI has grown in the field of Software-Defined Networks as, in recent times, the research communities are gravitating towards adopting the methods of AI in SDNs [33].

1. The minimization of latency and bringing the throughput in computer networks, supporting several routing ways, to its maximum is called the load balance function. SDN approach provides a due advantage when it comes to the discovering of the topology of the network. The use of Back Propagation

Neural Network (BPNN) made dynamic load balance possible and latency has been decreased by 19.3% compared to other methods [34].

2. SDN approach has a major concern of security and leaving programming systems vulnerable as complexity increases. The use of AI has been proposed in the past to overcome this issue. This is based on the integration of 'fuzzy interference system. and algorithms of both TRW-CB [35] and Rate-Limiting [36]. This system has shown better results as compared to others [34].

3. This collaboration has opened up possibilities for the creation of complex and intelligent applications [34].

Cognitive Radios as earlier discussed is another possibility brought about due to the integration of SDNs and AI. To distinguish CRs from software-defined radios, hardware like sensors and actuators are being

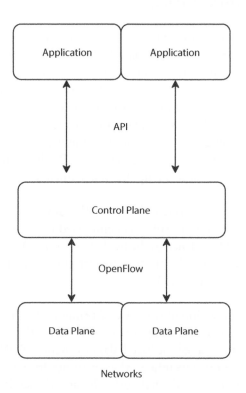

Figure 20.4 SDN architecture.

supplemented to help execute several applications. In 2004 [39], J. Polson proposed that in his concept, CRs would be able to:

1. create environmental awareness with the help of sensors
2. execute environmental interaction with the help of actuators
3. scan and observe to create a memory and a model of the environment
4. set goals for performance.

In the following years up till now, this idea has been revolutionized and worked upon further.

20.12   Artificial Intelligence in Network Function Virtualization

Telecommunication Service Providers (TSP) have witnessed the user traffic increase dramatically which demands expansions of the physical network. This, in turn, leads to high capital expenditures (CAPEX) and operating expenditures (OPEX). These costs cannot be met at the same rate due to an increase in competition with other TSPS. Network Function Virtualization (NFV) has been introduced with the same dilemma in mind. NFVs follow the concept of decoupling of network functions from hardware components and instead, running them on software [40].

When we see the working of both SDN and NFV, then it is observed that in the case of SDN, it helps in a smoother control of 5G by making a control plane which is different than the usual one used till 4G and in the case of NFV, there is efficiency in breaking down the network accordingly to the requirements of the user applications [21].

Many network functions would be virtualized in the future, getting executed via virtual machines in cloud data centers. Virtual Network Functions (VNFs) are being positioned as 'monoliths' which are single pieced software codes encompassing all implementations of network functions. BT and Telefonica are seeking the μservices-based architecture which means dismantling applications of larger sizes to its constituents, called μservices, and to deploy them into a network. As smaller components take less time processing, it makes it easier to handle. These comprise complex networking with mesh-like interdependencies, that is, they would need to communicate several times amongst each to complete and set up a service. AI comes into the picture where a model is made to resolve the issue using the generated date from the network [41].

20.13   Conclusion

As we are stepping into a world where almost everything is going digital, new challenges are being faced by the innovators in today's time, whether it be an investment in the idea, security of the user's privacy, etc. Every day, new methods are being implemented to get better than the past and the endeavor continues. We have already seen the birth of 5G and the communication world has begun moving towards the options beyond. Software-Defined Radios and Network Function Virtualization have been proposed to be integrated with AI to overcome their shortcomings. But it is safe to say that the future of AI is only just beginning.

References

1. Copeland, B.J., *Artificial intelligence| Definition, Examples, and Applications*, Britannica.com. Encyclopedia Britannica, https://journals.sagepub.com/doi/abs/10.1177/0008125619864925 (2019, accessed 25 February 2019)[Internet] https://www.britannica.com/technology/artificial-intelligence, 2017.
2. Haenlein, M. and Kaplan, A., A brief history of artificial intelligence: On the past, present, and future of artificial intelligence. *Calif. Manage. Rev.*, 61, 4, 5–14, 2019.
3. De Mauro, A., Greco, M., Grimaldi, M., A formal definition of Big Data based on its essential features. *Libr. Rev.*, 65, 3, 122–135, 2016.
4. Rappaport, T.S., The wireless revolution. *IEEE Commun. Mag.*, 29, 11, 52–71, 1991.
5. Baliga, B.J., *Silicon RF Power MOSFETs*, World Scientific, https://www.worldscientific.com/worldscibooks/10.1142/5725, 2005.
6. Asif, S., *5g mobile communications: Concepts and technologies*, CRC Press, https://www.routledge.com/5G-Mobile-Communications-Concepts-andTechnologies/Asif/p/book/9781498751551, 2018.
7. Williamson M. M., Throttling viruses: restricting propagation to defeat malicious mobile code. 2002, *18th Annual Computer Security Applications Conference*, IEEE, 2002, pp. 61–68, doi: 10.1109/CSAC.2002.1176279.
8. Dubendorf, V.A. and Dubendorf, V.A., *Wireless data technologies*, Wiley, New York, NY, 2003.
9. Ugweje, O.C., *Radio frequency and wireless communications*, The Internet Encyclopedia, https://onlinelibrary.wiley.com/doi/10.1002/047148296X.tie15112, 2004.
10. Wang, J., Li, R., Wang, J., Ge, Y.Q., Zhang, Q.F., Shi, W.X., Artificial intelligence and wireless communications. *Front. Inf. Technol. Electron. Eng.*, 21, 10, 1413–1425, 2020.

11. Wang, C.-X. *et al.*, Artificial Intelligence Enabled Wireless Networking for 5G and Beyond: Recent Advances and Future Challenges. *IEEE Wireless Commun.*, 27, 1, 16–23, 2020.

12. Caicedo, C.E. and Ph D. Student, *Software defined radio and software radio technology: Concepts and applications*, Department of Information Science and Telecommunications University of Pittsburgh, 2007.

13. Mitola, J.I., *Cognitive radio. An integrated agent architecture for software defined radio*, 0474–0474, Royal Institute of Technology, S-100 44 Stockholm, Sweden. , https://elibrary.ru/item.asp?id=5242514, 2002.

14. Rondeau, T.W. and Bostian, C.W., *Artificial intelligence in wireless communications*, Artech House, https://us.artechhouse.com/Artificial-Intelligence-in-Wireless-Communication-P1290.aspx, 2009.

15. Kaur, A., Aryan, P., Singh, G., Cognitive Radio Its Applications and Architecture. *Int. J. Eng. Innov. Technol. (IJEIT)*, 4, 11, 98–102, 2015.

16. He, A. *et al.*, A survey of artificial intelligence for cognitive radios. *IEEE Trans. Veh. Technol.*, 59, 4, 1578–1592, 2010.

17. Sharma, S., Nag, A., Cordeiro, L., Ayoub, O., Tornatore, M., Nekovee, M., Towards explainable artificial intelligence for network function virtualization, in: *Proceedings of the 16th International Conference on Emerging Networking Experiments and Technologies*, pp. 558-559, ACM, 2020.

18. Akyildiz, I.F. *et al.*, NeXt generation/dynamic spectrum access/cognitive radio wireless networks: A survey. *Comput. Networks*, 50, 13, 2127–2159, 2006.

19. Sahai, A., Hoven, N., Tandra, R., Some fundamental limits on cognitive radio. *Allerton Conference on Communication, Control, and Computing*, 2004.

20. Tang, Y.-J., Zhang, Q.-Y., Lin, W., Artificial neural network based spectrum sensing method for cognitive radio. *2010 6th International Conference on Wireless Communications Networking and Mobile Computing (WiCOM)*, IEEE, 2010.

21. Li, R. *et al.*, Intelligent 5G: When cellular networks meet artificial intelligence. *IEEE Wireless Commun.*, 24, 5, 175–183, 2017.

22. Ergen, M., *Mobile broadband: Including WiMAX and LTE*, Springer Science & Business Media, https://www.springer.com/gp/book/9780387681894, 2009.

23. Andrews, J.G. *et al.*, What will 5G be? *IEEE J. Sel. Areas Commun.*, 32, 6, 1065–1082, 2014.

24. Singh, S., *Eight Reasons Why 5G is Better than 4G*. Altran accessed (17.01. 2020) at: https://connect. altran. com/2018/03/eightreasons-why-5g-is-better-than-4g, 2019.

25. de Looper, C., *What is 5G? The next-generation network explained*, Digital Trends, https://www.digitaltrends.com/year- 2020, Retrieved May 5, 2020.

26. Hoffman, C., *What is 5G, and how fast will it be? How-To Geek web How-To Geek LLC*, https://www.howtogeek.com, 2019.

27. Stobing, C., *What Is MU-MIMO, and Do I Need It on My Router? How-To Geek*, https://www.howtogeek.com, https://www.howtogeek.com/242793/what-is-mu-mimo-and-do-i-need-it-on-my-router/, 2016.

28. Nordrum, A. and Clark, K., Everything you need to know about 5G. *IEEE Spectr.*, 27, 2017.

29. Segan, S., *What is 5G?*, PCMag. com, https://in.pcmag.com/cell-phone-service-providers/104415/what-is-5g, 2018.

30. Patel, K.K. and Patel, S., Internet of things—IOT: Definition, characteristics, architecture, enabling technologies, application & future challenges. *Int. J. Eng. Sci. Comput.*, 6, 5, 6122–6131, 2016.

31. Mohamed, E., The relation of artificial intelligence with internet of things: A survey. *J. Cybersecur. Inf. Manage.*, 1, 1, 30–24, 2020.

32. Katare, G., Padihar, G., Quereshi, Z., Challenges in the integration of artificial intelligence and Internet of things. *Int. J. Syst. Software Eng.*, 6, 2, 10–15, 2018.

33. Latah, M. and Toker, L., Artificial intelligence enabled software-defined networking: A comprehensive overview. *IET Networks*, 8, 2, 79–99, 2018.

34. Latah, M. and Toker, L., Application of artificial intelligence to software defined networking: A survey. *Indian J. Sci. Technol.*, 9, 44, 1–7, 2016.

35. Mikians, J. *et al.*, A practical approach to portscan detection in very high-speed links. *International Conference on Passive and Active Network Measurement*, Springer, Berlin, Heidelberg, 2011.

36. Viruses, Throttling. Restricting propagation to defeat malicious mobile code. 2007-01-16], http://www.hpl.com/techreports/2002/HPL-2002-172R1. pdf.

37. Solekhan, S. and Iqbal, M., Media Pembelajaran Pemancar Wireless Fm Menggunakan Raspberry Pi. *Simetris: Jurnal Teknik Mesin, Elektro dan Ilmu Komputer*, 11, 1, 257–262, 2020.

38. J.D. Ferguson, W.M. Kirschner, P. Witkowski, Artificial intelligence radio transceiver. U.S. Patent Application No. 16/206,056.

39. Polson, J., Cognitive radio applications in software defined radio. *Proceedings of the SDR Forum Conference 2004*, 2004.

40. Mijumbi, R. *et al.*, Management and orchestration challenges in network functions virtualization. *IEEE Commun. Mag.*, 54, 1, 98–105, 2016.

41. Sharma, S. *et al.*, Poster: Towards Explainable Artificial Intelligence for Network Function Virtualization, 2020.

Index

Also of Interest

Check out these published and forthcoming titles in the "Artificial Intelligence and Soft Computing for Industrial Transformation" series from Scrivener Publishing

Advances in Artificial Intelligence and Computational Methods for Transportation Safety
Edited by Naga Pasupuleti, Naveen Chilamkurti, B. Balamurugan, T. Poongodi
Forthcoming 2022. ISBN 978-1-119-76170-9

The New Advanced Society
Artificial Intelligence and Industrial Internet of Things Paradigm
Edited by Sandeep Kumar Panda, Ramesh Kumar Mohapatra, Subhrakanta Panda and S. Balamurugan
Forthcoming 2022. ISBN 978-1-119-82447-3

Digitization of Healthcare Data using Blockchain
Edited by T. Poongodi, D. Sumathi, B. Balamurugan and K. S. Savita
Forthcoming 2022. ISBN 978-1-119-79185-0

Tele-Healthcare
Applications of Artificial Intelligence and Soft Computing Techniques
Edited by R. Nidhya, Manish Kumar and S. Balamurugan
Forthcoming 2020. ISBN 978-1-119-84176-0

Impact of Artificial Intelligence on Organizational Transformation
Edited by S. Balamurugan, Sonal Pathak, Anupriya Jain, Sachin Gupta, and Sachin Sharma and Sonia Duggal
Forthcoming 2022. ISBN 978-1-119-71017-2

Artificial Intelligence for Renewable Energy Systems
Edited by Ajay Kumar Vyas, S. Balamurugan, Kamal Kant Hiran, Harsh S. Dhiman
Forthcoming 2022. ISBN 978-1-119-76169-3

Fuzzy Intelligent Systems
Methodologies, Techniques, and Applications
Edited by E. Chandrasekaran, R. Anandan, G. Suseendran, S. Balamurugan and Hanaa Hachimi
Published 2021. ISBN 978-1-119-76045-0

Biomedical Data Mining for Information Retrieval
Methodologies, Techniques and Applications
Edited by Sujata Dash, Subhendu Kumar Pani, S. Balamurugan and Ajith Abraham
Published 2021. ISBN 978-1-119-71124-7

Design and Analysis of Security Protocols for Communication
Edited by Dinesh Goyal, S. Balamurugan, Sheng-Lung Peng and O.P. Verma
Published 2020. ISBN 978-1-119-55564-3

www.scrivenerpublishing.com